THE CHINE ECONOMY
Past and Present

Ramon H. Myers

**Hoover Institution on War, Revolution
and Peace, Stanford University**

Wadsworth, Inc., Belmont, California

The Chinese Economy: Past and Present was produced by the following people:

Copy Editor: *Donna Maraget*
Interior Designer: *Cynthia Daniels*
Cover Designer: *Cynthia Daniels*

Library of Congress Cataloging in Publication Data
Myers, Ramon Hawley, 1929–
  The Chinese economy, past and present.
  Includes index.
  1. China—Economic conditions. I. Title.
HC427.M95   330.9'51   79-13173
ISBN 0-87872-231-9

Printed in the United States of America
1 2 3 4 5 6 7 8 9 — 84 83 82 81 80

To Ronald and Jennifer,
my son and daughter,
cited in order of age,
not any discrimination of sex.

Contents

Foreword

Civilization in Asia is a series intended to make available to college students and teachers the current state of scholarly thinking in various Asian subjects. The proliferation of specialized monographs of high quality during recent years makes it possible to write well-informed general summaries in many fields, and makes it essential to bridge the ever-widening gap between specialist knowledge and undergraduate education.

To write texts of the sort described is a task that requires the best scholarly awareness of the current state of the art, the ability to compress and summarize without distorting the subject, and a style of writing that is lucid and literate. Fortunately, the sound rationale for this series has attracted some of the best-qualified scholars in the field as its authors. These are all persons who have distinguished themselves by published research that gives them high reputations in the profession. That they have willingly devoted their learning and talents to provide sound, basic texts is a sign of their recognition of an urgent need.

Perhaps the most overriding concern shared by all who are involved in *Civilization in Asia* is that American education should continue, and increase, its efforts to bring all of humankind within the purview of our students, who must function intelligently and humanely in what is now undeniably one world.

Laurence G. Thompson
Series Editor

Preface

Contrary to popular belief, Chinese history has not been a continuity—one thing growing organically out of the last and on to the next. It has been a series of breaks or ruptures, each of which involved a novel mutation.

Consider these three major events within the past three hundred years: the Manchu takeover of China in 1644; Japan's victory over China in 1895; the Communist party seizure of China in late 1945.

Manchu rule over China laid the foundations for an unprecedented population growth and the expansion of the economy. China's defeat by Japan forced the imperial government to begin rapid, widespread modernization of the economy and society. The rise of the Communist party introduced a new socialist economic system geared to making China a world economic power by the year 2000. Just as these events led to sweeping political and social changes, so too did far-reaching changes occur in the tempo of economic growth and the structure of the economy.

China's economic history should be studied with the intention of answering several key questions. These questions relate to the historical discontinuities just mentioned.

The first question is, What kind of economic system enabled China to more than double its population between the late seventeenth century and the mid-nineteenth century to reach a total of nearly a half billion people? The reader should realize that such an achievement took place without the introduction and spread of modern technology—that is, mechanical instead of human power—and without a modern demographic revolution—that is, a rapid decline in mortality followed by a slow fall in the birthrate.

The second question is, Why should a country that had created printing, gunpowder, and advanced mathematics fail to recognize the advantages of modern technology until 1895 and then utilize only a little of it thereafter without really developing its economic potential? In other words, why was industrial development and a modern agricultural revolution so long in coming to China, and then when it did, why was it confined to a few, specific areas during the first three decades of this century?

The final question is, How did China after 1949 achieve such high rates of economic growth, for example, rapid growth of agricultural and manufacturing output and capital accumulation, from such a low per capita income base? China's unique economic growth record over the past three decades makes its performance very different from that of the advanced countries beginning their modern economic growth in the nineteenth century, the latecomers like the Soviet Union and Japan, and today's developing countries.

These three questions will be explored and answered in this text. Such an approach makes it possible to touch only lightly upon issues relating to causes of social protest, to whether or not living standards declined or improved, or to the oppressiveness of government economic policies. Occasionally I have introduced very simple economic analysis to show how state and private sector interacted, how markets worked, and to explain deflation, inflation, trade fluctuations, and the pattern of investment. This text should suitably complement general histories about China's recent past. Its focus upon salient historical and current economic development issues, such as making income distribution more equal, agricultural stagnation, and mobilizing savings should also make it useful to read in conjunction with courses on economic development and comparative economic systems.

Introduction

Part One

Economic Growth and Structural Change

1

Since the human race moved from food gathering in forests and fields to farming, two distinct epochs have evolved: premodern and modern economic growth periods. The premodern economic epoch, longer in time and more varied in its political and social institutions, had two major economic characteristics that distinguished it from the epoch that followed.

First, real per capita income remained stagnant for long periods or rose so slowly as to be imperceptible from one generation to the next. Often, real per capita income even plummeted and then remained stationary for some time. Its century-long trend might show growth, but certainly never more then .3 or .5 percent per annum, which meant that per capita income only rose 40 or 70 percent every one hundred years. Second, the economic structure of societies scarcely changed over time, and most economic activity depended upon agriculture, fishing, and forestry. The predominate sources of energy came from the sun, human and animal power, and organic materials.

All this changed when societies entered into an era of modern economic growth. Beginning around the mid-eighteenth century, England and Holland first broke with tradition. Modern economic growth quickly spread to northern Europe in the early nineteenth century and to southern and Eastern Europe in the late nineteenth and early twentieth centuries. By the mid-twentieth century nearly every state in the world had become committed to achieving modern economic growth for itself.

Two features distinguished this new epoch. First, per capita income began to increase on a sustained basis over time and typically rose to over 1 percent per annum. Second, various structural changes began originating in the economy as manufacturing, the most rapidly growing sector of the economy, adopted new sources of energy: more people abandoned farming to work in the cities; the proportion of output from manufacturing began to exceed that of agriculture in value terms. For these changes to be deep-rooted and enduring, societies had to borrow or create modern technology and science and then adapt to the organizations responsible for production and distribution.

Social scientists have not yet discovered laws that can predict when modern economic growth will occur or that explain why such growth takes place in some societies and not in others. Economic historians have identified some of the patterns that characterized the premodern epoch, and when data were available, these experts have measured some of the patterns that emerged when modern economic growth commenced and that appear common to nearly all countries. To be sure, some variations within the following five broad patterns can be observed since economic development often differs from country to country.

EPOCHS IN ECONOMIC HISTORY

First, if the growth of production for handicraft industries and agriculture only slowly increases over centuries, modern economic growth begins when the production of new industries and agriculture increases more rapidly than in the past. Typically, an industrial spurt occurs in manufacturing, which now produces goods by new sources of power and new methods.

Second, in the premodern epoch, population barely expands, and when it does, large numbers of people invariably die from wars, plagues, or famines, so that population again stagnates. Under modern economic growth a demographic revolution occurs. A sharp, sustained decline in the death rate among different age groups and by sex first takes place, later followed by a decline in the birth rate. This lag between the decline in death and birth rates means that more people survive birth and live longer, so that the rate of growth of population then increases and can even continue for as long as a century or more.

Third, before modern economic growth, societies channel very little of their current production to replace capital stock and add to it. Very low per capita income leaves little savings after consumption takes place. Extreme poverty and backwardness discourages capital investment. As modern economic growth commences, societies channel more resources to produce capital goods—machines, tools, structures, stocks of goods—so that the supply of capital rapidly expands. The economy consumes a smaller share of its current output, and more resources such as land, labor, and capital are freed for producing capital. At the same time savings in the new economic order increases.

Fourth, while the economic structure scarcely changes in the premodern epoch, the production structure rapidly alters as a modern economy grows. Agriculture, formerly the most important component of the economy, progressively contributes less capital to a society's gross national production, while manufacturing such products as iron, steel, machine tools, cement, and chemicals contributes more. A gradual deployment of the work force also accompanies this trend. The labor force employed in manufacturing and services grows whereas in agriculture it declines. As a result, the distribution of population radically changes. The proportion of people residing in cities rises as families leave villages for urban employment.

Finally, the pattern of income distribution that for centuries has remained unequal and unchanged begins to alter. Formerly, wealth and income were concentrated in the hands of a small elite, while the remainder of society held little wealth and divided the rest of society's income among its own members. With modern economic growth, income distribution at first becomes even more unequally distributed for an undetermined period. Finally, a point is reached when the economy's resources of land, labor, and capital have moved from low-income, low-productivity tasks to higher-income, higher-productivity tasks to reverse the trend toward an equal distribution of income.

Let us now turn to the Chinese economy over the past three hundred years and trace in a very general way the pattern of premodern economic development, identify when modern economic development commenced and the form it took, and then examine the features of modern economic growth that evolved after 1949.

PREMODERN ECONOMIC GROWTH: THE ANCIEN RÉGIME

Per Capita Income

We have no reliable information on the trend of per capita income between the late seventeenth and early twentieth centuries, that period of late imperial times commonly referred to as the Ch'ing empire (1644–1911). Reasonable estimates indicate that per capita income was very low and barely rose during the entire period. In 1933 per capita income was roughly 61 U.S. dollars and probably around 55 U.S. dollars in 1914–1918 (see table 1–3). In the early Ch'ing period per capita income could not have been very much below 55 U.S. dollars, but suppose it was as low as 25 U.S. dollars. Over a 250-year period the implied rate of growth still would have been only around .3 percent per year, a rate befitting the premodern epoch, and chances are the growth rate was slower. By the 1690s the economy recovered from the mid-seventeenth century rebellions and the Manchu invasion; it enjoyed prosperity during the next century, but then stagnated in the 1820s until the mid-century when rebellions rocked the empire. The 1860 to 1910 period was a time of recovery and of resumption of very slow growth until World War I when gradual modernization of the economy in the treaty ports commenced.

Meanwhile, the economy remained predominately agrarian. Judging from national income estimates of 1933, around two-thirds of China's output must have originated from agriculture, and nearly 95 percent of the population lived in villages and market towns. This teeming rural population depended upon the energy sources of sun, water, labor animals, and human labor. Inasmuch as traditional technology only improved slowly by the best farming practices, such as the planting of high yielding rice or cotton seeds, that gradually spread throughout one region and only sometimes to another, population or labor supply expansion, rather than per capita income or technological growth, gave this economy its very unique aspects.

Population Growth

Late imperial China faithfully tried to record its population. To this end the authorities devised a unique system for counting all households and recording the names and numbers of householders.

> After [the Manchus] entered China through the Shan-hai corridor, a law was passed during the Emperor Hsun-chih's reign to record population according to two units: the *p'ei* and *chia*. This law established 10 households into 1 *p'ei* with a leader, 10 *p'ei* into 1 *chia* with a leader, and 10 *chia* into 1 *pao* with a leader for every village, town, country, and prefecture. The name of every person and the number of male adults and every individual were recorded and listed in each *p'ei* register. Any person leaving [his or her residence] for another locality or any person leaving another locality to come to the residence [in question] was recorded, as well as the name of the locality.[1]

This record-keeping system fulfilled multiple purposes: to collect taxes, to identify criminals, to provide famine relief, and to conscript labor for public works and for the military. The ingenuity of the Chinese in pyramiding their organizations for information gathering and control is remarkable. Just as the state integrated the smallest socioeconomic unit—the household—into larger organizational units for the purpose of administration and policing, so too did it prescribe rules to identify institutions like temples, work places like mines, and types of occupations like manufacturing salt. As in any large-scale recordkeeping system, errors, omissions, and falsehoods could distort the true picture of population size. Therefore, the aggregate population totals produced by this record-collecting system for the Ch'ing period give only a rough approximation of the long-term trend. But when these aggregates are compared to the growth of population in Western Europe during its period of modern demographic transition (see table 1–1), a most interesting paradox can be observed.

TABLE 1–1. *Population Growth in Late Imperial China and Western Europe during Its Demographic Revolution: A Comparison*

Region	Base Period	Population	End Period	Population	Rate of Growth
Western Europe	1750	50–60,000	1850	152,600	.94%–1.10%
			1900	187,000	.74%–0.93%
China	1650	100,000[a]	1850	425,000	.70%
	1750	180,000	1850	425,000	.86%

[a] Estimated.

Source: Data for China compiled from Li Wen-chih, ed., *Chung-kuo chin-tai nung-yeh shih tzu-liao* [Historical Materials on Modern China's Agriculture] (Peking: San-lien shu-tien, 1957), vol. I, pp. 5, 8–9. The 1650 estimate was obtained by multiplying the number of able-bodied males (*ting*) by the average household size number (5), and then adding the numbers of families (estimated to have evaded corvée and tax rolls) times the average household size number (5).
Data for Western Europe compiled from E. E. Rich and C. H. Wilson, eds., *The Cambridge Economic History of Europe* (Cambridge: Cambridge University Press, 1967), vol. 4, pp. 63–67 for estimate of 1750; H. J. Habakkuk and M. Postan, *The Cambridge Economic History of Europe* (Cambridge: Cambridge University Press, 1965), vol. 6, p. 61 for 1850 and 1900 figures.

From the mid-seventeenth until the mid-nineteenth century China's population steadily grew to over 400 million people. How was this possible without China's experiencing a *demographic revolution*—that is to say, a decline in the death rate followed later by a fall in the birth rate as had occurred in Western Europe after 1750? The reason is perhaps that by the 1680s the country achieved peace. Poor harvests, epidemics, and famines naturally occurred but only on a very small scale during the eighteenth century. Fertility still remained very high, but the slight fall in mortality that resulted from moderated long swings in the death rate had produced a steady population growth nearly equivalent to that of Western Europe's during its demographic transition. Moreover, Western Europe's population acquired a different age and sex structure with very different fertility and mortality rates. In 1953 China's population still had the properties of a premodern society. The adult population was singularly deficient; the proportion of children under age fifteen was probably as high as 36 percent compared to only 20 and 25 percent in economically advanced countries.[2] The male-female ratio remained in favor of males rather than becoming equalized as in modern societies. The mortality and fertility rates still measured in the high thirties and low forties per thousand range.

Population Distribution

Where had population expansion occurred? Between 1787 and 1933 the greatest increase had occurred in the administrative areas of Manchuria, Shensi, Kansu, Hupeh, Hunan, Kwangsi, Szechwan, Yunnan, and Kweichow, or what Yeh-chien Wang has referred to as the "developing" areas.[3] Population in these areas rose from around 83 million to 212 million compared to an increase from only 209 to 274 million in the better-developed administrative areas: Chihli (Hopei), Shantung, Honan, Shansi, Kiangsu, Chekiang, Anhwei, Kiangsi, Fukien, and Kwangtung. The enormous population growth in the developing areas produced an increase in cultivated farmland from 16 million hectares in 1766 to 47.4 million hectares in 1933 compared to a growth from 42.6 million hectares to only 47.4 million in the better-developed areas. Population growth brought about new land settlement, and Chinese culture and society spread to what is territorially regarded as China today.

China's Macroregions G. William Skinner has recently presented another view of China's population distribution. He perceives China as made up of eight macroregions, each with a distinctive economic core area within it.[4] Figure 1–1 shows the specific economic core areas, whereas figure 1–2 presents these same eight macroregions superimposed upon the administrative provinces. This view of China's space has special merit. The country's economic system can be differentiated and analyzed on a geographic and economic basis. Secondly, population density patterns and regional population growth differences are clearly distinguished.

Table 1–2 shows how population growth and density changed over time within these macroregions. By the end of the nineteenth century the population had nearly recovered its all-time high, which had been achieved before the rebellions of the 1850s. The severe shortage of males resulting from the great loss of life prevented many families from being founded immediately, so that population growth increased more slowly in the remainder of the century. Meanwhile, population concentration became greatest in the lower Yangtze region, as in the first half of the century, followed by north China and the southeast coast. By 1953 population had passed the half billion mark with macroregional density patterns similar to that of the nineteenth century but much higher in every instance.

These macroregions can be distinguished according to the population concentration in cities and market towns that constitute the economic core. Except for the Yun-Kwei region, the economic core was either located in riverine valley lowlands or on plains that were characterized by the cheapest transportation within the region and the most advanced agriculture. Within these economic cores several

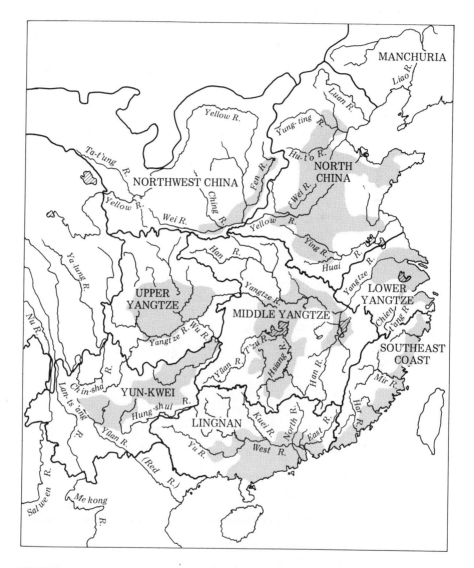

FIGURE 1–1. Economic Core Areas within the Macroregions

Source: Reprinted from *The City in Late Imperial China,* p. 214, edited by G. William Skinner with the permission of the publishers, Stanford University Press. © 1976, 1977 by the Board of Trustees of the Leland Stanford Junior University.

FIGURE 1–2. Provinces Divided into Eight Macroregions

TABLE 1-2. *Estimated Populations and Their Densities in Eight Macroregions*

Macroregion	Area (sq. km.)	Population					
		1843		1893		1953	
		(millions)	(density)	(millions)	(density)	(millions)	(density)
North China[1]	746,470	112	150	122	163	174	233
Northwest China	771,300	29	38	24	31	32	42
Upper Yangtze	423,950	47	111	53	125	68	160
Middle Yangtze	699,700	84	120	75	107	92	131
Lower Yangtze	192,740	67	348	45	233	61	316
Southeast Coast[2]	226,670	27	119	29	128	36	159
Yun-Kwei	470,900	11	23	16	34	26	55
Lingnan[3]	424,900	29	68	33	78	47	111
Total	3,956,300	406	103	397	100	536	135

Note. Total density derived from dividing aggregate population for each year by the total area for the eight macroregions.

[1] Excludes Manchuria.

[2] Includes Taiwan.

[3] Includes Hainan.

Source: Reprinted from *The City in Late Imperial China*, edited by G. William Skinner with the permission of the publishers, Stanford University Press. © 1976, 1977 by the Board of Trustees of the Leland Stanford Junior University.

cities dominated and were linked to other cities in a hierarchical pattern according to their size and trade. The marketing networks that flowed from these economic core areas outward within each macroregion were made up of medium- and small-sized towns, which were in turn linked to small market towns serviced by anywhere from 15 to 30 villages.* For the country as a whole in 1893, between 27,000 to 28,000 small market towns, about 8,000 larger market towns, and 2,300 very large market towns were functioning. In addition, 669 local cities, 200 large cities, 63 regional cities, 20 regional metropolises, and 6 central metropolises operated within these eight macroregions.

How much of the population lived in cities as opposed to villages or settlements of households without markets? In 1893 China's urban population ranged between 20.8 and 25.7 million persons and showed corresponding urbanization rates of between 5.3 and 6.6 percent. In fact the urbanization rate between 1843 and 1893 scarcely changed: 5.1 and 6.0 percent respectively. The urbanization rate was highest in the lower Yangtze followed by the Lingnan, northwest China, southeast coast, middle Yangtze, north China, upper Yangtze and Yun-Kwei macroregions. The urbanization rates within these macroregions did not neatly correspond with population size and density for the macroregion. Instead, the size of the market, division of labor, and level of technology within each macroregion combined to influence more strongly the level of urbanization. Therefore, areas like southern Kiangsu and northeast Chekiang contained the greatest urban population because of their advanced state of the arts, well-developed handicraft, and highly commercialized agriculture. The Lingnan macroregion contained the second highest urban population by virtue of the advanced economy within and around the Pearl River delta area.

Gilbert Rozman has pointed out that about three-quarters of Chinese *central places,* defined here as conglomerates of households and organizations in which significant central functions—such as politico-administrative, cultural, social, as well as economic—are performed, were equivalent to small market towns in the countryside.[5] These conglomerates differed from ordinary villages in that they contained a *periodic market*—that is to say, a place of exchange that opened during specific days and times of the month. This heavy concentration of small market towns in the countryside might have made China somewhat unique as a premodern society. The typical rural family did not exclusively farm; it engaged in many market transactions. Its members repaired structures and tools, spun thread, wove cloth, made decorative or useful objects from straw, bamboo, clay, and other

---

*These communities often were very large villages that permitted marketing on prescribed days of the lunar calendar.

materials, carted goods, and hawked wares. Probably only six out of ten households in villages—often less—obtained as much as 50 percent of their income from farming. The rest of their income came from activities linked to these market towns.

Employment

China's huge premodern population found employment mainly in agriculture, handicraft, commerce, and services. While roughly four out of every ten persons depended on the other six to feed them, employment outside of farming for those six or 60 percent of the population always had to be found. Sons of farmers could expect to receive land to farm when the family estate was divided. Sons with literary promise prepared for the imperial examinations, but few out of the majority could expect to become officials. Many young men simply drifted into handicraft, commerce, and services. A family would marry off its daughters during their late teens or would use their labor wherever possible.

Employment depended upon agriculture's prospering and expanding. Families took up farming by moving to frontier areas to clear and settle new lands. But new demand for crops and goods had to be found continually in older, developed communities in and close to the economic core centers of the country (see figure 1–1) to provide enough work for everyone. Meanwhile, officials constantly worried about unemployment. "All thieves come from the poor, and the poor all come from the unemployed" was an attitude widely held by Ch'ing officials.[6] And large pockets of unemployment were forever spreading. For example, opium smuggling along the Kwangtung coast in the 1830s induced many Chinese to transport and sell the drug. Official efforts to suppress this activity produced considerable unemployment. Also, in the 1890s many people who formerly serviced the inland man-made waterway—the Grand Canal—became unemployed when the court ordered that food grains from the south be shipped northward by sea. Finally, as some scholars now contend, the shortage of silver in the 1830s and 1840s caused prolonged deflation and widespread unemployment, thus creating powderkeg-like conditions by which the rebellions of the 1850s exploded. Whichever the case, the causes and consequences of unemployment in late imperial China remain an important, though little-studied, topic.

Land Distribution

The level of employment was in some way related to property ownership, especially land, which in turn bore some correspondence to the distribution of income. If landownership increased and equalized, so too did income, and conditions for maintaining high employment improved. The precise trends of wealth ownership during the Ch'ing period are unknown, but two broad changes definitely can be observed. In the mid-seventeenth century, land and other property were very unequally distributed.

Government-controlled Lands   State organizations might have controlled as much as 25 percent of the cultivated land in the mid-seventeenth century. The Manchus had seized vast tracts of land around Peking for their nobility; Manchu and Chinese troops set up garrisons (*t'un-t'ien*) around the country and confiscated nearby lands for their support; the imperial household (*nei-wu-fu*) also claimed vast areas, including the villages, as its own. This situation gradually changed over the next two hundred years, so that by 1887 at least 87 percent of all cultivated land was privately owned.[7]

Private Landownership   Just as claims to wealth shifted from the public to the private sector, so did claims to wealth within the private sector change. We cannot quantify this shift for eighteenth century China, but the process can be observed for Manchuria, where land gradually became cultivated during the nineteenth and early twentieth centuries by new migrants. When villages in south Manchuria first formed, only a few households had managed to clear and farm any land. Being wealthy, these households began to employ laborers and even lease some of their land to new arrivals. In a generation or so, many of these tenants had acquired land of their own, and even full-time laborers had acquired land or rented some. Meanwhile, few of the original wealthy households had kept their estates intact, since frequent cash demands for ceremonies such as marriages or funerals could only be met by selling land. Periodic division of property among male heirs further reduced their estates to fragmented holdings, either owned by outsiders or the heirs.

This same process occurred in villages founded in central and northern Manchuria. The fragmentation of a large estate can be observed in the case of the Chang household, which owned 1,080 hectares in K'o-shan county of Heilungkiang province in north Manchuria prior to 1911. By 1934 the Chang household owned none of this land. The estate had been sold off so that portions of it were claimed by 54 households, which ranged in size from 130 hectares to .13 hectares.[8]

Distribution of Wealth

In spite of the fact that more households gradually acquired claims to land and other property, this kind of wealth distribution still remained very unequal. Referring again to our Manchurian settlement illustration, when landownership distribution in villages settled prior to 1833 is compared to those settled after 1909, the pattern of land distribution in both village groups during the early 1930s was very unequal as measured by Gini coefficients of .78 and .85 respectively.[9] Wealth was frequently liquidated or redistributed through inheritance, but some households also accumulated wealth so that the overall pattern of wealth distribution still remained very unequal. Manchuria, being a frontier area, probably represented conditions of the late seventeenth century in China proper. Figure 1–3 shows land distribution in China for the mid-1930s according to a Lorenz curve and its estimated Gini ratio measure. The *Lorenz curve* measured distribution between perfect equality (any point on the straight diagonal line) and perfect inequality (a point near the intersection of the graph opposite the diagonal line). According to figure 1–3, 60 percent of the households owned only 18 percent of the cultivated land, and these farms were smaller than four acres in size. But for Taiwan in 1920, where rural institutions were like those of mainland China, 90 percent of the households owned only 40 percent of the land, and the Gini coefficient measured .76. As Taiwan and Manchuria were frontier areas settled later, these high Gini coefficients probably would have slowly declined as more time passed. Their examples suggest that in China wealth distribution since the late seventeenth century slowly became more equal, as gradual but steady economic development occurred. Yet even by the early twentieth century, the distribution pattern throughout China was still very unequal as figure 1–3 shows.

Many kinds of owners and managers operated rural land: lineages, village councils, charitable estate supervisors, temples, schools, villagers and, of course, absentee owners like merchants, moneylenders and the literati. Exactly how much rural land was held only by absentee landowners is uncertain. The wide range of owners just mentioned suggests that the proportion of land held by absentee landlords might have been smaller than generally believed. But land was the most sought-after, prized asset because investors expected its rate of return over time to be higher than what could be earned by purchasing any other asset. In this agrarian society people who owned land invariably were the more wealthy, so that we can reasonably say that, prior to 1900 at least, income distribution closely approximated land distribution.

Income Distribution in the Ancien Régime

What was the pattern of income distribution in China during the final phase of the Ch'ing period? It too was very unequal. What made this so was the existence of a privileged class with easy access to wealth. The literati or gentry, by virtue of passing one or more imperial examinations, acquired official titles that enabled its members to hold office, manage public projects and institutions like schools, and

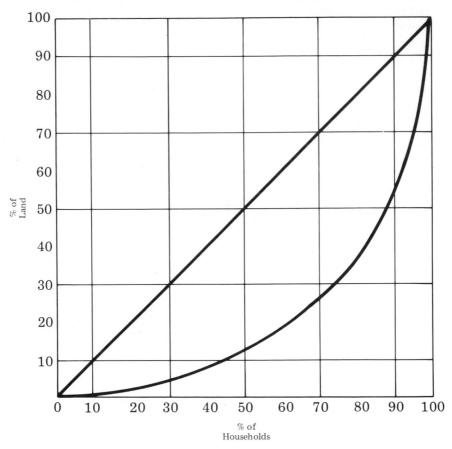

% of Households		% of Land	
35.61	98.66	6.21	81.68
59.60	99.38	17.63	87.39
72.77	99.62	28.26	90.15
80.76	99.82	37.43	93.32
88.98	99.93	50.60	95.95
95.18	99.98	66.14	98.25
97.35	100.00	74.52	100.00

FIGURE 1–3.   *Land Distribution in China (1936)*

Note: Gini Ratio (ratio of enclosed area between Lorenz curve and diagonal reference line to total area under diagonal) equals .5728.
Source: Ch'uan-kuo t'u-ti tiao-ch'a pao-kao kang-yao [Summary Report of the National Land Survey] (Shanghai, 1937), p. 32.

supply their professional services as secretaries, teachers, scholars, and physicians. Their activities did not stop there. Whenever members of the literati entered into the state bureaucracy, they increased not only their prospects for earning "illegal" income, but also their access to information concerning the acquisition of wealth. Merchants sought them out as silent partners in their investments. Relatives, friends, and even strangers approached the gentry to lend money against lucrative collateral assets like land. But even those literati who failed the imperial exams gained close connections with officials and acquired similar jobs.

Chung-li Chang's pioneering investigation gives some very rough magnitudes for various ways by which the gentry earned their income.[10] In the 1880s the annual income flowing to this class came to around 645,225,000 taels. Roughly 52 percent of this sum came from property rents and mercantile services such as banking and commerce. Income from holding office, including regular and extra income, amounted to only 121 million taels or 19 percent of their total income. The gentry totaled 1.5 million people, and with families, their total number amounted to about 7.5 million or 2 percent of the population. Chung-li Chang's very rough estimate of the Gross Domestic Product (GDP) for this period amounts to 2.7 billion taels, which means that about 24 percent of the GDP accrued to only 2 percent of the population. Simon Kuznets's investigations for U. S. income distribution between 1919–1938 showed that the top 1 percent of the U.S. population received 15 percent of the *national income*—that is, the Gross Domestic Product minus depreciation spending.[11] The top 5 percent received 30 percent of U.S. national income. However, for China of the 1880s the top 2 percent perhaps earned about 30 percent of national income. As roughly 3 percent of Chinese households owned about 25 percent of all land in the mid-1930s, both land and income distributions were indeed very unequal.

EARLY MODERN ECONOMIC DEVELOPMENT

China's stinging defeat at the hands of Japan in 1895 finally forced the Ch'ing imperial government to bring the country into the modern world. The imperial state firmly committed itself for the first time to far-reaching reforms to make the country militarily strong and wealthy. These reforms quickly nurtured a favorable climate for private business owners in the early 1900s. Many Chinese entrepreneurs stepped forward to create modern manufacturing enterprises in the many cities located along the coast and inland waters. Joining with this new class were foreign business entrepreneurs with their investments and firms. Competition and cooperation between the two groups increased the pace of modernization.

The state, weakened by political revolution, all but collapsed after 1911. It revived in 1928—for only a decade—to create in several provinces the beginning of a modern economy with an infrastructure of communications, uniform weights and measures, standardized currency, modern educational institutions, and research institutions by which business firms could improve production and distribution. But a decade was too short for the business owner and farmer to reap any tangible rewards. China was also beset by Japanese aggression in Manchuria and suffering like so many other countries from the world-wide depression. The Japanese invasion in 1937 ended the state's short-lived development efforts, and for the next decade China was engulfed in war and revolution. The state progressively became weaker as inflation paralyzed its organizations and corruption became more rampant.

In this early modern period after the turn of the century the organizers of production within agriculture and handicraft had worked as usual to expand production. After World War I, their efforts began to founder because of disturbances in world markets where China traded and because of the on-again, off-again civil war with its numbing effects on the economy at home. During the next two decades farm and handicraft production wildly fluctuated without any upward or downward trend. By the 1940s the production trend was one of persistent decline.

Economic Dualism

The economic development characteristics of this 1895 to 1949 period were the following. China had experienced a rapid industrial spurt after 1900, but this modern development was confined to the treaty ports, which first opened to foreign trade in the mid-nineteenth century. Modest railroad development also took place, but the trunk lines were built mainly in the north. Some telegraph communications had been constructed, and modern banking institutions under foreign and Chinese management also had emerged with the treaty ports. However, scarcely any real economic change had occurred in agriculture and handicraft. Their production very slowly expanded until World War I, and then appears to have stagnated thereafter. Thus, a small modern sector had evolved by 1937, but without exerting any profound influence on the rest of the economy. This pattern of *dualism*—a small modern sector growing alongside a large, unchanging agricultural and handicraft sector—persisted until 1949. Under these circumstances, per capita income increased only slowly, often erratically, while population slowly expanded.

Manufacturing Sector, 1914–1933   The gradual changes prior to 1949 and the more rapid changes after 1949 are presented in statistical form in table 1–3. Since economists prefer rates of growth or changes in ratios to analyze and assess economic change or the lack of it, table 1–3 is given in percentages. For the moment, let us examine only economic change between 1914–1918 and 1933.

TABLE 1–3.   *Estimates of Chinese Economic Growth*

	1914–1918	1931–1936	1952–1957	1972–1977
Economic Indicators				
GDP (billion 1933 yuan)	24.26	29.13	37.97	102.52
Population (millions)	440.0	500.0	602.0	897.0
GDP per capita (yuan/person)	55.1	58.3	63.1	114.2
Average Annual Rate of Growth				
GDP		1.08%	1.27%	5.00%
Population		0.75%	0.89%	2.00%
GDP per capita		0.33%	0.38%	3.00%
Sectoral Share				
Agriculture	65.9%	62.9%	53.6%[1]	33.0%[2]
Manufacturing	16.2%	18.9%	18.5%[1]	39.0%[2]
Services	17.9%	18.2%	27.9%[1]	28.0%[2]
Gross Domestic Investment				
1933 Prices	—	5.0%	16.0%	20.–23.%

[1] Data for 1958.

[2] Data for 1977.

Source: Data for 1914–1918, 1931–1936, and 1952–1957 compiled from K. C. Yeh, "China's National Income, 1931–36," in The Institute of Economics, *Conference on Modern Chinese Economic History* (Taipei: The Institute of Economics, Academia Sinica, 1978), pp. 125–58.
Data for 1972–1977 are estimates by author based on extrapolation of 1952–1958 data according to various rates of growth.
The growth rates for the expansion of China's GDP and GDP per capita for the first half of the twentieth century are nearly the same as those estimated by Subramanian Swamy in his essay, "The Response to Economic Challenge: A Comparative Economic History of China and India, 1870–1952," *The Quarterly Journal of Economics* 93, no. 1 (February 1979): 25–46.

Between World War I and 1933 the GDP is estimated to have grown slightly more rapidly (24.26–29.13 billion yuan) than population (440–500 million) so as to generate a faster growth of per capita income than during the Ch'ing period—an increase of nearly .3 percent per annum.* The motor force for this growth was the rise of the small modern manufacturing sector in the treaty ports. As the sources of growth were confined to these port centers, the expansion of income accrued mainly to the port cities' residents—particularly to the wealthy ones. Income distribution, therefore, became more unequal as little or no improvement in countryside income took place. As can be seen in table 1–3, the manufacturing sector's contribution to GDP rose by several percentages, as did services, and thus reflected this development, whereas agriculture's contribution slightly declined.

The growth of the modern sector was also reflected in the expansion of industrial output between 1916 and 1933: pig iron rose to 471,000 tons in 1933 compared to 199,000 tons in 1916; coal output stood at 22.1 million tons compared to 9.5 million tons; cement at 737,000 tons compared to 105,000 tons; electrical power at 2.1 billion kilowatt-hours compared to .11 billion kwh; and railway freight of 4.77 million tons per kilometer compared to 2.94 billion ton-km.

Agricultural Sector, 1914–1933 While the supply of food grains and industrial crops easily kept pace with population expansion from the 1870s to World War I, the agricultural sector did not grow commensurately with the modern sector. Between World War I and the mid-1930s wheat production climbed to 23.5 million metric tons compared to 20.4 million metric tons—only a .9 percent growth rate. Rice production rose from 43.2 to 50.0 million metric tons or a .9 percent growth rate, and cotton declined from 800,000 to 500,000 metric tons. More significantly, as very large output fluctuations occurred between these terminal years and some crops expanded while other declined, agriculture probably barely kept pace with population growth.

Capital Formation, 1914–1933 The reader should carefully note in table 1–3 several characteristics of Chinese economy between 1914 and 1933: the country's population size and growth and the economy's capacity to save and finance capital goods production. First, by World War I China's enormous population surpassed the level it had attained in 1850 before rebellions rocked the empire and before an estimated twenty to fifty million people perished. In spite of civil war, disease, and famine, which occurred intermittently in different provinces during the 1920s, population continued to grow slowly at a rate of around .7 percent per year. This population growth probably just began to exceed the long-term population growth rate of the Ch'ing period.

---

*These Gross Domestic Product estimates exclude the valuation of economic activities of Chinese nationals abroad and the remittances they sent home. Gross National Product estimates include such valuation.

Secondly, while the accuracy of the 5 percent gross domestic capital formation in 1933 can be questioned (see table 1–3), it roughly conforms to the capacity of the economy to save at this time. The country was exceedingly poor, and some of the current output was being used to wage war or support the military. The bulk of savings was channeled to the small modern sector, where combined with foreign capital, it produced the investment in capital formation required to establish factories, mines, and railroads.

Employment and Income Distribution

By 1913 China's population was around 430 million, and it probably reached 500 million in 1933 (see table 1–3). As the share of population below fifteen years of age had also expanded, the pressures to provide employment and maintain living standards mounted. These new demands were not met after 1911. When the imperial government fell and subsequent efforts failed to establish a constitutional government fully in control of the country, regional warlords and their armies caused havoc. Meanwhile, during this interwar period the world economy did not grow as it had in the late nineteenth century, and violent shifts in world demand for China's exports caused more production difficulties at home. Finally, the goverment could no longer contain the devastating effects of natural disasters as it did during imperial times. These new forces eroded the favorable spread effects of the treaty ports and produced severe economic fluctuations. As a result, unemployment in the 1920s rose, and a 1933 yearbook source tried to estimate the total as follows:

> The progress or decline of our country's industry and commerce depends upon the annual repetition of calamities abroad, domestic disorders, and natural disasters. These factors have ruined our economy, impaired industry and commerce, caused production to stagnate and made the problem of unemployment more serious. According to statistics in 1925 the total unemployed in the country came to 168,332,000. The proportion of able-bodied workers of the total population was estimated at 70 percent or about 305,266,000 persons. Various statistical reports show rural workers to number 87,218,000, coolie laborers [unskilled] 34,887,000, industrial workers [semi and skilled] 1,744,000, handicraft workers and artisans 13,082,000 to make a grand total of 136,931,000. As this industrial work force was smaller than the number of able-bodied workers, the total number of unemployed was around 168,335,000 persons.[12]

As crudely estimated as this 1925 unemployment figure is, it is conceivable from the general reports of that year that unemployment had reached one hundred million or more—roughly one out of every three able-bodied workers. As questionable as these figures are, they suggest high unemployment levels, which are not contradicted by the vivid descriptions of unrest and misery of this decade. Unemployment continued to remain high in the 1930s and through the 1940s.

Under these conditions, income distribution was bound to become more unequal. Stagnant production in the countryside and the slow expansion of the modern sector in the treaty port cities caused more income to be concentrated in the hands of the wealthy. Those in the countryside who lost their sources of income and could not find work incurred debts and ultimately sold some or all of their land. Between 1929 and 1933 some redistribution of landownership occurred as a result of such sales, and land distribution in this brief period probably became more unequal. These general conditions of hardship and uncertainty continued and even worsened through the war years and the hyperinflation period that followed.

MODERN ECONOMIC GROWTH: THE ECONOMIC REVOLUTION

If slow, faltering, modern economic growth characterized the first three decades of the century, rapid, modern economic growth became a reality after 1950 as table 1–3 clearly shows. Gross domestic product expanded very rapidly in the early 1950s and slowed only slightly after 1957. The growth rate of per capita income also increased rapidly at first (1952–1957) and then stabilized at around 3.0 percent (1957–1970). By 1977 per capita income was about twice that of the 1950s. If a 3 percent growth rate for per capita income is maintained until the year 2000, China's per capita income would again double. As the gross domestic and per capita estimates in table 1–3 are expressed in 1933 yuan prices, a conversion into U.S. dollar figures produces very low figures. Therefore, if we refer to estimates in 1977 U.S. dollars by the CIA, the 1977 U.S. dollar per capita income figure is 370. If this amount roughly doubled by 2000, China's per capita income would be only $740, still a very low per capita income level and a very poor country.

This rapid growth from a very low per capita income platform was made possible by the rapid expansion of modern manufacturing. Its contribution to GDP rose from 18 percent in the 1950s to nearly 40 percent over a two-decade period, while agriculture's contribution rapidly fell (see table 1–3). Between 1949 and 1977 the annual rate of growth for all industry was about 13 percent, while the growth rate for agriculture was around 4 percent. Thus, the rates of growth of all economic sectors have been swift enough to label this period as an "economic revolution."

The spurt in industrial production along with the rapid structural changes in the economy could not have occurred without a great increase in capital stock. To allocate such a high proportion of current output for capital goods production means a very high ratio of savings to GDP. Depending upon the prices used to estimate capital, this ratio rose to around 20 percent by the 1970s (see table 1–3). This is indeed a high ratio to maintain at such a low per capita income level.

Population Growth and Distribution

By 1949 China's population was still premodern in character and in excess of a half billion people. About 10 percent resided in cities—a slight increase over the late nineteenth century urbanization rate. Certain regions had attained very high population densities, and remote regions in the northeast, northwest, and southwest were rapidly filling up. What changes occurred to this population as modern economic growth commenced?

Between 1949 and 1977 the rate of growth of the population more than doubled—from .71 percent before 1933 to 2.01 percent in the 1970s—(see table 1–3), and is not likely to fall below 1 percent for the rest of this century. The implications of such growth for an already-large Chinese population are profound. In fact, such a sustained growth at even 1 percent from 1980 to the year 2000 could produce a population as low as 1,175 million or as high as 1,480 million depending upon how fertility and death rate changes.

Until 1957 the Chinese managed to record their population, but political campaigns and violent policy changes disrupted their reporting system. Attempts followed in 1964 and again in the 1970s to count people accurately, but a reliable official statement of total population for the mid-1970s is still not available. A count of provincial population totals for mid-1976 shows 893.9 million, and various estimates range from 938.1 to 968.0 for the end of 1976.[13] The CIA estimates 950.7 million. For general purposes let us examine the implications of a 950 million population for 1976.

Population in the 1950s grew at more than 2 percent per year, and only by the mid-1970s did the annual growth rate decline, perhaps to around 1.6 percent. An analysis of Chinese mortality and fertility rates based on the population structure for 1953 produces the following results. The death rate, around 34 per thousand in 1949, has dropped to around 9 per thousand; the birth rate, which stood at 45 per thousand, has fallen to around 25 per thousand. Because of the very rapid growth produced by this disparity from an already-huge population, the 1976 population still had premodern characteristics: About 37 percent of the population was still under fifteen years of age, with males slightly in excess of females. Perhaps not until the year 2000 will the population in China assume truly modern attributes. By then, the death rate should be around 8 per thousand and the birth rate around 20 per thousand; the proportion of the population under fifteen years of age will be only 28 percent. But the population will stand at around 1,328 million and increase at a natural rate of around 13 percent, which means adding around 17 million people to society each year.

Did the spatial distribution of China's population radically change over this modern period as it did during the eighteenth and nineteenth centuries? Two policies affecting population distribution have been initiated and carried out by the Chinese government: (1) encouraging large-scale migration to the northeast, northwest, and southwest, and (2) sending urban youth to the countryside to live and work. The former began as early as 1951 and continues to the present. The latter dates from the Great Cultural Revolution period (1966–1969) but in late 1978 seems to have been halted. Between 1953 and 1970, perhaps as many as 12.2 million migrants moved to Sinkiang, Kansu-Ningsia, Heilungkiang, Inner Mongolia, and Tsinghai.[14] Estimates vary, but as many as 10 million young people have left the cities, at one time or another, to work in the countryside, although many secretly returned.

The urban population, sparked by a great outpouring from the villages to the cities, rapidly mushroomed until 1956. The share of total population living in cities rose from 10 to 14 percent. In 1957 the government desperately clamped down on the rural-to-urban migration, and reduced it to a trickle. No figures on urban population size have been published since 1956. Since the rate of population growth in cities very likely is below that of the countryside, no more than 20 percent of the population probably live in cities today.

Employment and Income Distribution

The new socialist government created in 1949 did not bring about full employment immediately. In fact, urban unemployment remained as high as 5 million until 1958 because of the spillover of rural people seeking work in cities. State-initiated institutional and organizational reforms have made possible very high, if not nearly full, employment in this labor-abundant economy. Mobilizing this huge population to work remains one of the impressive achievements of the People's Republic of China (PRC).

Government Control of Labor   Partitioning cities into "wards" and ultimately into "blocks" has given the new regime the urban organizations wherewith to record all families. Further, every economic unit to which a worker is attached pays income and distributes ration coupons. In the countryside the commune administrative unit contains the brigades and production teams that record each worker's compensation; these teams also mobilize the work force. As every able-bodied worker is attached to some kind of economic unit or administrative body, full-scale mobilization and allocation of the work force according to plan has become possible. While some evasion does occur and widespread shirking often exists, urban and rural commune organizations still have been able to find work for their members when political upheavals were not taking place, as was the case between 1966 and 1969 and again from 1975 to 1977. Estimates of the urban and rural workforce size vary greatly because no reliable information on population size, rural and urban share of population, and labor participation rates is available. Therefore, different assumptions are adopted to estimate these figures. Because of the regime's effective organizational controls, rural workers since 1957 rarely wandered into the cities, and employment has been found for them and their urban counterparts. For this reason, as rural industry rapidly develops, China will adhere more to a premodern employment structure than other developing countries will. The rate of urbanization will rise only very slowly, and the towns and small cities in and near communes will continue to retain their labor.

Property Redistribution   The land reform between 1947 and 1952 eliminated the ownership of real estate and land in excess of roughly a half acre. It did not eliminate outright the farmers euphemistically referred to as "rich and middle peasants." In Kiangsu province even by 1952 the households of middle peasants operated farms 40 percent larger than did the poor families who had little land at all to farm. But private, family farming disappeared by 1957 because all households were compelled in the previous year to give their tools and farm animals to village cooperatives and to forego the income from land they once owned. The redistribution of property transformed every household into a wage-earning unit, or team, whose labor force size dictated the income the household could now earn.

Equalizing Income Distribution   The new team farming system, under which households farmed the land in production teams, operated with a much more equal distribution of income than had been the case under the old family farming system. Several attempts to measure income distribution for rural communities in the 1950s have produced Gini coefficient values ranging from as low as .17 to only .25— very low indeed compared to prewar measures for land distribution.[15]

Although property rights were also redistributed in cities and all households were ultimately compelled to earn only wage income plus interest on savings deposits in branches of the People's Bank, large wage differentials among city residents still existed.

Recent visitors to China have reported monthly wages in Shanghai machine tool plants ranging from a low of 42 to a high of 124 yuan per month. At the same time the rural-urban wage differential undoubtedly was lower than in the prewar period, yet considerable difference still existed. The average urban industrial worker probably earned around 50 yuan per month in the early 1970s. When this amount is compared to a monthly wage of 42 yuan per month for workers on the most advanced communes, the rural-urban income difference is very small. But the advanced communes make up less than 5 percent of the countryside's communes. The monthly worker's wage in a very poor commune is about 12 yuan per month. The average monthly wage in much of the countryside is perhaps still only one-third of the urban worker's monthly income. In spite of such differences, whether we point to factories in cities and compare towns with the countryside, wage differentials have been reduced from that of the prewar period. When we consider the elimination of property income that took place during the 1950s, we can conclude that income distribution since 1949 has become more equal.

SUMMARY AND COMPARISONS: CHINA'S UNIQUE ECONOMIC DEVELOPMENT PATTERN

The bird's eye view of economic development given so far demands some final remarks. For convenience, we have identified three distinct phases of economic development: (1) premodern economic development, (2) early modern economic development, and (3) modern economic growth or the economic revolution. We can now compare the key features of each of these phases with those in other countries' economic development experiences to highlight unique aspects of Chinese economic history in recent times.

China's traditional growth phase, the period of *premodern economic development,* of course, dates well before the late seventeenth century, but from this time onward certain facts become more obvious. Population expansion began with a very unequal distribution of wealth and income. But slow steady economic growth reversed this distribution ever so slightly. State policies helped to achieve this, and the private sector vigorously responded to these as well. The result was that population growth rarely was interrupted by severe Malthusian checks arising from extreme pressure upon food grain supply and attendant shortages of goods and services. Unlike continental Europe prior to 1750, which did experience great fluctuations in population growth caused chiefly by poor harvests, malnutrition, and disease, the Chinese population steadily expanded to over 400 million people by 1850 without violent swings in population growth. The reasons for this remarkable growth pattern will be examined in later chapters.

Some claims to property rights shifted from the public to the private sector, and even within the private sector the proportion of property-owning households rose. While many Chinese still found earning a living difficult even by the late nineteenth century, a higher proportion of people now owned land and were integrated into villages and market towns than had been the case in the late seventeenth century. But per capita income probably increased very little, if at all, by the mid-nineteenth century. The dislocations to the economy caused by the Taiping rebellions very likely reduced per capita income slightly. Then, between 1870 and World War I per capita income barely increased, if at all, as population slowly recovered and once again assumed its traditional rate of growth.

To be sure, the GDP produced by factors of production still originated mainly from agriculture and handicraft where labor-intensive methods predominated, and where the primary sources of energy were human, animal, and solar. Furthermore, the structure of interest rates for loanable funds remained unchanged over the period. Nor did any great change occur in relative prices for goods or services or for factor services such as rent, wages, and profits. This is to say that scarcities both in factor and product markets were continually offset by subtle and pervasive adjustments from the demand and supply sides of the two markets.

The story is quite different in Europe prior to 1750. Already for the high Middle Ages waterpower had become widely used. A large share of agricultural output went to support livestock, and thus, the further development of animal power was made possible. By the seventeenth century a long-term decline for interest rates had occurred. By the same period the continent began experiencing a profound revolution in the structure of prices because of the great influx of precious metals from the New World. Directly associated with this change in prices was a shift in terms of trade between agriculture and industry, so that many industries earned more profits. Changes in relative prices for factor services and for goods and services encouraged technological change and the production of more capital goods. By 1750 the old European economic order was rapidly breaking up.

In 1895 China entered a new phase—early *modern economic development*. This period saw the influence of foreign trade and capital in the country and a commitment by the imperial government to initiate reforms aimed at speeding up economic growth. But this gradual economic development did not bring about far-reaching change for all of the economy. China's new pattern of economic growth probably best resembles that of some Eastern European countries after the 1880s: Modern manufacturing grew very rapidly; modest advances in infrastructure development occurred, such as transportation and communications; yet agriculture remained backward and either grew slowly or stagnated. This pattern certainly was characteristic of China until 1937 when war disrupted economic growth altogether.

Contrary to some opinion, China's new dependency upon foreign markets and the activities of foreign business leaders in the country did not hinder, but rather stimulated economic growth in the early modern period. The failure of China to unify itself and protect its territorial sovereignty from foreign encroachment was rooted in the inability of a new generation of leaders to solve the political problem of how to establish a new constitutional government that could manage this huge country. As later chapters will demonstrate, the parties organizing production and distribution in the newly emerging modern sector did so under extremely adverse conditions. Farmers and merchants in the traditional sector meanwhile had to cope with difficulties beyond their powers to resolve. What is perhaps unique in China's case during this short-lived phase is that the modern sector was able to develop at all and that it did so without assistance from the state. In other developing countries, like Japan, where the state became committed to launching modern economic growth and political stability was the rule rather than the exception, the pattern of early modern economic development was very different from China's: improvement of agriculture alongside the rapid growth of modern manufacturing; rapid expansion of a modern infrastructure to promote economic development such as education, transportation, and public health. Therefore, China is a special case, and the gradual modernization that did occur in no small measure made possible the economic revolution that followed after 1949.

The final phase of economic growth in China—the period of *modern economic growth*—has captured much of the world's interest. Certainly nothing quite like it had ever occurred in China's past. Since 1949 the country began to have unprecedented growth rates for manufacturing, agricultural production, population, and per capita income. These ingredients combined to produce a sharp shift in the former economic structure that had heavily depended upon agriculture and handicraft. In this newly emerging economic structure manufacturing contributed a rising share to gross domestic production, and the share of agriculture declined. Even more remarkable was that while restructuring of the economy rapidly took place, the pattern of income distribution became more equal instead of unequal as had been typical for both early- and latecomers to modern economic development. Furthermore, the structure of employment still remained very traditional with the rate of urbanization rising only very modestly.

These features of China's recent past take on a different perspective when compared to the economic development pattern of other modernizing countries on a quantitative basis. Table 1–4 presents a quantitative comparison of the rates of total product (GNP), population, and product per capita at the initial period when rapid economic development began in China, in developed countries, and in less-developed countries.

One of the central findings of Simon Kuznets's study of how developed countries achieved modern development is that modern economic growth begins when the rate of growth of product or per capita income expands rapidly on a sustained basis. A glance at table 1–4 shows that for the West European countries, the United States, Canada, Australia, and even Japan and the USSR, sustained growth was also the case during the nineteenth and twentieth centuries. Even though the rate of population expansion quickened because mortality declined more rapidly than fertility, total product grew more rapidly than population. Very simply put, a revolution in production and distribution had taken place because of the application of modern technology to manufacturing and agriculture. As a result, the traditional economic structure began to change. Employment in manufacturing and services grew, but agricultural employment declined. The contribution of manufacturing and services to the GNP rose whereas for agriculture it fell.

The reader should note that in table 1–4 the developing countries beginning their modern economic growth before or after World War II obtained very high rates of growth for total product, population, and per capita income. In some instances, their growth rates even exceeded the rates of the developed countries. But the time period for comparison is not always the same. Jamaica, Ghana, Philippines, Egypt, and India achieved rapid growth rates within only fifteen years or so. They might not be able to sustain these rapid growth rates for the remainder of the century. Of course, the same possibility might occur in China, which—except for the USSR and Jamaica—achieved the highest product per capita growth rate.

What makes the rates of growth for China so impressive, however, is that China began its modern economic growth from a very low per capita income—even lower than Japan's, and India's. The developed countries initiated their modern economic growth from a per capita income level far higher than 200 U.S. dollars, and even today's developing countries began from a level much above 100 U.S. dollars. Whether China can continue to adopt modern technology so that its rapid economic growth can continue is problematic. The future growth prospects in the country will be discussed in the final chapter. China's

TABLE 1-4. Rates of Growth of Total Product, Population, Product per Capita, and Estimated Product per Capita at Initial Date of Period of Modern Growth for China, Developed Countries, and Less Developed Countries

Country	Period	Duration of Period (years)	Rates of Growth — Total Product	Total Population	Product per Capita	Estimated GNP per Capita (1965 U.S.) at Base Date of Period
China	1952–1972	20.0	72.9%	24.1%	37.0%	61%
United Kingdom	1801/11–1831/41	30.0	32.1%	15.4%	14.5%	227% (1765–1785)
France	1831/40–1861/70	30.0	26.3%	3.9%	21.6%	242% (1831–1840)
Belgium	1900/04–1925/29	25.0	19.6%	6.0%	12.8%	326% (1865)
Netherlands	1860/70–1890/99	30.0	20.3%	11.7%	7.6%	492% (1865)
Germany	1880/89–1905/13	24.5	32.9%	13.5%	17.0%	302% (1850–1859)
Norway	1885/94–1905/14	20.0	24.9%	9.2%	14.3%	287% (1865–1869)
Sweden	1885/94–1925/29	20.0	38.8%	7.1%	29.6%	215% (1861–1869)
Italy	1885/99–1925/29	30.0	24.6%	6.5%	16.9%	271% (1895–1899)
Japan	1885/94–1905/14	20.0	39.8%	11.4%	25.5%	74% (1874–1879)
United States	1869/78–1889/98	20.0	50.7%	13.5%	32.8%	— —
Canada	1870/74–1890/99	22.5	50.0%	24.7%	20.3%	474% (1836–1843)
Australia	1861/69–1890/99	29.5	41.8%	13.2%	25.2%	508% (1870–1874)
Argentina	1900/04–1925/29	25.0	45.1%	36.9%	6.0%	760% (1861–1869)
Mexico	1925/29–1963/67	38.0	57.0%	40.2%	12.0%	443% (1900–1904)
Jamaica	1950/52–1963/66	13.5	59.0%	30.0%	22.3%	215% (1925–1929)
Ghana	1950/54–1963/67	13.0	110.5%	18.5%	77.7%	232% (1950–1952)
Philippines	1950/54–1963/67	13.0	49.1%	30.6%	14.2%	263% (1950–1954)
Egypt	1945/46–1963/66	17.5	77.8%	36.7%	30.0%	181% (1950–1954)
India	1952/58–1963/67	17.5	65.4%	27.4%	29.8%	117% (1945–1949)
India		10.0	41.4%	26.1%	12.2%	77% (1952–1958)
European Russia	1860–1914	53.0	30.2%	13.8%	14.4%	— — —
USSR	1913–1958	45.0	35.7%	6.4%	27.4%	— — —
	1928–1958	30.0	53.8%	6.9%	43.9%	— — —

Source: Simon Kuznets, Economic Growth of Nations: Total Output and Production Structure (Cambridge, Mass.: Belknap Press of Harvard University, 1971), pp. 11–14, 24, 30–31, 38–40.

low per capita income in the 1930s and early 1950s means that per capita income had to be very low in the late seventeenth century. Consequently, the expansion of the economic system with steady population growth cannot have taken place from a level of per capita income very much below 50 U.S. dollars. For the premodern economic phase, then, the same growth rate for total product and population of around .2 or .3 percent seems to have been plausible. This rate implies an increase of total product by 30 or 40 percent every century, but scarcely any significant improvement in per capita income.

QUESTIONS FOR DISCUSSION

1. When the developed countries began their phase of modern economic growth, income distribution seems to have become slightly more unequal. Why? Only after sustained per capita income growth did income distribution begin to equalize. Why? What was the likely long-term trend of income distribution in China from the late seventeenth century until the 1930s?

2. What are the characteristics of modern economic growth? How typical has China's economic growth experience been in the last quarter century? What are the necessary conditions that must be met for China to sustain its modern economic growth?

3. What were the general characteristics of China's population in the 1930s and 1950s? Had these features changed since the late nineteenth and early twentieth centuries? What are the implications of such a population structure for economic growth?

4. How could China have gradual modern economic growth during the first three decades of the twentieth century with a savings to the Gross Domestic Product ratio of only 5 percent?

5. What factors account for the low urbanization rate in late imperial China? How would these factors influence the distribution of income and employment?

NOTES

1. "Ch'ing-shih kao" [A Draft History of Ch'ing History], Shih-huo-chih [Food and Commodities] (Taipei: Kuo-fang yen-chiu-yuan, 1961), vol. II, pt. 1, p. 1443.

2. Leo A. Orleans, Every Fifth Child: The Population of China (Stanford, Calif.: Stanford University Press, 1972), p. 127 for a discussion of the 1953 population structure.

3. Yeh-chien Wang, Land Taxation in Imperial China, 1750–1911 (Cambridge, Mass.: Harvard University Press, 1973), p. 87.

4. G. William Skinner, ed., *The City in Late Imperial China* (Stanford, Calif.: Stanford University Press, 1977), pp. 211–20. The following paragraphs rely exclusively upon Skinner's important work.

5. Gilbert Rozman, *Urban Networks in Ch'ing China and Tokugawa Japan* (Princeton, N.J.: Princeton University Press, 1973), pp. 14 and 104.

6. Lo Ehr-kang, "T'ai-p'ing t'ien-kuo ko-ming ch'ien ti jen-k'ou ya-p'o went'i" [Population Pressure prior to the Taiping Rebellion], in *Chung-kuo chin-tai-shih lun-ts'ung* [Collected Essays on the Modern History of China] (Taipei, 1958), vol. 2, p. 69.

7. Li Wen-chih, ed., *Chung-kuo chin-tai nung-yeh-shih tzu-liao* [Historical Materials on Modern China's Agriculture] (Peking: San-lien shu-tien, 1957), vol. I, pp. 62–63.

8. Jigyōbu rinji sangyō chōsakyoku, *Tochi kankei narabi ni kankō hen* [A Ccmpendium on Land Relationships and Customs] (Hsinkyo: Manshu tosho kabushiki kaisha, 1937), pp. 157–60.

9. Ramon H. Myers, "Socioeconomic Change in Villages of Manchuria during the Ch'ing and Republican Periods: Some Preliminary Findings," *Modern Asian Studies* 10, no. 4 (1976): 616. The *Gini coefficient* measures the ownership distribution for a population or group of owners. A high coefficient indicates inequality of distribution whereas a low coefficient value shows the opposite.

10. Chung-li Chang, *The Income of the Chinese Gentry* (Seattle: University of Washington Press, 1962), pp. 196–98.

11. Simon Kuznets, *Economic Growth of Nations: Total Output and Production Structure* (Cambridge, Mass.: Belknap Press of Harvard University, 1971).

12. P'eng Tse-i, comp., *Chung-kuo chin-tai shou-kung-yeh shih tzu-liao* [Materials on the History of Handicraft Industries in Modern China], 4 vols. (Peking: San-lien shu-tien, 1957), vol. III, p. 66.

13. John S. Aird, "Recent Provincial Population Figures," *China Quarterly* 73 (March 1978) : 1–44.

14. Leo A. Orleans, *Every Fifth Child*, p. 91.

15. Mark Blecher, "Income Distribution in Small Rural Chinese Communities," *China Quarterly* 68 (December 1976): 797–816.

SELECTED READINGS

1. Albert Feuerwerker. *The Chinese Economy, ca. 1870–1911,* Michigan Papers in Chinese Studies No. 5. Ann Arbor: Center for Chinese Studies, University of Michigan, 1969.

2. ———. *The Chinese Economy, 1912–1949,* Michigan Papers in Chinese Studies No. 1. Ann Arbor: Center for Chinese Studies, University of Michigan, 1968.

3. Robert F. Dernberger. "The Role of the Foreigner in China's Economic Development, 1840–1949." In Dwight H. Perkins, ed., *China's Modern Econo-*

my in Historical Perspective. Stanford, Calif.: Stanford University Press, 1975, pp. 19–48.

4. Dwight H. Perkins. "Growth and Changing Structure of China's Twentieth-Century Economy." In Perkins, ed., *China's Modern Economy,* pp. 115–66.

5. Alexander Eckstein. *China's Economic Revolution.* Cambridge: Cambridge University Press, 1977, chapter 6.

6. Leo A. Orleans. *Every Fifth Child: The Population of China.* Stanford, Calif.: Stanford University Press, 1972, chapters 2 and 6.

7. Simon Kuznets. *Economic Growth of Nations: Total Output and Production Structure.* Cambridge, Mass.: Belknap Press of Harvard University, 1971, chapters 1, 7, and 8.

Analytic Frameworks

China's unique pattern of economic development requires an explanation. Two principal theories—one from Marx, the other by Malthus—are used to explain China's economic history during the past half millennium. These theories, however, are directed at two questions that are quite different from those of this study. The first question addresses the long-standing concern of why capitalism never evolved in China as had been the case in Western Europe. The second question asks why the Chinese economy after the eleventh century merely grew larger in size but never developed any different kind of system of production and distribution. Both questions are interrelated. Could the weakness of capitalism itself be the reason why the Chinese economic system expanded while its technology, economic organizations, and market structures hardly changed? On the other hand, could capitalism never develop from within the Chinese economic system to fundamentally alter it because apparently the preconditions for capitalism were too weak or because some set of relationships discouraged its evolution?

The visions of Marx and Malthus have dominated the historiography interpreting why capitalism has not emerged in China or why the economy and society simply reproduced themselves and expanded, but never really basically changed their form. The important relationships at the heart of these two different approaches deserve discussion in the next section. However, since this text is more concerned with the question of how this economy expanded to such a huge size before modern economic growth commenced, a different analytic framework is needed. Furthermore, the same broad framework ought to apply to the other two questions: Why did modern economic growth come so late to China, and when it did, why did it falter? And why was modern economic growth after 1949 so rapid in this poor and technologically backward society? The final section outlines an alternative analytic framework to answer these questions.

THE MARXIAN ANALYSIS

Marx postulated that two basic socioeconomic relationships were fundamental for understanding different stages of history: the mode of production and its corresponding system of distribution. The *mode of production* was that particular system of how the means of production—capital and other resources—were controlled and used by socioeconomic units or classes in society. The output of goods and services produced by a particular mode of production then had to be distributed between classes in society. This *distribution*, moreover, was mainly determined by which classes controlled the means of production and how much of the *surplus*—that amount above the necessary and allowable consumption of goods and services by those not in control of the means of production—was to be retained by the dominant classes. If we understand the mode of production and how the economic surplus was distributed and used, we are then in a position to interpret the key turning points in human history and the essential characteristics of the stages of history themselves.

Feudalism

Let us take the case of late imperial China, the Ch'ing period or that historical stage commonly referred to as "feudal" (*feng-chien chih-tu*) by Marxist scholars.[1] The mode of production of late feudal China was one of land relationships in which state officials and their assistants, landlords, merchants, and moneylenders controlled the means of production, namely land. Although land was freely purchased and sold, these four dominant groups gradually accumulated considerable land and the wealth associated with it. The masses of poor farmers, artisans, and laborers claimed the remainder—small, scattered plots—and depended upon their labor to earn a living. The powerful, wealthy feudal classes extracted chiefly rent and taxes from the masses as income, but these sources were supplemented by interest payments and extra income from monopoly-determined prices and monopsony-set wages from the rest of society. The surplus squeezed out of this economy by the feudal classes was expended partially for luxury consumption, but chiefly for supporting inefficient state organizations, the bureaucracy, and the military.

Early in the Ch'ing period the ruling classes did limit their extraction of surplus; in fact, they redistributed some of it as subsidy or support for the poor to reclaim and farm new land, restore and construct new water control and irrigation projects, and improve the economic infrastructure of roads, communities, and cities. This modest redistribution greatly encouraged the growth of the private sector. The Ch'ing rulers even eliminated the corvée so that for the first seventy-five years the economy prospered and population grew. But later in the period, this redistribution of surplus diminished, and the extraction of surplus became more severe—especially when the court had to suppress rebellion or military disturbances in one of its frontier regions.

Protocapitalism

Yet capitalism in a weak form had already sprouted and produced small buds. In medium and large towns some merchants organized silk weaving and dyeing, contracted master weavers to hire workers, and paid wages to these employees. Workers congregated at certain streets to hire themselves out so that a free-floating proletariat was emerging. In some villages managerial landlords (*ching-ying ti-chu*) hired workers to farm crops and later marketed the goods for a profit.[2] Another variant of this emerging cash-commodity nexus was wealthy *tenant-farmers*—individuals who rented land, hired laborers to work their fields, marketed the crops, and thus earned enough to pay rent and wages, as well as to receive a handsome profit to repeat the economic cycle.

Chinese Marxist scholars in the 1950s marshaled historical evidence to illustrate that these examples of protocapitalism had been evolving; the thrust of their research, naturally enough, was to confirm Mao Tse-tung's widely quoted statement that "the development of a commodity-exchange economy within Chinese feudal society nurtured an incipient capitalism, and had it not been for the influence of foreign capitalism, China would have developed into a capitalistic society."[3] But by the 1840s capitalism still remained stunted, fully incapable of provoking any crisis in the feudal order. How much time would have had to pass before these new production relationships could have challenged the feudal classes that constrained them is difficult to say. But by that decade Western capitalism had penetrated China.

The first Opium War of 1842 opened the door for Western trade.[4] First, the arrival of English merchants, then—soon afterward—the coming of businesspeople from other countries, and ultimately, the establishment of modern enterprises that produced for local consumption carried China to a new historical stage: a semicolonial and semifeudal social and economic system (*p'an chih-min-ti p'an feng-chien*). Complex changes in the mode of production and use of economic surplus gradually took place. The feudal classes still retained their claims to land, although by a musical chairs process of ownership and use turnover. Foreign business leaders needed the assistance of some Chinese who could provide services and assist them in their commercial transactions of buying and selling in the new city-port centers. As a result, a new Chinese business class called *compradores* soon emerged and in turn used its newly acquired wealth to set up its own firms, which often competed with the foreigner.

Bureaucratic Capitalism

The new Chinese capitalist class took advantage of commodity exchange and naturally purchased land so that both old and new means of production came under the control of new socioeconomic classes: Foreign and Chinese capitalists allied with feudal groups of landlords, merchants, and moneylenders. By the second quarter of the twentieth century a new official class comprised of members from the National People's party (Kuomintang) had begun to unify the country and modernize the economy. These bureaucrats frequently sought out wealthy Chinese business operators for loans and assistance and in turn favored the businesses with information and monopoly rights for trading and banking. Many bureaucrats also became extremely wealthy by starting their own businesses and purchasing land in order to join this new ruling class alliance. The 1930s and 1940s were thus called the era of "bureaucratic capitalism."

The economic surplus obtained by these new groups continued to grow but only a small portion of it went for promoting the growth of the modern industrial sector in the city-ports. Much of the surplus was used for unproductive purposes: squandered by the Ch'ing state on enterprises that failed to take off; wasted by warlords and their armies; drained overseas as loan repayment and indemnity transfers to foreign states, and profits for overseas business leaders; and spent for luxury consumption by the higher income groups.

Meanwhile, the new commodity exchange had produced new economic class relationships and spawned new crises. Among these new economic relationships were merchant-capitalist-organized industries such as cotton cloth weaving, food processing, and silk reeling, for which numerous rural hands were hired as wage earners. Another form was new cash crop farming such as tobacco and groundnuts by tenants and tenant-farmers who also hired their wage workers. In the cities a new industrial work force—made up of women in the cotton textile spinning industry and men in food processing, mining, and manufacturing—expanded.

Foreign trade meant cheap imports that displaced many handicraft industries and hurled artisans into the reserve army of unemployed. New trade opportunities encouraged agriculturalists and merchants to produce for export and thus gave rise to these new economic relationships. But the new trade ties also brought dependency, frequently followed by sudden, sharp shifts in international demand or by a domestic business recession which forced more persons into the ranks of the unemployed.

Meanwhile, the same exploitative arrangements in the marketplace, so familiar during the feudal period, persisted—sometimes worsening when the wealthy themselves were economically hard pressed. The consequences of severe economic exploitation, the decline in domestic handicraft, and the vicissitudes of the economy combined to produce rising unemployment, the loss of land by the poor, and the impoverishment of the bulk of the population. This trend allegedly took place at the same time that the economic surplus was being misallocated and squandered. On the demand side of the market, people were too poor to provide a strong, effective demand for goods and services. The very low per capita income made the mobilization of savings for investment impossible. The wealthy classes extracting the economic surplus either wasted or misused it so that on the supply side of the market few resources were mobilized for developing the modern sector. Class conflict in town and country became more severe as a result, and countless labor strikes and peasant protests erupted in the 1920s.

Development of Chinese Socialism

As China became more dominated by foreign control and was bled of its wealth and energy, socioeconomic decline and rising unemployment became widespread. When war broke out in 1937, the country could offer only feeble resistance to the Japanese aggressors and quickly yielded its principal cities and vast areas to enemy control. But in certain sections of the north and northeast new, administrative areas under the control of the Communist party and its military units began to emerge. These Communist groups initiated a new "democratic economic management" in which both feudal classes and the masses of farmers and poor were mobilized to increase production and resist the Japanese.[5] By 1949 this party and its army had successfully unified the country under its control, and China had entered a new historical stage: socialism.

Crucial to the Marxian analysis of long-term Chinese economic development are two considerations. First, the socioeconomic groups that controlled the means of production extracted a large economic surplus by means of their effective control over prices and incomes. Their monopoly control over organizations of distribution allowed them to charge prices much higher than those that would have existed under more competitive conditions. Similarly their monopsonistic control over resources allowed them to pay much lower incomes to workers than would have been the case had more competitive conditions prevailed. Second, these socioeconomic groups used only a small portion of the economic surplus for productive investment. Expenditures for ceremony and luxury consumption, in addition to sheer waste, left very little for accumulating capital or increasing the supply of the means of production. As a result the economy expanded only very slowly. Meanwhile, successive crises and disturbances to production cast more people into the ranks of the unemployed and impoverished society.

One study tried to measure the amount of economic surplus generated in 1933—a year when statistical data were most abundant.[6] The analysis measured the share of property income in *net domestic product* or the profits, rents, and interest accruing to those groups owning the means of production. It also attempted to estimate that portion of production value lost because of unemployment or factors of production at the time.

The study's findings showed that roughly one-third of the net domestic product could be regarded as economic surplus and this amount would fall to one-quarter if the economy could have achieved full employment. Of the total potential surplus two-thirds originated from agriculture and the remainder from outside it. How was this surplus used? Very little of the surplus was reinvested in agriculture; most of it went to the government or to expenditures for luxury goods.

Marxists argue that one of the major ways the new Communist state in 1949 launched rapid economic development was to redistribute this surplus by passing part of it to low-income groups to raise their consumption and investment levels, and by allocating the rest to investment in capital formation and to the revival of the war-torn economy. Redistribution of this economic surplus was drastic. The Communist party introduced land reform and later nationalized industry and much of commerce, and thereby expropriated nearly all property and its income from the former property-owning classes.

THE MALTHUSIAN ANALYSIS

Malthus observed that a complex relationship among technology, population, and available resources in any society inevitably produces two distinct trends. If technology improves, society's capability to produce more goods and services from a given resource base will increase. Rising living standards, however, encourage greater procreation and population expansion. The time eventually comes when population numbers press against the available resource base and the productivity of new entrants into the labor force steadily declines. Gradually, lower living standards for all result. The advent of either war, disease, or famine that arise from social and economic conditions of overcrowding and acute resource scarcity finally alter the balance between population and resources because of the loss of life and reduction in population growth itself.

Thus technological change leads to population growth, but ultimately population expansion outstrips the resource base unless technological change is continuous and successively raises labor productivity to keep producing a large economic surplus. If technology fails to increase resource productivity, the resulting imbalance between population and the available resource base can only be brought into a new equilibrium by various *Malthusian checks* to limit population growth and even reduce it. These checks are dreaded wars, plagues, and famines. This vision of Malthus certainly has influenced interpretations of China's economic past.

A Modified Neo-Malthusian Model

Mark Elvin has produced the most sophisticated interpretation of the relationship of long-term technological change, production, and population growth for China. His view owes much to the Malthusian legacy.[7] In all fairness to Elvin, however, we should not call his analysis entirely neo-Malthusian. Yet the important variables that Malthus postulated as critically interrelated also play a key role in Elvin's interpretative schema. Elvin was interested in what factors accounted for China's failure to take advantage of the important technological advances made during the eleventh and twelfth centuries— the Sung period—and to achieve modern economic development like that of Western Europe after the fourteenth and fifteenth centuries. Instead, China merely expanded to an incredible size and only refined a technology that essentially had originated by the twelfth century.

In 1313 Wang Chen's *Treatise on Agriculture* described the machine to reel silk. It could spin 130 pounds of thread every 24 hours, and some machines driven by water did even better. Every section of the country used these machines, and in many areas people relied upon them to manufacture hemp. Yet five hundred years later the same type of spinning machine was still in operation for silk spinning and cotton spinning; inferior implements were still being used. Scarcely any technological advance had occurred. This pattern of development illustrated the lack of technological progress in all areas of production and exchange.

Part of the reason for the absence of new inventions was that China turned inward after the fourteenth century and cut itself off from contact with other countries. Another reason was the emergence of new philosophical orientations that tried to establish some linkage between humankind's ordering of the terrestrial world and its comprehension of the cosmos.[8] This new orientation discouraged speculating and questioning about natural phenomena. But perhaps the most important reason, according to Elvin, was the improvements in transportation and marketing that continually corrected for any sharp change in relative prices that would have reflected critical resource scarcity and a production bottleneck.

The proliferation of small market towns across the rural landscape made more and more villages able to support themselves and to exchange with each other.[9] Merchants and their brokers moved from one market to another to respond to changes in demand and supply. If raw cotton became expensive in one area, merchants found ways to import it from another area so that the spinning and weaving of cotton cloth, alongside farming, continued in the village. Likewise, in other commodity lines, the market worked effectively to circumvent resource and commodity scarcity. For this reason, artisans had no incentives to tinker and discover new implements and techniques that would have made their tasks more profitable. Large relative price changes rarely occurred to provide a strong inducement for the discovery of labor-saving techniques.

The final factor was the creation of a large, free-floating work force formerly composed of a servile work force on rural manors in the rich alluvial lands of east central China. This work force liberated itself in the seventeenth century, fled to other provinces, and opened up new lands to farm. Food supply increased, and trade and market expansion quickly followed. This institutional change gave more people the incentive to produce for the market and expand the margin of cultivation into wasteland areas.

High-Level Equilibrium Trap   How did technology, population, and the resource endowment interact as a result of these concurrent developments? In brief, the population slowly grew as a result of the improvement in social status of large segments of society and the general peace and order restored by the new Manchu rulers after the 1680s. Gradual improvement of technology and the diffusion of the best technical practices in farming and handicraft enabled labor productivity to remain constant. As certain resources became scarce, market adjustments created substitutes so that production bottlenecks never became serious. Economic growth was slow but always accompanied by steady population expansion. This process could continue for some time, but not without a gradual reduction of the actual surplus that the labor force produced or the potential it could produce. The reason for this reduction was that technology had merely been refined but never substantially improved. The remarkable market organization and institutional changes that occurred after the seventeenth century and that supported huge population growth without fundamental economic development have been conceptualized by Elvin as a "high-level equilibrium trap."[10] This concept applies only to agriculture and can be described as follows.

The term *high-level* means that the Chinese economy had achieved impressive improvements in traditional technology alone so as to obtain very high productivity from its resources—especially land. In the 1930s Chinese crop yields were not too far below Western and Japanese crop yields, in spite of the fact that China was one of the largest food grain and fiber producers in the world. In rice, for example, Chinese yields were nearly 70 percent of Japanese rice yields, the world's highest at that time due to modern technology.

The concept *equilibrium* means that the Chinese economy had passed through stages of expansion whereby subsistence needs for the population had been adequately met. Ultimately a point would be reached when the maximum output that technology could produce would support a huge population only at subsistence. Until this equilibrium point was reached, however, the available surplus per head of population would diminish, and the potential surplus that could have been produced—had the best practices been utilized everywhere—also would decline. If population increased beyond this point, the familiar Malthusian checks soon limited population growth and then reduced it to the equilibrium level or below.

The notion of *trap* means that unless modern technology can be introduced, traditional technology becomes exhausted and produces no actual or potential surplus beyond the equilibrium point (see E_t in the figure in note 10). This trap occurs precisely where long-term population, technology, and resource endowment equilibrium has been reached. Elvin believes that by the end of the nineteenth century China was fast approaching its high-level equilibrium trap.

AN ALTERNATIVE EXPLANATION

The Marxian analysis postulates that socioeconomic class relationships are shaped by which classes control the means of production, how much of the economic surplus they can extract, and how they use that economic surplus to strengthen their political and social networks of support. Their efforts to claim this surplus are opposed by other classes, so that intense class struggle, especially rivalry to acquire power and achieve high status, occurs from time to time. Therefore, to understand how class relationships change is to understand history.

Malthusian analysis postulates that the relationship between population growth, technological change, and the resource endowment decidedly shapes the long-term development pattern of society.

When rapid population growth produces certain resource scarcities, these scarcities can be offset by technological changes that promote the development of alternative resources. If such technological changes fail to occur, some equilibrium balance must be restored between population and society's resources. To understand the mechanisms by which this new equilibrium balance is achieved is to understand the economic history of mankind before the modern era.

Both analytic methods have inspired much controversy in Chinese economic history. This text offers an alternative analytic framework that focuses upon the three problems already described in some detail. First, what accounts for China's ability to have expanded its population and productive capacity to such a huge magnitude without experiencing modern economic growth? Second, what accounts for China's protracted response to adopt modern technology from the West, and then when the country did begin to take advantage of it, how did modern economic growth spread? Finally, what accounts for the rapid growth rate achieved by the Chinese economy after 1949 from its appallingly low per capita income platform? The following section describes this analytic framework, and in the final section of this chapter the framework is applied to each of the central questions to elucidate how the historical evidence is organized and interpreted in succeeding chapters.

The Analytic Framework

Three basic relationships shape the history of how a society has organized its resources to produce goods and services, how its resources were used and allocated for such production, and how the final output was distributed between current consumption and future economic growth.

The first relationship involves that of state and society. The second is that of economic organizations and markets. The third is the relationship between technology and economic organizations. When we examine each of these relationships, it is essential to identify the important social groups that make the basic economic decisions. At the same time we want to analyze the important values or norms that shaped the political, economic, and social culture of each group. Having done this, we can discuss all three relationships in terms of how the Chinese economy organized its resources for production and distributed that output between current consumption and investment for future economic growth. But let us first note the historical context within which we discuss those social groups crucial for making the decisions that influence our three broad relationships.

Any economy's goods and services can be increased by enlarging the supply of resources such as land, labor, and capital and/or by making each of these resource units produce more by raising its productivity. Economic growth in the premodern epoch was characterized by the gradual expansion of society's resources with hardly any increase in resource productivity. On the other hand, modern economic growth is characterized by the sustained increase in productivity of resources, as well as by the expansion of resource supply—especially capital goods. We will see in the final chapters of this text that China's modern economic growth has been achieved principally by the expansion of resource supply and almost no growth of resource productivity. In China over the past three centuries our three basic relationships have interacted primarily to expand the supply of resources: first, very slowly prior to 1900; more rapidly after 1900; and then with breakneck speed after 1949.

Relationship of State and Society   In China the public sector or state historically possessed enough power to influence the behavior of society or the private sector. Except for periods of disunity, the state typically took the lead to initiate modest change or far-reaching transformation of society. Within the public sector the monarchy and its supporters—or in more recent times a political party and its organizations—used state power to control the distribution of property rights in society and even redistribute those rights as it saw fit. Social groups in the private sector responded by trying to preserve their property rights and, whenever possible, to expand these rights. If the state could also create a beneficial economic environment for the private sector, private social groups would receive powerful incentives to conduct their economic activity more efficiently and more vigorously.[11] Let us examine some of these state initiatives in more detail.

When the state passed new laws curtailing economic privilege or expropriated the wealth of certain groups, the distribution of property rights in society naturally changed. Such redistribution might compel groups who lost their special privileges to rely more upon the market to earn their living just as everyone else did. It also might entail the transfer of wealth from one group to others who formerly had little or no wealth. Whichever the case, if the state successfully makes the distribution of wealth more equal, it has given more members of society the opportunity to use their new wealth as they see fit and, in particular, to increase their property rights still further.

But to preserve or increase one's property rights means that one must acquire and try to increase a supply of resources to earn income. Many more people in society can do this if the state creates a favorable economic environment and does not compete with the private sector for resources to use for purposes that will hinder private individuals from pursuing their goals. To this end the state might do one or more of the following.

The state might introduce legal and fiscal reforms that will make property rights more secure and impose a lighter tax burden on property owners if they produce for the market. The state can direct its efforts toward expanding and improving the economy's infrastructure and consequently creating a favorable atmosphere for greater private individual economic activity. Examples of such state efforts include controlling water resources, standardizing the money supply, building roads, and promoting education. State power also can be used to subsidize the private sector in acquiring better access to resources—such as to assist households to reclaim and farm new lands or to render assistance when households have suffered from natural calamities. The state can make modern technology available to the private sector through policies of employing foreign experts, purchasing capital from abroad, establishing research institutes, and reforming the education system. Finally, the state can promote market expansion and activity by increasing the money supply to ensure that liquidity demands can be satisfied or by curtailing growth of the money supply to prevent inflation from disrupting the economy.

The powerholders in the state, whether an individual or a group, perceive how society and the economy ought to be organized. They formulate their policies to achieve their desired ends according to certain values. These values can stress the maintenance of social order and harmony and justify policies that adopt symbols, slogans, and actions to preserve the existing social hierarchy and ensure that society adheres to and complies with the cultural norms and ethical standards of the prevailing culture. In the case of imperial China, Confucianism embodied these values; for contemporary China, it is socialism. Such values place paramount importance upon social groups accommodating to policies of the state. But when rulers, like Mao Tse-tung in contemporary China, urged voluntaristic action by members of society to achieve goals set down by the state, they stressed different values— one governing state policies and the other, a newly transformed set of values, governing social relationships and behavior for all members of society.

Relationship of Economic Organizations and Markets   Economic organizations are made up of households or members representing such units, each with a hierarchy of decisionmakers having power to determine how to organize resources for production and exchange. These organizations can range from the simple household, such as the family farm to complex units like a company or bank. Economic organizations usually have the freedom and power to acquire claims to property rights and exchange these claims with each other. Their opportunity to take such action, however, depends upon policies of the state that regulate how much income and wealth they can acquire.

Economic organizations relate to each other through networks of markets, which can be open and competitive or closed and under monopoly control. In highly competitive markets, economic organizations must produce at the lowest unit cost and sell according to market demand. In markets where certain organizations possess considerable economic power to influence costs and price, the market values will diverge from those that would prevail had competitive conditions existed. Organizations can earn significant profits under both market conditions, but where organizations possess economic power their profits will be higher and will persist for longer periods. While it is not clear which market conditions are more likely to promote innovations in production and exchange, the prospects for financing innovations or technological change seem to be brighter where profits are high and stable over time.

Because economic organizations, whether simple or complex, must competitively bid for resources to carry on production, many will negotiate and establish contracts to minimize risk and to make certain they can hire resources at favorable terms. In particular, units that produce in part for self-sufficiency, as well as for the market, must hire certain resources that they currently lack so that production can be undertaken more efficiently. In premodern China households relied upon customary law procedures to engage in resource exchange, such as the leasing and renting of land or borrowing and lending credit.

When markets widen because of foreign trade, economic organizations gain greater access to new sources of technology and low-cost resources. New organizations will invariably appear in the marketplace to take advantage of these external sources, and they will create new methods of production and exchange, such as the modern factory in the treaty ports along the China coast.

Where economic organizations interact in markets to adjust quickly to eliminate scarcities, relative prices will remain stable over time, and windfall profits for firms will be rare. Windfall profits can be a sufficient but not a necessary condition for innovations. An economy also requires a cultural ethos that promotes tinkering and experimentation so that individuals will come forward with inventions and innovations to transform existing methods of production. Where market scarcities persist and become serious, commodity production might be adversely affected, and population welfare even decline. But should organizations recognize what items are responsible for causing acute resource or commodity scarcity, and should they earn sufficient profits because of the new market condition, they might be induced to find substitutes to offset these scarcities.

The members of those households belonging to economic organizations possess economic and social cultural values that govern their decisions and work behavior. If such values stress a strong work ethic, place a high value upon saving, and praise the virtue of accumulating wealth, households will take predictable actions to organize production and exchange for the market. Even where certain households adhere to social values emphasizing gift exchange, conducting elaborate ceremonies, and performing religious ritual, these beliefs still reinforce the economic cultural norms of hard work, thrift, and accumulation. This was the case of Confucian culture, which placed a high value upon the ritual and ceremony practiced by all households, and which served to inculcate in the individual the economic values to orient him or her to work for the corporate group, the household.

Relationship of Technology and Economic Organizations The relationship between technology and economic organizations must be viewed within the context of society's available resource endowment. Economic organizations must select between available technologies and choose one that will make maximum use of their abundant resources and conserve their scarce resources. In labor-abundant, land-scarce societies economic organizations will select those technologies that will make use of abundant labor and save the scarcer resource, land. If new technology becomes available that can augment scarce resources because new forms of capital can be used in production, new production possibilities are opened up for our labor-abundant, land-scarce economy.

SUMMARY AND APPLICATION OF THE FRAMEWORK

In premodern times an economy achieved growth by the gradual expansion of its supply of resources—land, labor, and physical and human capital. Only in the more recent, modern epoch have certain societies rapidly increased their supply of these resources, and such resources became far more productive than ever before because of the application of modern science and technology that were embodied in new physical and human capital. The combination of rapidly expanding resources—especially capital—with their increased productivity accounts for why modern economic growth in the West and in Japan has been rapid and sustained over long periods.

The Marxist and Malthusian analytic models provide some insight into why China's historical pattern of economic growth radically differed from that of other countries. Yet these frameworks cannot satisfactorily answer the three questions posed in this text. The framework that is applied in subsequent chapters postulates that the policies initiated by the state are crucial for understanding how society and economy in the private sector will be influenced and shaped. The economic organizations outside the public sector pursue their goals, but at the same time they are responding to state policies, they will also try to make the most of their market networks. These market networks function to provide signals and information to economic organizations that will enable them to select from among the available technologies the most efficient methods for production and exchange.

The more successfully the state can increase the opportunities for economic organizations to acquire income through the redistribution of property rights and improvement of the economic environment, the more vigorously will economic organizations strive to increase their supply of resources to carry out production and exchange to earn income. The improvement of any technology that permits economic organizations to eliminate critical scarcities and use their abundant resources more efficiently will then assist them to increase production and support a larger population.

State policies, the response and behavior of economic organizations, and the availability of new technology interact to expand the supply of resources and very possibly even to increase their productivity. In succeeding chapters this framework will be applied to three central questions in order to advance our understanding of Chinese economic history—both past and present.

Why Growth without Development during the Ch'ing Period?

The chapters in Part II attempt to answer this question. By focusing on state policies that encouraged economic organizations of the private sector to rely upon market activities, we can see how the Chinese gradually increased their supply of resources to expand production and exchange. While the productivity of these resources scarcely increased over time, the Chinese managed to expand the output of goods and services to match their steady population growth so that living standards comparable to those of the recent past were always maintained. This pattern of development differed from that of most European countries whose population and general life style for nearly four centuries remained frozen at levels approximate to those in 1300.[12]

First, the state initiated new laws that chipped away at the old privileges enjoyed by local elites who had long derived most of their income from large land estates. Such privileges included their paying less tax to the state and performing little or no corvée labor for state public works. These new laws protected the servile laboring classes farming these estates and repealed the land tax and corvée-exempt privileges of the local elite. Second, the state instructed its local officials to subsidize poor families to reclaim land for farming. Third, the state spent considerable funds to restore irrigation and water control over rivers, rebuild road systems, and revive grain storage facilities for relief when harvests failed.

For over two centuries the Ch'ing state followed these guidelines to manage the economy. First, the court monitored seasonal food grain and fiber prices to observe which areas began to suffer severe shortages. After noting prolonged price increases that suggested emerging scarcities, the court ordered merchants to ship commodities to the suffering areas and even cancelled tax payments. Second, the state gave up trying to investigate increases in land values in order to determine if the land tax should be raised. Therefore, the land tax remained fixed over time, and the real tax burden on the people only increased when the state permitted the occasional levying of surcharges on the original land tax quotas. Third, the state tried to regulate the supply of money in order to prevent a shortage of coinage—of either silver or copper, since the country's money supply relied on both.

State policies successfully redistributed income to poorer households, encouraged former servile laborers to become farmers and property owners, and created a beneficial economic environment that greatly promoted the growth of farming and handicraft. Consequently, by the early eighteenth century the economy was already prospering and continued to do so for at least another century.

A turning point arrived, however, in the late 1820s when the state had difficulty in increasing the supply of money to overcome a mounting silver shortage. The subsequent economic deflation spread throughout the southeast provinces, and unemployment in agriculture and commerce worsened.

The response of the private sector to these state policies is examined in chapter four. Economic organizations, such as the typical rural household, produced for and exchanged in highly competitive markets. Certain regions specialized in rice, silk, cotton, wheat, and tea production. Merchants and their brokers moved such raw materials and their processed goods through various markets to final destination for consumers and even for export. Within these competitive markets sellers sold their products at their lowest cost, and prices fluctuated according to the forces of supply and demand. Profit margins for suppliers remained low unless windfall profits accrued because of unusual foresight and good fortune.

The pervasive practice of customary law enabled households to exchange their resources with each other to eliminate specific scarcities that prevented the households from producing to their full potential. The formal and informal contracts households negotiated with each other for resource exchange mitigated against uncertainty and

risk and enabled households to achieve a more balanced supply of resources to undertake production and exchange than would have been
true otherwise.

The Chinese possessed a strong work ethic, practiced frugality,
and typically only spent heavily for religious ritual and gift exchange;
this behavior was in accordance with family ancestor worship and kinship rules to maintain solidarity and continuity of descent group and
lineage.

The households that did achieve an elite status because one or
more members successfully passed some of the imperial exams also
earned considerable income and were able to amass much wealth.
These elite usually maintained a high propensity to consume and frequently engaged in lavish gift exchange as part of the expected code of
social behavior to advance in career and win support from colleagues.
Yet this elite also used their own funds and expended much time and
energy to organize projects that produced an economic environment
favorable for local community development.

Wealth continually was being redistributed within the private
sector and rarely remained in any single household for more than one
or two generations. Part of the reason was because of the two kinds of
elite expenditures just mentioned: gift giving and spending for community projects. But perhaps the principal reason was the inheritance
system so well defined by customary law. Households were supposed
to divide their property equally between their eligible male heirs, and
this usually occurred sometime during the typical household cycle of
early growth, maturation, and decline.

Exceptions to this general pattern, of course, often occurred. In
wealthy areas where certain lineages had managed to acquire great
wealth, leading households organized schools and hired tutors to prepare the more promising children for the imperial exams. These lineages, then, exported considerable human talent and skill when the
educated members became officials and clerks to other provinces
where they built networks of political ties that transcended geographical boundaries.

But because product markets operated so effectively to prevent
commodity scarcity from becoming serious, because factor markets also functioned smoothly to permit households to exchange resources to
eliminate their resource scarcities, and because most households continually redistributed their wealth, the Chinese economy did not experience any trend for unequal income and wealth distribution over
time. At the same time the structure of commodity prices remained
rather constant, and even the monetary returns to land or rent, to
moneylending or interest, and to organizers of production and exchange or profit appear to have been roughly the same over time.
Under such circumstances, then, the households that invested in capi-

tal formation merely saved and invested just enough to maintain a fairly constant ratio of capital-to-income over time.

All signs seemed to point toward the supply of resources to grow gradually without any major increase in the productivity of any resource. Such market development was bound to discourage the kinds of innovations in organization and technology that came to characterize northwest Europe in the eighteenth century and even earlier. Somehow China lacked the cultural ethos for experimentation and the desire to transform nature. Without innovations or technological change to increase the productivity of resources, the Chinese economy merely became larger, supported more people, but did not undergo any structural change. Nor were new organizations created that might have acquired a different momentum of their own to initiate either new innovation or technological change.

Not unsurprisingly then, the public sector remained small and even receded in importance as the private sector grew to awesome size. Even the outbreak of massive rebellions in the 1850s failed to alter this pattern of social and economic development. The Chinese economy quickly recovered by the late 1860s, and in spite of new trade contacts with foreign countries, the economic structure remained unaltered until the first Sino-Japanese War in 1895 and 1896.

Why Was Modern Economic Growth Retarded? Again we must look to the behavior of the state for an answer to why economic modernization was delayed until nearly the twentieth century. The Ch'ing monarchy, for complex reasons, deliberately delayed making any commitment to modernize the economy until after China was defeated by Japan in 1896. Until then most Ch'ing officials firmly had believed in their economy's superior performance and viewed any widespread adoption of modern machinery with great apprehension. They feared that modern machinery would displace labor from transport and handicraft; further, such machines even violated local religious customs. Therefore, most officials argued that the potential, socioeconomic dislocations might prove too disruptive for community stability and peace—especially so soon after the violent rebellions that had rocked the empire in the 1850s and early 1860s. But after China suffered an ignominious military defeat by Japan, its leaders reversed themselves and recognized that far-reaching legal and fiscal reforms had to be quickly introduced by the state if China were not to perish in the modern world.

Yet when the state began to launch modernization, why did modern economic growth thereafter advance so slowly? The simple reason is that China lost its political unity after 1911 and state power enormously weakened so that it could not promote rapid economic development. The premature collapse of the Ch'ing state ushered in lawlessness and disorder whereby the economic environment became less favorable for encouraging the growth of modern enterprise. Even when the Kuomintang party finally established control over several central provinces in 1927, it tried merely to unify the country immediately under its authority without first obtaining sufficient economic power and administrative control over the countryside under its aegis to mobilize full support for its modernizing efforts. As a result the state never became strong enough to garner enough tax revenues from agriculture by which to modernize the economy at the same time it was trying to extend its political control over the rest of the country.

Part III describes how the state made only the most feeble of efforts to promote modern economic growth between 1865 and 1949. In spite of these weak state initiatives, a small number of entrepreneurs began to organize production on an entirely new basis by making use of modern technology. Their economic-cultural values were common to all households of the day. More and more of them crowded into the new city-ports because they perceived that high profits could be earned from foreign trade and from the production of the same kinds of goods China eagerly imported from abroad, namely, products such as machine-made cotton yarn and cloth, dyes, flour, machines, and cement. Rather than cooperate with state bureaucrats to launch modern enterprises approved and demanded by the state, these business leaders took their own bold initiatives to invest in food processing, textile manufacturing, and banking. During and after World War I they even extended their investment to producing machine tools and chemicals. The many city-port economies dotting the coast and up the great inland waterway of the Yangtze became the enclaves for modern enterprise, which supplied only limited markets elsewhere in the country. Chinese factories and firms produced for their buyers in and just outside these city-port enclaves or for export, and yet beyond them lay the huge economy of agriculture and handicraft of only imperial times.

Although violence raged outside these city-port enclaves of prosperity and modern economic growth, Chinese business owners continued to perform remarkably well despite extreme adversity. The modern banking, trading, and manufacturing networks created by the foreigner and Chinese business organizer somehow managed to grow in spite of war, deflation, the invasion by Japan, and the great post-World War II inflation. During the 1927–1937 decade the Nanking government did mobilize some tax revenue and established research institutes, colleges, roads, rural cooperatives, and banks. By 1937 this small infrastructure already had begun channeling modern technology to some rural areas, but the Japanese invasion of that same year terminated such progress before its influence could produce any substantive, observable change.

The agricultural sector, meanwhile, entered a period of profound crisis. After World War I farm producers found it increasingly difficult to adjust to the numerous disruptions of the product and factor markets in the countryside. On the demand side of the market, the foreign demand for Chinese exports rapidly declined so as to reduce the demand for products produced by rural handicraft. Meanwhile, on the supply side the warlord armies, bandits and units of the Japanese military imposed new financial burdens on the farmers. As a result of contracting demand and periodic disruption to supply, farm prices fell or violently fluctuated so that farm income was greatly reduced. Even more disastrous was the rural unemployment that followed upon these market disturbances—particularly the world depression's adverse impact upon the Chinese market and the great outflow of silver that occurred in 1934 and 1935 when the U.S. Treasury began buying silver. Throughout this entire period the state was too helpless to do anything to stabilize these market fluctuations, so that economic conditions for the farming classes greatly worsened.

The small modern sector that successfully emerged had received its growth impetus from foreign trade, the presence of the foreign business operators, and the dynamism of Chinese entrepreneurs. But without a strong state to provide social stability and improve the economic environment, the modern sector remained too weak to provide enough effective demand to increase employment and incomes in the countryside and encourage the modern transformation of agriculture. The Chinese economy became characterized by a huge agricultural sector stagnating alongside a small, but slowly expanding modern sector with its own very small, modern infrastructure.

Why an Economic Revolution after 1949? In Part IV we again look to the role of the state and the response of newly created economic organizations to increase the supply of resources rapidly enough to produce rapid modern economic growth after 1949. The Communist party had quickly established its control in villages and cities through its policies of large-scale redistribution of property and income from land reform and the nationalization of all urban industries. The party then established new economic organizations in agriculture and industry that achieved far greater participation of the work force than in former times. These new organizations successfully mobilized households to work on capital projects, restricted their consumption, and increased their savings. The result was a very high accumulation rate of capital with almost all labor fully employed.

At first the state spent heavily to employ foreign technicians from the Soviet Union and imported Soviet machinery to build the most modern enterprises of machine-tool, iron, and steel production. Several decades later China borrowed from other foreign countries to construct chemical fertilizer plants and petrochemical factories. This transfer of modern technology was achieved through foreign trade or purchased by exports, so that the state gradually acquired the modern industrial capacity to supply other regions and related industries with new equipment and engineering design to improve their industrial production. This technological transfer did not occur smoothly or at once. It occurred at particular phases when the Chinese leaders became committed to relying upon foreign trade to modernize their industries.

The economic organizations in agriculture and industry, of course, underwent a monumental change in management and structure. All organizations became linked to statewide agencies of control and produced according to a fixed economic plan. Each organization, large or small, balanced its budget and maintained a high reserve fund for capital accumulation. The welfare of households slowly rose only when the state lowered the prices of consumer goods, expanded the supply and variety of consumer goods without raising their prices, and permitted households to use their savings to buy these new goods. As all private property except household structures and family household belongings have become the property of the state, household members only can earn wage income.

The state had achieved a balance between a high accumulation of capital and the gradual improvement of consumer welfare, but by the late 1970s China's leaders began to express great concern about the absence of productivity growth in the economy. After experiencing more than a decade of political turmoil in which higher education and scientific research had virtually come to a standstill, the Communist party reversed many of its former policies and instead reverted to many of the strategies used in the 1950s to modernize both industry and agriculture. In other words, China now looks to the West for borrowing modern technology and expanding its foreign trade in order to pay for the kind of imports that will transfer some of this new technology. The state manages many large-scale organizations as did imperial administrations of the past. China's historical legacy of economic statecraft has undoubtedly contributed toward enabling the party to mobilize the country's resources and expand their supply at an unprecedented rate to achieve a modern economic revolution. China's central problem now is to make those resources much more productive so as to sustain the rapid economic growth already underway.

QUESTIONS FOR DISCUSSION

1. How has the concept of "economic surplus" been used to explain Chinese economic history in recent times?

2. What are the key functional relationships that postulate that China was fast approaching a "high-level equilibrium trap" by the end of the nineteenth century?

3. What state policies might be initiated to promote modern economic growth in a premodern society? In the Chinese case was an unresponsive private sector the chief cause for slow modern economic growth?

4. In what way can market structures influence the rate of investment?

5. Is there any relationship between state economic policies to transform the Chinese economy after 1949 and those of late imperial China? If so, what are the alleged relationships?

NOTES

1. One of the best descriptions of this historical stage and those that followed is Hu-pei ta-hsüeh cheng-chih ching-chi hsüeh-chiao yen-shih-pien [Department of Political Economy Education and Research of Hupeh University], comp., *Chung-kuo chin-tai kuo-min ching-chi-shih chiang-i* [A Commentary on Modern Chinese Economic History] (Peking: Kao-teng chiao-yü ch'u-pan-she, 1958).

2. For a discussion of these early forms of rural capitalism see Ramon H. Myers, "The 'Sprouts of Capitalism' in Agricultural Development during the Mid-Ch'ing Period," *Ch'ing-shih wen-t'i* [Problems in Ch'ing History], 3 no. 6 (December 1976): 84–89.

3. Mao Tse-tung, *Mao Tse-tung hsüan-chi* [The Collected Works of Mao Tse-tung], 5 vols. (Peking: Jen-min ch'u-pan-she, 1955), vol. II, p. 620.

4. For a recent discussion of the significance of this war for Chinese economic-social change see Dilip K. Basu, ed., "The Opium War," *Ch'ing-shih wen-t'i* 3, supp. 1 (December 1977): 1–91.

5. Department of Political Economy Education and Research of Hupeh University, comp., *Chung-kuo chin-tai kuo-min ching-chi-shih chiang-i*, pp. 525–46.

6. The definition of economic surplus and the analysis of the components producing this surplus can be referred to in Carl Riskin, "Surplus and Stagnation in Modern China," in Dwight H. Perkins, ed., *China's Modern Economy in Historical Perspective* (Stanford, Calif.: Stanford University Press, 1975), pp. 49–84. See in particular the diagram on p. 53, which shows the components of spending and income giving rise to economic surplus.

7. Mark Elvin, *The Pattern of the Chinese Past* (Stanford, Calif.: Stanford University Press, 1973), chapter 17.

8. For a comprehensive and provocative statement of how this new philosophical orientation arose see Thomas A. Metzger, *Escape From Predicament: Neo-Confucianism and China's Evolving Political Culture* (New York: Columbia University Press, 1977).

9. Mark Elvin, *Chinese Past,* chapter 16.

10. Ibid., p. 313. In the diagram of Elvin's high-level equilibrium trap in agriculture, the schedule OT represents the long-term potential agricultural output that can be produced by the best practices of traditional technology. The schedule OS shows that output required to sustain the labor force at subsistence. The P_1 P_2 P_3 P_4 schedules show labor productivity, which always rises and declines because of the law of diminishing returns to the constant factor—land. At OM labor input, MC output supports the labor force with a small surplus of BC and a potential surplus of AB per head. At ON labor input, the actual and potential surplus has declined (GH and FG respectively). At E_t the high-level equilibrium trap has been reached. See also a modified presentation of this same analysis by Robert F. Dernberger, "The Role of the Foreigner in China's Economic Development, 1840–1949," in Perkins, ed., *China's Modern Economy*, pp. 24–25.

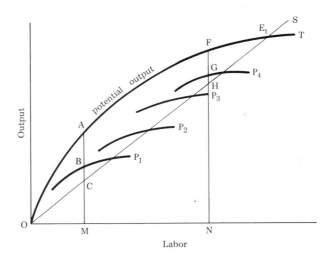

11. Professor Thomas A. Metzger of the University of California (San Diego) suggested this relationship to me.
12. This view is advanced in Emmanuel LeRoy Ladurie, "Motionless History," *Social Science History* 1, no. 2 (Winter 1977): 115–36.

SELECTED READINGS

1. John K. Fairbank, Alexander Eckstein, and L. S. Yang. "Economic Change in Early Modern China." *Economic Development and Cultural Change* 9, no. 1, pt. 1 (October 1960): 1–6.
2. Mark Elvin. *The Pattern of the Chinese Past.* Stanford, Calif.: Stanford University Press, 1973.

Premodern Economic Growth: The Ancien Régime

Part Two

The State
and the Economy

3

An economic system is an abstraction by which we can understand the real world—either past or present. Every economic system—whether primitive, feudal, bureaucratic, capitalistic, or socialistic—performs four key functions: (1) It determines what kind of goods and services to produce; (2) it establishes the quantity of these goods and services; (3) it undertakes the distribution of incomes by which these goods and services can be allocated; and (4) finally, it selects the resources from current production that will be invested to produce capital so that the system can either reproduce itself or expand.

These four functions are decided either by individuals or by households and groups that hold power and control the political and economic system. Whether the society in question is small or large, simple or complex makes no difference as far as the necessity to fulfill these functions is concerned. The four functions still must be performed if the economic system is to feed, shelter, and clothe its people. How are decisions to carry out these economic functions made?

ECONOMIC ORGANIZATIONS AND MARKETS AS AN ECONOMIC SYSTEM

Three basic kinds of systems allow for such decision making. The first occurs through command; the second is by the marketplace; and the third is by a combination of these two. In order to describe how these systems operate to produce the decisions by which the four functions can be performed, the reader should refer to figure 3–1, which shows the various circular processes by which units in society and economy make decisions so that the economic system can fulfill its four functions.

An economic system has two types of markets and three kinds of components (see figure 3–1). The first type of market, the *product market,* is made up of the myriad marketplaces—formal or informal—

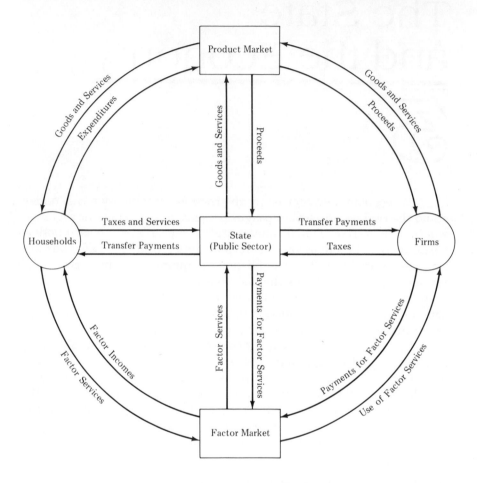

FIGURE 3–1.   The Circular Flow Schema of an Economic System

where goods and services are exchanged between buyers and sellers. Second, the *factor market* is comprised of markets—again formal or informal—where the services offered by factors of production are bid for and hired by units or firms that will use these services for the production of goods and services for final consumption. Both types of markets can be further clarified when we note that *formal markets* are the identified places or establishments where suppliers and buyers converge and where exchange takes place. By *informal markets* we designate simply the transactions between suppliers and buyers in which exchange occurs.

The three components of an economic system include two broadly defined units: households and firms (see figure 3–1). The *household* is the basic socioeconomic unit of human life where individuals and groups related through blood ties live, work, and play. Households earn incomes with which to purchase goods and services for final consumption. In order to earn income, they sell their *factor services* (see figure 3–1), which can consist of labor, the use of assets such as land or structures, the use of funds such as savings, and the use of their special skills and talents for organizing production such as entrepreneurship.

Units or firms that organize production and distribution perform certain tasks. The organizers of firms hire factor services with which to produce a complex assortment of goods and services (see figure 3–1). By the same token, these organizers pay incomes for the use of factor services such as wages for labor, rents for land and structures, and interest for loanable funds. Finally, production organizers receive salaries out of their profits, which serve as the payment for their special skills and talents. Depending upon the state of technology and the arts, many firms can exist to produce and distribute goods and services for final consumption.

In simple, early economic systems firms and households are one and the same. But the different functions to be performed can be distinguished by the circular flows within every economic system. That is to say, only through the organization of production and exchange can goods and services be produced and finally sold to buyers. Buyers, on the other hand, can only buy with the income they earn from the system of production and exchange or from the factor markets.

The unit of account, store of value, and medium of exchange called *money* facilitates exchange in both markets and enables households and firms to make their valuations for spending and buying purposes. Prices of goods and services and of factor services are thus expressed in this unit of account.

Historically, most economic systems must incorporate the activities of the state, the third component of the circular flow schema (see figure 3–1). Hypothetically, the state bids for, hires, and pays for factor services and also produces goods and services for its own consumption or to sell—perhaps at zero price—to households and firms. The sources of revenues for the state are households and firms that pay taxes and/or supply services at zero price, for example, corvée labor. The state also may redistribute some of the income it receives and, instead of spending for itself, transfer some of it to households or firms. Examples of such transfers include famine relief, tax reductions, subsidies, and welfare payments.

Our three economic systems can be studied separately. First, the *command economy* is the system in which a small group holding political and economic power makes the decisions as to which goods and services will be produced, their quantities, their distribution, and the amount of current output used for investment in capital to make the system grow. In a feudal system the king and the nobility held sufficient power to allocate a large share of society's resources—factor services and final goods and services—to waging war. In a socialist system like the USSR, the powerful Communist party's central committee through its planning commission sets a very high priority on production of capital goods to expand the economy. Meanwhile, the scarce supply of consumer goods and services must be rationed, which in turn has lasting effects for living standards and income distribution. In command economies market prices are controlled or strongly influenced by the state. Taxes and transfer payments serve as instruments to achieve market equilibrium—that is, to match the available supply with demand to clear the market.

The second kind of economic system is the pure *market system* in which prices are free to fluctuate according to the forces of supply and demand. If certain prices rise because the demand for the merchandise has increased relative to supply, some producers will respond by increasing their purchases of factors to supply more of the goods in demand to the market, while other producers will reduce their supply to the market. Households will adjust their spending according to preferences—some buying more of the goods whose prices rose, some buying less. The major impulses determining what to produce and in what quantities come from household spending. The distribution of wealth and income in turn influence household spending. Consumer sovereignty determines the expansion of the system—the kinds of goods and services produced and their quantities.

In the third type of economic system, a *mixed economic system* operates. State authority to regulate, tax, and spend can exert moderate influences upon income and expenditure streams. These influences shape the profit opportunities perceived by firms. They also influence household decisions to spend, to save, and to allocate factor services among alternative uses. Market forces continue to predominate, so that a complex blend of household and business expectations interact to determine outcomes in the marketplace.

Our circular flow schema in figure 3–1, then, can be simple or complex depending on the actual economic system being examined. Let us now turn to the late imperial economy of the Ch'ing government (1644–1911) and examine the existing economic system within a geographical and temporal context. That is to say, we want to describe the geographical environment within which economic organizations and their markets functioned. We then will turn to a discussion of how this economy's activities changed over time as reflected by changes in such key economic indicators as price, income, and employment. Meanwhile, the reader should keep in mind the abstraction of the economic system just mentioned in order to later identify and understand how the components of the system relate to each other in the real world of premodern China.

THE SPATIAL CONTEXT

Although the Ch'ing military and bureaucratic forces unified and ruled a territory comprised of eighteen huge provinces, this political unit—really an empire—was not a national economy and never became so even when Ch'ing rule was ultimately overthrown. By a *national economy* we mean a system of uniform monetary standard and uniform weights and measures, a fiscal system in which tax revenues are re-allocated by the state to different regions, and an interregional and interprovincial trade system whose flows vitally affect the economic activities within all regions and provinces. For example, the copper content of copper cash coins was never uniform. As early as the 1820s, foreign silver coins circulated alongside Chinese copper cash and silver taels in Kwangtung and Fukien provinces to serve as money. Grain-measuring units, as well as the unit of land, varied in every county of the empire. The Board of Revenue merely set tax quotas that each province had to submit annually to Peking, and the state never re-allocated tax revenues for national economic purposes. A few luxury goods, food grains, and iron products were among the items exported by provinces, but the share of total provincial production value derived from such exports probably did not exceed 2 or 3 percent. Thus, if the Ch'ing economic system was not a national economy, how can it be described?

Three Large City Classes

The reader should now refer to figures 1–1 and 1–2, which show the eight physiographic macroregions with their economic core areas nestled upon fertile plains or in alluvial valleys, alongside estuaries, or spread out upon the delta basin of large rivers like the Pearl, the Min, or the Yangtze. The concept of *physiographic macroregion* refers to a distinct region populated around and in river basin areas and characterized by a hierarchy of cities—each of varying and relative size—linked by well-defined transport networks. The term *economic core area* refers to a zone within the physiographic macroregion characterized by higher population density, greater urbanization, and more commercial exchange. In these economic core areas were three large city classes: the large national metropolises, the regional metropolises, and the large regional cities; with a few exceptions, these economic centers depended almost entirely upon their macroregion for their raw materials as a source of supply and a market to sell their finished products. For 1893 G. William Skinner has estimated that only 89 such large cities in all of China had a total population of roughly 11,906,000 or about 45 percent of the total urban population.[1] Within these cities were special areas designated for handicraft production and the sale of goods and services. Producers and merchants congregated in these locations to do business. A typical urban scene in Ningpo near Hangchow (Chekiang) is described by the American traveler Robert Fortune in 1843:

> Rope-making is carried on extensively in the suburbs near the river, and some strong cables and ropes for junks are made from the bracts of the palm, formerly noticed, and from the bark of the urticaceous plant, commonly called hemp by the English in the north of China. There are, of course, the usual quantity of curiosity shops, containing bamboo ornaments carved into all possible forms; specimens of ancient porcelain, which are said to "preserve flowers and fruit from decay for an unusual time," lacquered ware, and other ornaments brought by the junks from Japan, many beautifully carved rhinoceros' horns, bronzes, and other articles to which the Chinese attach great importance, purchasing them at exorbitant rates, apparently far beyond their value. But what struck me as being most unique, was a peculiar kind of furniture, made and sold in a street, generally called "Furniture Street" by foreigners who visit Ningpo. There were beds, chairs, tables, washing-stands, cabinets and presses, all peculiarly Chinese in their form, and beautifully inlaid with different kinds of wood and ivory, representing the people and customs of the country, and presenting, in fact, a series of pictures of China and the Chinese.[2]

While Fortune was impressed with the quality of workmanship in Ningpo, his account conveys both the diversity of production and marketing and the specialization carried out in certain sections of the city. The reader should realize that the owners and operators of the firms that produced marketable goods usually lived next to or above their place of business. They sold their wares directly to consumers or to merchants who arranged to sell the products elsewhere. These production firms purchased raw materials or semi-assembled items from other firms. To enable firms to handle the stream of raw materials and semiproduced goods entering a large city like Ningpo, merchants and their brokers operated in medium and small cities, as well as in intermediate and small towns. Because the materials and goods had to pass from one local stopover to another before arriving in Ningpo and cities like it, merchants greatly relied upon brokers to make purchases in the small cities and towns considered on the basis of size to be in a descending hierarchy below the three large city classes. A Japanese commentary describes the importance of these brokers in integrating the complex production and distribution structure of Chinese firms:

> Merchants rely upon brokers to carry out their transactions between markets and the sources of supply. Merchants will go to markets, where brokers supply the goods they will need to have at a particular time to sell in their markets. Some merchants have agents or hire the services of shopkeepers to be brokers. Ordinary merchants do not have agents, and therefore they are in trouble if they cannot buy and sell at a definite time. To avoid uncertainty and reduce risk, most merchants delegate their buying and selling to brokers.[3]

Not all regional cities of large size lay strictly within the economic core areas of each macroregion as figure 3–2 shows. For example, the regional city of Kuang-yuan, while still part of Szechwan province and within the periphery of the upper Yangtze macroregion, lay outside the economic core area. Within that economic core were fourteen greater cities and twenty-four local cities—all located on rivers that provided convenient transportation between them. Firms organized the production and distribution of a flow of raw materials and final goods and services within and between all thirty-eight of these cities. At the same time the economic core area, characterized by its high urban and rural population density, traded through similar merchant-broker networks with its peripheral area, which contained some large cities like Kuang-yuan, more very small cities, and countless market towns. The small market towns because of their superfluity upon the rural landscape and their importance for village economic activities, deserve further mention.

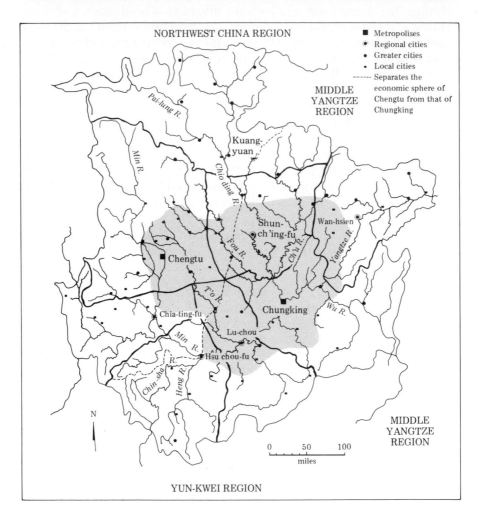

FIGURE 3-2. The Upper Yangtze Regional City Trading System (1893)

Note: The dotted line bisecting the region separates the economic sphere of Chengtu from that of Chungking.

Source: Reprinted from *The City in Late Imperial China*, p. 292, edited by G. William Skinner with the permission of the publishers, Stanford University Press. © 1976, 1977 by the Board of Trustees of the Leland Stanford Junior University.

Small Market Towns

In villages and small market towns the majority of households in China lived and worked. Whether in the economic core areas or the peripheral areas of macroregions, these households were both consumers and producers. As a multiproducing unit, a household was continually allocating the labor and skills of its members to many different occupations. This meant that considerable handicraft, processed farm products, and manufactured items for clothing and shelter were produced in villages and exchanged in periodic markets located in very small market towns. The area serviced by standard marketing centers gradually came to support larger populations and in many instances assumed a hexagonal spatial form, which thereby provided minimal transportation costs to all producing units.[4] Such a marketing area beyond the town usually contained between fifteen to thirty villages where considerable specialization and exchange within and between villages occurred. Therefore households sold their factor services in formal factor markets and more often on an informal basis to other households or firms. They also purchased goods and services from each other, but more importantly, they did all of this in the small marketing towns.

In the typical small marketing towns, some handicraft might be produced, but quite often various stores sold goods, and establishments such as barbershops, inns, teahouses, moneylender shops, and apothecaries supplied their services. The following is a description of the small market town of Wu-li-pao in I-tu county of central Shantung province during the late 1930s. The facts given about Wu-li-pao are similar to those of the tens of thousands of small marketing towns across China even for the earlier period of Ch'ing rule:

> The farmland and agriculture of Wu-li-pao could not support the livelihood of all the inhabitants; it barely supported about half their number. Therefore, it was the markets of Wu-li-pao that provided a livelihood for the other half.
>
> Wu-li-pao had periodic markets open on the first and sixth and fourth and ninth day of every lunar month. A small market opened on the first and sixth days; a large market opened on the fourth and ninth days. The largest market, for mountain berries and fruit, was located on a plaza off the South Road near a Buddhist temple. On the east side of this temple there was a vegetable and hog market at a vacant lot. A market catering for daily necessities was located on the main thoroughfare of the town. From June until October when farming was most active, a market opened for short-term farm hands in the courtyard of the temple. A market for silk co-

coons opened at the same location as the large market in very early summer. At the end of summer around 2,000 muleteers would convene at Wu-li-pao, and it was said that the noisy sounds of the mules could be heard as far away as the walls of the county seat.

The large market for mountain berries and fruit was the main market of the town. The bountiful producing areas supplying these goods to the market were located in the hills and mountains to the southwest of the county.[5]

The 231 households of around 1,500 persons in this small market town supported themselves through farming, handicraft, commerce, and services. Like those in all such communities in China, Wu-li-pao households sold and hired their factor services, organized their production and exchange, and bought their merchandise at the marketplace. Households in nearby villages did the same—except they could also depend upon Wu-li-pao for borrowing credit, hiring farmhands, selling their goods, and buying whatever items they needed. These small market towns and their satellite villages enabled households to engage in a sort of division of labor whereby household resources could be specialized in one or several production activities.

Stretching beyond the medium and small cities were these small market towns with their clusters of villages in which most of the people lived and worked. Just as a continuum of different-sized cities, market towns, and villages existed in the economic core areas of each macroregion, so too did this continuum characterize the peripheral areas around each economic core area. The economic core area and its peripheries were self-contained economic units quite capable of producing the goods and services its inhabitants needed. To be sure, special resource endowments afforded some economic core areas the opportunity to achieve fame in ceramics, textiles, or iron products, and some export to other regions followed as a result.

THE TEMPORAL CONTEXT

How did this economic system change through time? The statistics bear repeating: If per capita income in 1933 was between 60 to 100 U.S. dollars depending upon which year's prices are used, per capita income in the late seventeenth century could not have been very much lower. Therefore, as population by 1850 had more than doubled, total product too had to increase at least by the same amount if per capita income was not to decline. A strong possibility exists that during the 1830s and 1840s per capita income declined, but such an assertion is entirely speculative and impressionistic. The serious loss of population and total product during the 1850s means that per capita income in the 1860s either remained the same or declined slightly, so that until 1933 when population rose to around 500 million, total product also increased, but if the rise in per capita income did occur, it was probably very inconsequential.

The Ch'ing economic system, then, expanded spatially and grew larger over time, but it did not experience modern economic growth. This is to say that the economic core areas of eight macroregions must have grown in size and most certainly must have come to support larger populations. Although their peripheral areas, too, expanded in size as new villages formed and older ones grew in size, they were more poor and backward. This economic system had cycles and trends of growth specific to itself. The most important was the *harvest cycle*. Good harvests caused prices of food and industrial crops to stabilize or decline. Users of these goods in handicraft or commerce had lower costs and could profit. Supplies to market towns and cities of all sizes increased. Urban economic welfare improved. Households dependent chiefly upon wage income found their purchasing power increased. Poor harvests, on the other hand, caused scarcities, raised prices throughout the economic system, and thus reduced the monetary gains of many Chinese living in cities and towns. The localized short-term scarcities produced by a poor harvest rarely lasted for long. Markets in the economic core areas conveyed price signals of these scarcities to the periphery or to other regions, and merchants usually responded by increasing supply. In the advent of several years of very poor harvests in which food and industrial crop prices would have skyrocketed, the state intervened by ordering officials to dispense from grain reserves or pay merchants to import grain to reduce prices.

Price Increases and Market Adjustment, 1700–1820

Long-term economic trends can only be examined by the movement of prices in the product and factor markets. In the first three decades of the Ch'ing period, trade was just slowly reviving. Severe commodity price fluctuations, which obviously represented acute shortages of goods and services, continued. Yet the trend of prices was downward. Only after 1700 did prices, as represented by such commodities as silk and rice, slowly and inexorably rise. The violent price fluctuations of the late seventeenth century no longer were evident; instead, short-term price fluctuations of three or five year's duration— like in the harvest cycle—became more frequent. But throughout the eighteenth century all prices gradually rose, as if pulled upward by periodic shifts in demand relative to supply, so that the trend line is persistently tilted upward.

Did relative price changes occur? Was the supply of some goods becoming relatively scarce? Our commodity price information so far is insufficient to say yes or no, but the historical record sometimes hints of scarcities. Yet adjustments in the marketplace invariably followed to partially eliminate these shortages. The supply of timber in north China declined, so that the court had to obtain wood from as far away as Szechwan. As the cost to produce salt by firewood, coal, or natural gases slowly rose, more producers turned to solar heat and thus offset this rise in cost. Whether all commodity scarcities were so alleviated is not known, and the historical record does not expressly dwell on any serious scarcity.

Meanwhile, did relative changes in factor service prices occur? If the ratio of land rent to its price rose over time, rental income rose relative to other factor costs. If interest rates moved upward relative to other costs, suppliers of loanable funds gained appreciably. The historical record does not mention any such factor price changes and thus suggests that like the product market, adjustments continually occurred in the factor market to eliminate specific scarcities.

Between 1780 and 1820, however, the rate of price increase slackened; prices moved more slowly upward. The state had suppressed the great White Lotus rebellion in five provinces of the far west between 1796–1804, had spent about 120 million silver taels to do so and thus greatly depleted its treasury reserve. Had the state at that time increased taxes in order to spend more and thereby compete with households in the private sector for resources to supply its armies, household spending in the marketplace undoubtedly would have been reduced. If resources had been bid away from the private sector by the state, households would have had to sacrifice this output. If they used their savings and competed with the state, market prices would have risen. As no sharp upswing in prices occurred, how did the state obtain the resources it needed to suppress the rebellion? It spent from its huge accumulations, and therefore, these large-scale expenditures must have had a favorable and stimulative effect upon employment and production. Only in the districts adversely affected by warfare did production decline.

Economic Contraction, 1825–1850

The economic situation greatly changed after 1825. For the first time a clear indication shows that prices in the late 1820s and early 1830s declined, rose moderately in the mid-1830s and then declined in the early 1840s. Meanwhile, silver began flowing out of the country, especially from the provinces of Kwangtung and Fukien. Estimates place the outflow between 1827 and 1849 at 133.7 million yuan of silver, and probably more was smuggled out in payment for opium. Officials complained to the court that the shortage of cash was paralyzing trade. The court responded by instructing various prefectural governors to use their reserve silver and buy copper cash currency in the market; thus the state injected silver into the marketplace and eased its shortage. The memorials exchanged between the provinces and the court during these decades mention that economic contraction was taking place in different economic core areas because of the scarcity of coin. What was the relationship, then, between prices in this economic system, and the supply of money that made possible the circular flows between firms and households in the product and factor markets?

In an economic system the value of goods and services produced and exchanged must equal the value of the money supply times the average times per year a unit of money changes hands. This identity relationship can be expressed as:

$$MV = PQ$$

where M is the money supply; V is the average times per year a unit of money changes hands or "velocity"; Q is the quantity of goods and services; and P their unit prices. This identity relationship simply shows that a change in M and/or V will be reflected by a change in P and/or Q. The causal link between the two sides of the equation is the change in spending relative to the supply of available money in the system.[6] In the 1820s the quantity of M had declined because silver slowed out of the country. More households and firms also began to hoard silver because they expected its value to appreciate later as it became more scarce. Buyers in both factor and product markets reduced their spending as a result; prices declined—as the historical record confirms—and total product very likely declined. The result was a prolonged deflation for the economic system until 1850 when the Taiping rebellion broke out.

Price Deflation The deflationary process worked in the following way: Merchants in the economic core area cities used silver to advance to their brokers to buy raw and semiprocessed materials from small cities and market towns. The producers of such goods as silk, tea, sugarcane, and betel nut, depended upon these silver advances to hire laborers and prepare their deliveries. When merchants could not buy silver or hoarded it, the producers reduced their spending. If the flow of silver from cities to the countryside declined, the supplies produced in villages and market towns also declined. Commodity exchange between cities in the economic core areas and between villages and towns in the periphery contracted. Managers of handicraft firms, landlords, and wealthy farmers ceased hiring the same number of workers and tenants they once did; the flow of cash wages to households declined. Household spending for luxury goods then declined, and fewer ceremonies were performed. Less funds were available for maintaining temples, schools, and bridges. The persistence of such a serious deflation and the multiplying effects of contracted spending caused unemployment to rise. Market towns and cities no longer flourished as they had formerly. Unemployed people began migrating from one district to another.

Unequal Income Distribution   Another new trend in the 1820s and 1830s probably caused a temporary shift in income distribution toward inequality. Households paying the land tax typically sold their food grain and industrial crops for copper cash, which they then used to buy silver to pay their land tax. When silver became scarce relative to copper cash, its value expressed in copper greatly increased. Households had to spend more of their farm proceeds to obtain silver to pay their land tax. As some households could evade this tax by not registering their land, a higher tax burden shouldered by some people meant that income distribution after taxes had become more unequal.

Water Control Problems   A final trend caused considerable disruption of markets and unemployment, especially in north China. In the 1840s the Yellow River shifted its course, causing great property damage; frequent floodings from spring rains every year thereafter continued to inflict misery and property loss upon the countryside. The break in the walls of the Hung-tse reservoir in the 1820s in north Kiangsu province forced grain shipments up the Grand Canal to be delayed. This in turn caused distress in the capital and threw out of work many Chinese who were operating the canal. Whether these new troubles in water conservancy originated from official corruption—as is sometimes alleged—or from intractable engineering difficulties that had just arisen is still a matter of great controversy.

Reduced Population and Production, 1850–1865

The rebellions that broke out in the 1850s and early 1860s were put down with great loss of life. The loss of so many able-bodied workers (*ting*) made it impossible for households and firms to produce the same output as before. Agriculture, in particular, depends upon sequential operations being completed on time, and for this, much manpower must be on hand. Any withdrawal of labor from soil preparation, planting, irrigating, or weeding will reduce output. The famous German traveler, Von Richthofen made this same point while observing the barren countryside outside of the once flourishing city of Hangchow in Chekiang province in 1869:

> This area, which has been allowed to go fallow, once supported a very large population and contained some really rich land. Even now most of it is not being cultivated. The reason for this

seems to be that the method of land use in China depends upon the available population of a certain size, which, if too small, cannot even farm a small area of land. Moreover, the limited labor supply of the Chinese and their undeveloped tools seem to be the principal reasons for that tightly knit organization of labor which works so hard. The scale of cultivated land in this country seems to be in a fixed relationship with the quantity of fertilizer that a certain number of people can produce. If any of these people are lost due to sickness or war, the production of fertilizer declines. Then that potential farming land diminishes in size. So if half of your population dies, half of your land will never be farmed.[7]

But given time, these lands again filled with villages and their market towns, which were linked to larger cities like Hangchow by river or overland roads. Very soon population again grew, total product expanded, and prices resumed their slow, upward drift.

By 1900 many parts of the country were bursting at the seams with villages, yet only 6 percent of the population still lived in cities of any size. Very little had changed in this economic system in spite of the opening of some forty port cities to foreign trade and the granting of special privileges to foreigners to live and do business in these cities. Why after nearly a half century of growing foreign trade and influence, the economy resisted such outside influences is an issue that needs explanation. We know that the Ch'ing economy expanded both spatially and temporally. But why this cluster of huge macroregions with their relatively independent economic core areas merely enlarged without undergoing real change also deserves examination. The activities in markets and the behavior of a component part of the economy, the state, now deserve close scrutiny.

THE PUBLIC SECTOR: THE STATE

Superimposed upon the economic system was the state and its organs of administration and units of production and distribution. The capital, Peking, controlled the eighteen large provinces through an extensive bureaucracy. The state carried out certain economic functions, but its involvement in the economy was small and its contribution to GDP probably no more than 6 or 7 percent. The state's economic functions at the provincial (sheng), department (fu), and county (hsien) levels were to collect taxes, maintain certain establishments producing goods for the court, provide certain services to the populace, and manage the supply of money or copper currency.

County Government Functions

In the *hsien,* the lowest echelon of government, the *yamen* or official office governed through informal associations like merchant guilds, the local constabulary (*ti-pao*), and the household record and policing agency (*pao-chia*). The *yamen's* chief economic task was to collect the land tax, other taxes such as the salt tax, and levies on certain goods in transit or sold in markets. The *yamen* retained a share of these revenues for its administrative costs and salaries and remitted the rest to the department and province levels of government.

The *yamen* also could manage granaries, initiate public works, and supervise water control and conservancy organizations. To this end, *hsien* officials tried to arrogate operating costs to the users and beneficiaries of these projects. By insisting that the private sector shoulder the costs and manage those organizations and projects designed to benefit the local communities, *hsien* officials, rather than the state, regulated and supervised such functions.

State Jurisdiction

State agencies carried out ceremonial functions, maintained a modest defense force, operated a transport system—Grand Canal, communicated with eighteen provinces, and adjudicated criminal and civil court cases. These state agencies used general tax revenues to finance their activities, which in effect provided services to the economy; in part, they also arrogated some of the operating expenses to local areas. For example, the military units stationed around the empire were given special lands (*t'un-t'ien*) by which to feed and support the troops and their families. These households served as soldiers and part-time farmers.

Within the imperial court the imperial household (*nei-wu-fu*) controlled rural estates mainly in Manchuria and managed factories—some located as far south as Soochow in Kiangsu province—to produce commodities for the court. The *nei-wu-fu* collected taxes from its estates and even owned certain monopolies, like the production and sale of ginseng, a perennial herb, so that the court had its private source of revenue in addition to general tax revenues collected from the provinces. Sometimes the *nei-wu-fu* even transferred revenue to other state organs when rebellions in various areas had reduced general tax revenues. Overall, however, the *nei-wu-fu's* share of the private sector economic activity remained minuscule.

The state operated salt and copper monopolies mainly by co-opting merchants to organize their production and exchange. It also established provincial granaries for the purpose of stabilizing food grain prices and preventing famine. In fact the emperor demanded from his officials monthly reports of weather and grain prices in order to monitor agricultural conditions throughout the empire. Finally, during the early decades of Manchu rule, the state seized nearly 560,000 hectares of land in twenty-nine counties around Peking and gave the confiscated lands to high-ranking officers and nobles for supporting their livelihood. These lands were then worked by Manchu and Chinese bond servants and operated by estate managers. The former Chinese landowners were never recompensed for their property loss. But in the next one hundred years most of this land was gradually sold or mortgaged by its Manchu owners to Chinese merchants and moneylenders, so that by the late nineteenth century the majority of new owners were Chinese farmers and urban wealthy.

These operations were the major economic activities of the state—other than its collecting of tax revenue. In other words the Ch'ing state, as we will see, extracted very few resources from the economy so that its contribution to GDP was extremely low. Whenever the state did bid for factor services—as it did when hiring workers for its textile mills in Soochow and factories elsewhere—it had to pay a competitive wage or else close down the factories. Such closings characterized the last half of the Ch'ing period. Yet the state impinged on the economic system in several other ways.

First, the state managed granaries and water conservancy works. Its operation of these organizations greatly determined the prosperity of agriculture in certain economic core areas such as the north China plain, the middle Yangtze, and the upper reaches of the Yellow River area around Sian in southern Shensi. Second, the state exercised some control over the money supply, which in turn influenced prices. During the eighteenth century the state had managed to solve a copper coin shortage, but by the 1820s its failure to prevent the decline in silver, or find suitable money substitutes for silver, produced serious deflation. Third, through various legal reforms and cash subsidies the state encouraged the clearing and settling of new farm lands early in the Ch'ing period and thus gave a vigorous impetus to the private sector to expand its activities. These three important functions by the public sector not only modulated in a very flexible way the behavior of the private sector, but encouraged the private sector to use its resources in a most efficient way.

Let us first examine how the state obtained taxes from the product and factor markets and what effect these taxes had upon households and firms. We then will analyze the policies initiated by the state to encourage the private sector to produce more for the marketplace. Finally, we will observe the key state economic organizations and how they influenced the economy.

The organizational chart in figure 3–3 shows the fiscal system at the end of the Ch'ing period. However, if we exclude the special bureau for collecting the tax on goods being shipped (*Likin* bureau) and its director and the office for foreign affairs (Tsung-li Yamen) and its attendant agencies, the chart accurately shows the fiscal system in the early and mid-Ch'ing period. The Board of Revenue collected taxes from the empire but only supervised the provincial governors in this and other tasks. This board directly controlled the state granaries, the treasury, and the mint—all located in the capital. But note the overlapping control by the emperor himself over the head of the grain transport agency and over the provincial governors. In each province the governor supervised offices for grain collection and shipment, general financial affairs, and salt. The Board of Revenue, then, supervised and coordinated the shipping and storing of grain, collecting of taxes, minting of currency, and managing of salt production and distribution throughout the empire.

Tax Revenue

In the early Ch'ing period the court collected the land and head tax, which was unified in 1713, the salt tax, and customs duties. By the mid-nineteenth century three sources of revenues were added to these: the *Likin* tax—that is, a tax on goods in transit—foreign customs duties, and the sale of official titles. Earlier the Manchus had tried to survey all land to establish a new land tax base. For example, Ch'ing officials in Shantung and Honan began to survey the land, but they soon recognized the task was impossible to complete on the scale of an entire province. They had to report that too much wasteland was neither owned nor reclaimed. They pointed out that such land could be surveyed and registered only after households cleared and farmed it and a tax levied to encourage the new owners to use the land in its highest productive use. In 1663 the state tried for the third and last time to launch a countrywide land survey, but officials abandoned the project after they failed to obtain land records from the landowners and the costs simply became too prohibitive to continue.

The court then hit upon a scheme that it considered would legitimize its rule, elicit popular support, and still raise sufficient revenue for the Board of Revenue. It eliminated the traditional corvée labor system in which households formerly supplied a quota of work days for public works to the state each year—depending upon their number of able-bodied workers (*ting*) between sixteen and sixty years of age. The court ordered that the labor supplied by each household be commuted to an amount of silver and then added to a lump sum tax— depending upon the amount and quality of land. In effect each area paid an assigned land tax quota, which was allocated among households—depending upon the amount of land they owned and registered with the land tax office. Households paid this tax in silver, and by

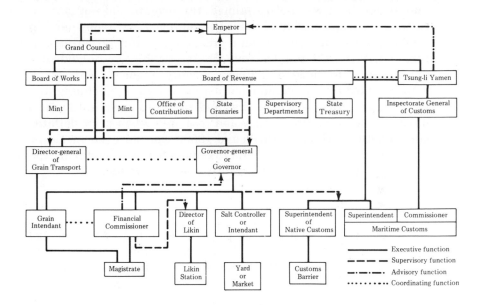

FIGURE 3–3. Fiscal Organization of the Ch'ing Economy

Source: Yeh-chien Wang, *Land Taxation in Imperial China, 1750–1911* (Cambridge, Mass.: Harvard University Press, 1973), p. 14.

1736 the state collected this kind of land tax in all provinces except Shansi, Taiwan prefecture (part of Fukien province), and Kweichow. Every household was supposed to register its land at county tax offices when it sold land or cleared and farmed new land. Many owners evaded registering land, even though they ran the risk of litigation that might later reveal their true ownership status to official eyes. By the twentieth century, surveys showed that as many as one out of three or two out of five households never paid land taxes.

The land tax accounted for at least three-quarters of state revenue. If new land was not reclaimed, tax revenue did not rise. As the state never reassessed land values or surveyed for landownership, the land tax did not increase as land productivity, and agricultural prices rose. Therefore, the gap between the tax paid by households and the market price for food and fibers steadily widened. This is vividly demonstrated by the examples of Soochow and Sung-chiang districts in Kiangsu province where the land tax burden definitely declined during the eighteenth century and rose only when price deflation occurred between the late 1820s and 1850.[8] The state sometimes levied a surcharge on the existing land tax quota for an area during the late nineteenth century when it urgently needed revenue.

Incentives for the Private Sector

After the Manchus seized power, they initiated various policies to encourage the Chinese to find employment and produce for the market. In 1649 provincial officials were ordered to "mobilize all the people without property and homes. Even if they had not been registered in a household or given registration status, they were to be enrolled into the *pao-chia* system, encouraged to reclaim land that was not owned, and given a deed granting ownership in perpetuity."[9] In 1690 the court sanctioned that because—"there were great areas of wasteland in Szechwan and many homeless people, they should be given the right to settle and reclaim this land and then given ownership rights in perpetuity." Again in 1706 the government decreed that—"there was a great amount of uncultivated land in Hupeh and Hunan. The people should reclaim and farm this land. The local gentry of these provinces should also supply work animals and seeds to enable people to cultivate the land."

The government also changed the laws that under the previous Ming government (1368–1643) had favored the rich with special privileges. We have already noted the elimination of the corvée obligation, which wealthy families had always evaded. In 1657 all literati below the *chü-jen* and *kung-sheng* ranks had to pay the commuted silver payment for corvée from which they had previously been exempted. The holder of *chü-jen* rank had successfully passed the provincial imperial exams. Holders of *kung-sheng* title had graduated from district or prefectoral colleges. In 1658 the government ruled that all literati or gentry with degrees would be regarded as criminals if they were found falsifying the amount of land they owned or delaying to pay their taxes over eighty silver taels. By chipping away at upper class special privileges and subsidizing the poor to acquire landownership in these early decades of rule, the Ch'ing government gave incentives to many households to resort more and more to the marketplace to sell their factor services and produce in order to earn income to accumulate wealth.

Key Economic Organizations

Granary System   The government provided two important economic services to the private sector. The first was a system of granaries; the second was to establish water conservancy projects. In 1655 the government ordered that granaries for stabilizing the prices of food grains (*ch'ang-p'ing-ts'ang*) be built in every prefecture (*chou*) and county (*hsien*). Officials were to use government funds and private contributions to buy various food grains after the autumn harvest. If a harvest was poor, the government sold its grain below market price and granted loans to farmers short of seeds or food in the spring. These borrowers would repay after the fall harvest. The economic reasoning behind this scheme to stabilize rural income made sense.[10] But two parallel developments slowly undermined the system by the late nineteenth century. The first was that officials often used granary funds for other purposes, while they still produced written accounts showing fictitiously stored grain. The second was the growth of grain markets and the operations of grain merchants to speculate and thereby stabilize price (see chapter four). This purchase and sale strategy to stabilize food grain prices depended on officials having correct information of price trends and current grain stocks. Provincial officials reported conditions of weather, harvest, and grain prices each year to the throne until the end of the Ch'ing dynasty. As late as 1821 granaries in northeast Shantung province loaned grain as food and seed to soldiers and farmers; in 1833 granaries in southern and northeast Chihli (Hopei) province dispensed grain during the spring. These actions indicate the state granary system still functioned reasonably well even in the early nineteenth century.

Water Conservation Projects   The prosperity of the economic core areas of each macroregion depended upon agriculture and, more importantly, upon effective control of unruly rivers, manmade canals, and numerous sluices that irrigated fields. Without these controls, spring flooding and torrential summer rains might ruin the harvest and thereby create severe food and fiber shortages the next spring and cause unemployment. In the late Ming period water conservancy projects everywhere were in decline. The Ch'ing government immediately tried to restore them and build new ones. Officials mobilized the rich and the farmers to build embankments and dikes where the Han River crosses the Yangtze; they built another water control system above I-ch'ang along the upper Yangtze River (see figure 1–1), where that river flows across a low plain occupied by ten counties; another system of dikes was built along the Hsiang River near Hankow city in Hupeh province; in Nan-hai and Hsun-te counties of Kwangtung province, officials built embankments to protect the rich mulberry-rice area; in P'u-t'ien county of Fukien, another large control system was constructed; flood control systems also were constructed near Hui-chou city south of Lake T'ai-hu in Chekiang and along the Min River where it flowed across the fertile Ch'eng-tu plain in northwest Szechwan.[11] These are but a few of the many projects officials restored.

Treasury funds and official support were the key elements responsible for restoring and building these new multipurpose systems, which controlled flooding and allocated water on demand. After the projects had been completed, officials shifted the burden of the maintenance of these systems upon the local gentry and, in effect, exchanged privilege for responsibility. The local gentry had to make these systems operable by undertaking dredging, repairing embankments, and shoring up sluices every year. They worked with landowners and farmers in informal organizations whereby owners of land and tenant-farmers supplied materials and labor to keep these systems in repair. Households were assessed money and labor according to the amount of land they owned, so that the annual maintenance costs were apportioned according to the ability to pay. But without initial state efforts to allocate funds and resources to these enterprises, the conditions for prosperity in the key economic core areas could not have been established.

In 1687 the Grand Canal finally resumed operations. Long out of use, this vital transport link had enabled the Ming state to collect a grain tax in many areas and ship it to Peking to feed the capital. The Ch'ing government too continued to collect this grain by levying an impost upon areas in Shantung, Honan, Kiangsu, Ahwei, Chekiang, Hupeh, Hunan, and Kiangsi provinces. Each year this grain was collected in Hui-an and T'ung-chou cities for delivery up the Grand Canal to Peking to feed the capital. As much as 400,000 metric tons may have moved along the Canal each year. This grain transfer required at least 6,000 boats to move in fleets of 30 to 100 ships from Kiangsu to Chihli every year. Along the Canal the government set up sixty-one military stations with an undetermined number of soldiers to protect the Canal and supervise the shipment of grain. These troops received about 450,000 hectares of land to farm in order to support themselves and their families. County officials along the Canal—assisted by the soldiery—saw to the annual task of mobilizing nearby villages to maintain the Canal. The state once again used its resources to restore an important transportation link and then arrogated most of the costs of maintaining the system to local officials and organizations.

Salt Monopoly   States have always heavily taxed or made the subject of monopoly control the essential commodities for which the demand is strongly price-inelastic. The Chinese state from earliest times had tried to control salt production and distribution because of the large tax potential that could be tapped. The Ch'ing, therefore, took over the salt monopoly of the Ming and merely refined the system. The country contained many salt-producing areas, but the following description of the Liang-huai salt-producing region along the seacoast above the Yangtze River extending to Yen-ch'eng city shows how the monopoly actually worked.

Farmers and fishermen worked in the Liang-huai salt-yards to produce a brine that was then boiled to make crystallized salt. Peddlers and merchants purchased this salt at the yards and then shipped it to two depots, I-cheng and Huai, situated on the Huai and Yangtze Rivers. Other merchants then moved the salt into other provinces to sell to consumers. The merchants dealing with the Liang-huai salt-yards were under the informal control of twenty-four wealthy merchants (*tsung-shang*) who were responsible for seeing that each merchant obtained a license (*chu-tan*) to ship salt each year and that he registered in a tax register at the Liang-huai headquarters under the name of the head merchant who had guaranteed him. Merchants paid the state for the right of a license to produce and distribute salt. Rather than incorporate nearly a half million salt workers and traders into the bureaucracy, the state officials "allowed them to retain a private or semi-private status and also [become] involved in a complex web of cooperation with powerful merchants whose interests sometimes conflicted with its own."[12] Salt monopoly officials had to prevent smuggling of salt from the yards and increase production to keep pace with demand without the merchants earning such exorbitant profits that they might try to corrupt officials. To meet these ends they urged merchants to police their salt-yards, increased the allowable weight of salt that could be shipped, and permitted salt boats to move with greater frequency. As a result the 140,000 metric tons of salt produced at Liang-huai in 1645 had risen to 225,000 metric tons in 1726 and became 305,000 metric tons in 1800. Salt tax revenues also rose, and in 1800 the taxes from Liang-huai alone amounted to 6 percent of all tax revenue collected from the empire.[13]

Control of Copper and Silver Currencies   The government sought control of copper production because this metal was one of the major sources for currency used in the economic system. Yunnan province supplied about 90 percent of the copper produced in the country, and about 80 percent of the copper mines were located there. Between 1740 and 1811 Yunnan exported 2,100 metric tons of copper to Peking and 5,500 metric tons to provincial mints for the minting of coins. Several merchants would purchase a certificate for opening a mine and sell their copper to a state agency that shipped it from Yunnan. The profits to be earned by having special rights to copper mines were particularly lucrative in the eighteenth century, and merchants from Hunan, Hupeh, Szechwan, and Kwangtung invested as much as 100,000 to 200,000 silver taels and employed as many as 5,000 workers in some of the largest mines. As production costs were still low during this period, Yunnan satisfied the country's demand for more copper, but early in the nineteenth century costs began to rise because of the difficulty of pumping water from these mines, and output stagnated.

For the product and factor markets to have functioned properly and for the state to have interacted with these markets, a monetary system had to facilitate exchange, provide a unit of account, and maintain the store of value. Like the Ming before it, the Ch'ing government established a bimetallic system of two currencies: copper and silver. In 1644 the new government created two separate offices in Peking for minting copper coins—one for paying Manchu Banner military units, the other for paying hired workers of state enterprises that produced goods for the court.[14] In the major cities of fourteen provinces the government also operated mints to produce copper coins for the private sector. The metal composition of these coins was roughly 50 percent pure copper, nearly 40 percent a mixture of copper and lead, and the remainder a combination of lead, iron, silver, tin, and sand. These copper coins served as the unit of account and the medium of exchange for daily transactions in both the product and factor markets. Farmers used copper cash to exchange for silver to pay their land tax. Managers of handicraft production and farmers hiring labor paid wages in this currency. Households used it for buying at the marketplace.

The state increased the supply of new copper coins rapidly in the late 1640s and 1650s and then more gradually until 1720. Thereafter the annual issue of coin fluctuated between 230 and 430 million copper wen. The supply of copper coins, however, failed to keep pace with the demand for this currency. The problem was that many people saw a profit in collecting copper coins and melting them to make copper products for sale. The shortage of copper became so serious as to force the state to pass laws prohibiting such activity and to increase copper production from the mines in Yunnan. These measures succeeded during the eighteenth century, but by the second quarter of the nineteenth century, the government sometimes had to revert to paper issue and to mint coins that contained far less copper and more lead and iron.

During the Ming period silver had become an important component of the money supply. As China produced little silver, foreign trade accounted for the growing abundance of the metal in domestic commerce. Silver imports of increasing quantity originated from Chinese merchants exporting silk, tea, and other items to Manila. Spanish merchants in Manila then shipped these goods to Mexico in exchange for silver. This trans-Pacific trade, involving China, the Americas, and Manila as a crucial entrepôt center, allowed the supply of silver to increase enormously in China. During the eighteenth century silver continued to pour into China in huge quantities—probably at the annual rate of between two to four million silver dollars.[15] The state made silver the unit of account for its transactions, kept its tax surpluses of silver in the treasury, and used silver for all intergovernment money transfers. Local officials used silver in their financial dealings. Merchants relied almost exclusively upon silver for funding their advances to brokers to buy raw materials and goods.

The state very early decreed that the official exchange rate at the mint between silver and cash would be one silver tael being equal to one thousand copper cash expressed in the unit of the wen. Of course, on the free money market the exchange between silver and copper was determined by the available supply of each currency and the demand for it. This system operated much differently from the standard bimetallic currency system in which individuals had the option to exchange a currency at the mint according to the fixed mint ratio. The Ch'ing government tried to maintain the silver-copper coin exchange rate at the one silver tael to one thousand copper wen ratio, but it had no control over the supply of silver because the balance of foreign trade and private hoarding primarily determined its domestic supply at any time. On the other hand, by the early nineteenth century the government faced difficulties in increasing the supply of copper currency. In fact long before—during the 1730 to 1780 period—the copper-silver exchange rate fell and remained below the mint rate. The reason was that copper coins steadily were being withdrawn from circulation for commercial production, and foreign trade brought larger quantities of silver bullion into the country. But from the late 1820s until the late 1840s the reverse occurred, and the copper-silver exchange rate rose as silver became scarce and copper supplies increased. The price deflation that commenced was never satisfactorily solved by state monetary efforts. The state not only failed to introduce a form of money in lieu of silver but was unable to increase the supply of silver sufficiently to restore the old mint ratio.

STATE AND ECONOMY IN THE NINETEENTH CENTURY

The 1820s to 1840s was a period in which the state faced many new difficulties unprecedented in the dynasty's history: scarcity of silver, decline of prices and spending, rising unemployment, engineering difficulties for key water conservancy projects, and troubles in the salt and copper monopolies. Were these economic and technical problems caused only by the decline of bureaucratic efficiency and rising official corruption? One study has argued that bureaucratic norms worked well to elicit honesty and dedication to duty. Taking the reforms of the salt monopoly by T'ao Chu in the 1820s as an illustration of official response to crisis, Thomas Metzger has shown that many difficulties in the salt monopoly were effectively dealt with by official measures.[16] More of these issues deserve further study before any alleged official corrupt behavior can be clearly established as the cause of China's economic problems. At this stage of our understanding, we can say only that a unique concatenation of domestic economic troubles began to plague the economy and government in the late 1820s and seemed to have set the stage for massive social uprisings in the 1850s.

By 1865 the empire was again at peace. For the next three decades the state reverted to its time-honored policies of encouraging the private sector to reclaim and farm more land, to stabilize the harvest by transfer of grain stores, and to maintain a balance between the supply of and demand for currency. The throne was continuously bombarded by memorials from provincial officials seeking permission and financial support to launch new projects such as weapons factories, shipyards, iron and steel mills, modern textile factories, and Western-style schools. A great debate began to rage among officials on how much reform the government should initiate, what kind of reforms these should be, and what were the true costs and benefits of these reforms. The majority of Ch'ing officials recognized that managing these new projects involved the state more deeply in the affairs of the private sector and created new difficulties for it. They speculated about the serious socioeconomic dislocations—particularly unemployment—that might arise in the key economic core areas should more resources be used by the state to develop these modern projects. Sufficient tax revenue never seemed to be available anyway to allow the state to bid resources away from the private sector in order to carry out these ambitious programs. Such difficulties were pointed out by factions at the court and cliques of officials in the provinces. It is no wonder, then, that official conservatism remained deeply rooted and court factions apprehensive about modernizing the economy. The day-to-day difficulties of maintaining law and order in this great empire and seeing that the economic system satisfactorily clothed, sheltered, and fed the country's huge population were serious enough concerns without having to deal with the unexpected problems that might arise from far-reaching changes of the economic order.

QUESTIONS FOR DISCUSSION

1. What functions did the Ch'ing economic system perform?
2. What spatial characteristics did the Ch'ing economic system have? How could a society with such a low rate of urbanization provide income and employment for so many people working in agriculture?
3. Why was deflation such a real threat to the stability of the Ch'ing economy? What economic processes took place when deflation occurred?
4. Although the ever-normal granary in China was based upon a sound economic principle, what practical difficulties were likely to arise to prevent it from stabilizing rural incomes?
5. Why did the Ch'ing land tax system fail to supply more tax revenue as agriculture developed?
6. Describe how Ch'ing officials operated large state monopolies. Are these monopoly enterprises similar to the ones you are familiar with in modern times?
7. Can the Ch'ing economic system be called a "command economy" or a "mixed economy"?

NOTES

1. G. William Skinner, ed., *The City in Late Imperial China* (Stanford, Calif.: Stanford University Press, 1977), pp. 286–87. The population estimate for these eighty-nine large cities is derived from the mean figures for these three groups of large cities.
2. Robert Fortune, *Three Years' Wanderings in the Northern Provinces of China* (London: John Murray, 1847), p. 78.
3. Tōa Dōbunkai, *Shina keizai zensho* [A Compendium of the Chinese Economy], 12 vols. (Tokyo: Tōa Dōbunkai, 1910), vol. 7, pp. 224–25.
4. John C. H. Fei has shown that the optimum shape of the market area tends to be hexagonic and transportation costs within such a spatial form can be optimally minimized. It is not surprising that such market structures so often characterized rural China so as to support a densely populated empire. See John C. H. Fei, "The 'Standard Market' of Traditional China," in Dwight H. Perkins, ed., *China's Modern Economy in Historical Perspective* (Stanford, Calif.: Stanford University Press, 1975), pp. 238–41.

5. Kokuritsu Pekin daigaku fusetsu nōson keizai kenkyūjo, *Santō no ichi shūshichin no shakai teki kōzo* [The Social Structure of a Market Town in Shantung Province] (Peking: 1941), p. 9.

6. The relationship between spending and the supply of money in the Ch'ing economy can be observed in the diagram below. The vertical axis represents nominal money income (current purchasing power or money supply); the horizontal axis represents the supply of money. The line *AB* denotes the demand for money and shows that the higher the nominal income, the larger the quantity of money demanded. The supply of money is fixed for the system at *MM*. When the supply contracts to *M'M'*, an excess of demand given supply exists at ab. Households and firms will spend less to establish a new equilibrium at Y_1. This condition will be associated with either lower product and lower prices or the same product and even lower prices.

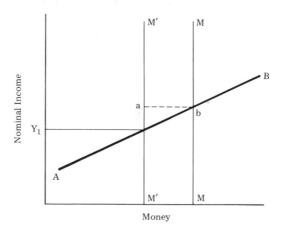

7. Ferdinand Von Richthofen, *Shina ryokō nikki* , 2 vols. [A Daily Journal of Travels in China] trans. by Ehihara Masao (Tokyo: Keiō Shuppansha, 1944), vol. II, pp. 79–80.

8. Ts'ui-jung Liu and John C. H. Fei, "An Analysis of the Land Tax Burden in China, 1650–1865," *Journal of Economic History* 37, no. 2 (June 1977): 373–74.

9. Li Wen-chih, "Lun Ch'ing-tai ch'ien-ch'i ti t'u-ti chan-yu kuan-hsi" [An Essay on Land Ownership Relationships in the Early Ch'ing Period], *Li-shih yen-chiu* [Historical Research] 5 (1963): 79. I am indebted to Professor Thomas A. Metzger for directing my attention to this important article.

10. The economic reasoning for this scheme is as follows. The demand for food grains is generally price-inelastic. In the diagram below the price per unit of food grain is shown on the vertical axis and the quantity of grain on the horizontal axis. The hypothetical EE demand curve shows unitary elasticity of demand in which any change of price and quantity along the *EE* curve will yield total proceeds for farmers that remain unchanged. We

superimpose an inelastic demand curve *DD* upon *EE*. The government's task is to buy and sell grain to stabilize the price and output at *OP* and *OM*. If a good harvest shifts the supply to *OT*, prices will fall to *OR*. Government purchases of *MT* grain should raise the price to *OP* and allow only *OM* quantity of grain to be sold. If the harvest is poor, the quantity normally would be *ON*, and the price would rise to *OQ*. But the government now sells and loans grain, attempting to lower the price to *OP* and increase the supply to the market to *NM*. Government actions will not bring about instantaneous market adjustments, but over a period of time, farm income can be stabilized at the value of *OP* price multiplied by *OM* quantity of grain sold.

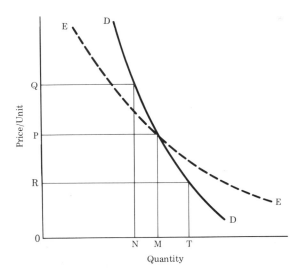

11. Morita Akira, *Shindai suirishi kenkyū* [A Study of the History of Water Control During the Ch'ing Period] (Tokyo: Aki Shobo, 1974), pp. 417–97.

12. Thomas A. Metzger, "The Organizational Capabilities of the Ch'ing State in the Field of Commerce: The Liang-huai Salt Monopoly, 1740–1840," in W. E. Willmott, ed., *Economic Organization in Chinese Society* (Stanford, Calif.: Stanford University Press, 1972), p. 19. My discussion of the salt monopoly is based on this excellent account.

13. Ibid., p. 18.

14. When Manchu military forces conquered China, they consisted of eight organizations referred to as eight "Banners." These Banners eventually were merged to form the Army of the Green Standard (*Lu-ying*), which was then distributed throughout the empire to perform military duty and maintain order.

15. Ch'uan Han-sheng, *Chung-kuo ching-chi shih lun-tsung* [Collected Essays on Chinese Economic History] (Hong Kong: Hsin-ya yen-chiu-suo, 1972), vol. I, pp. 438–39. Pioneering research upon this trans-Pacific trade and the importance of silver imports on the expansion of the Ming and

Ch'ing economies have been discussed in numerous articles by Professor Ch'uan Han-sheng.

16. Thomas A. Metzger, *The Internal Organization of Ch'ing Bureaucracy* (Cambridge, Mass.: Harvard University Press, 1973), pp. 53–54, 58–61, 75–76, 78–79.

SELECTED READINGS

1. Yeh-chien Wang. "The Secular Trend of Prices during the Ch'ing Period (1644–1911)." *Journal of the Institute of Chinese Studies of the Chinese University of Hong Kong 5,* no. 1 (December 1972): 347–68.

2. ———. *Land Taxation in Imperial China, 1750–1911.* Cambridge, Mass.: Harvard University Press, 1973, chapters 1 and 2.

3. Thomas A. Metzger. *The Internal Organization of Ch'ing Bureaucracy.* Cambridge, Mass.: Harvard University Press, 1973, chapter 1.

4. Yang Lien-sheng. "Government Control of Urban Merchants in Traditional China." *Tsing Hua Journal of Chinese Studies,* n.s. 8, no. 182 (August, 1970): 186–206.

5. Ts'ui-jung Liu and John C. H. Fei. "An Analysis of the Land Tax Burden in China, 1650–1865." *Journal of Economic History* 37, no. 2 (June 1977): 359–81.

6. Hsiao Kung-chuan. *Rural China: Imperial Control in the Nineteenth Century.* Seattle: University of Washington Press, 1960, chapter 5.

7. Frank H. H. King. *Money and Monetary Policy in China: 1845–1895.* Cambridge, Mass.: Harvard University Press, 1965, chapters 1 and 5.

8. G. William Skinner, ed. *The City in Late Imperial China.* Stanford, Calif.: Stanford University Press, 1977, pp. 275–351. In the same volume see John R. Watt. "The Yamen and Urban Administration," pp. 353–90.

9. ———. "Marketing and Social Structure in Rural China," pts. I, II, and III. *Journal of Asian Studies* 24, no. 1 (November 1964): 3–43; 24, no. 2 (February 1965): 195–228; and 24, no. 3 (May 1965): 363–99.

10. Thomas A. Metzger. "The Organizational Capabilities of the Ch'ing State in the Field of Commerce: The Liang-huai Salt Monopoly, 1740–1840." In W. E. Willmott, ed., *Economic Organization in Chinese Society.* Stanford, Calif.: Stanford University Press, 1972, pp. 9–46.

The Private Sector
of the Economy

Under the Ch'ing economic system the household was the basic producing and consuming unit. Some households that pooled their savings established stores, handicraft firms, and small factories, but the number of such partnerships probably accounted for less than 10 percent of all households. As producing and consuming units, Chinese households had to make two very different kinds of decisions. First, they could earn income by selling their factor services. For example, laboring to earn wages, leasing property or assets to earn rent, and lending money to earn interest brought the household considerable income. Such actions required that alternative buyers for these services be evaluated and a decision made as to whom to sell factor services. Second, households earned income by organizing the production of goods or services to sell to other households. Households might hire labor and rent land to grow food or fibers for the market. They might operate a store, manage a factory, or engage in commerce. These two sources of income permitted households to buy the goods and services they needed in product markets.

Equally important, households also changed in size and form, enlarging when births exceeded deaths, contracting when deaths exceeded births. Households invariably went through a cycle of forming, enlarging, dividing, perhaps even declining and expanding again or disappearing entirely. In each cycle the household tried to build relationships with kin of the same patrilineal descent group. Of course, when their best interests dictated, households transcended kinship ties and established relationships with other units. Depending upon its power or weakness, the descent group—the clan or lineage—always remained an important network for economic gain and social advancement. The economic dynamics of village and city life can neither be appreciated nor understood unless the household cycle and descent group is always kept in mind. Let us now turn to examine the production and exchange of rice, cotton cloth, silk, and tea as illustrative of how production and exchange worked during the Ch'ing period.

PRODUCT MARKETS

Rice Production

Between 1933 and 1936 the land under rice cultivation occupied about 26 percent of the total farmland. As rice cultivation had declined somewhat after 1900, probably just under a third of the total cropped area grew rice in the eighteenth and nineteenth centuries. Three factors contributed to the importance of rice. After the eleventh century, farmers began producing two crops—rice followed by a coarse grain—each year in some areas because of the availability of an early maturing rice seed imported from Vietnam. This seed required more water and better fertilizer to mature early, and when the rice was properly planted, farmers could harvest a second grain crop every year. Moreover, this hearty seed produced good yields even on inferior soils. Farmers gradually improved their irrigation and fertilizer methods over the same period. The result was that the *crop index*—that is, the sown areas divided by farmland multiplied by 100—slowly rose as did rice yield. More food meant more people. By the eighteenth century the densely populated areas in the Lingnan area, along the Fukien coast, and in the lower Yangtze barely produced enough rice for their inhabitants.

The following excerpt from a memorial by General Ho T'ien-p"ei in the summer of 1729 shows how this difficulty had been overcome:

> Secret investigations have revealed that most rice is produced in the southeastern provinces, and that merchants are daily involved in its distribution. If on occasion there is an insufficient supply of rice for the year, it becomes extremely important for merchants to obtain rice from neighboring provinces. For example, the rice for Fukien is obtained from Taiwan and Chekiang; rice for Kwangtung is obtained from Kiangsi, Kwangsi, Hunan, and Hupeh; further, it seems that all the rice for Kiangsu and Chekiang comes from Kiangsi, Hupeh, and Hunan. There are no restrictions at all on the export of rice from these neighboring provinces. Each year the rice flows out from these areas in an endless stream. Even when the people on the coast are likely to be short of rice, no scarcity will arise.[1]

The annual average rice deficit for these areas ranged between 900,000 to 1.4 million metric tons each year.[2] Perhaps as much as a million metric tons of rice annually moved from surplus areas to deficit areas. Tens of thousands of brokers, shippers, and merchants brought this rice from surplus areas to the more populated centers chronically in need of rice. How did this rice market system work? Let us examine only one small segment of this market: Hunan and its marketing links to southern Kiangsu on the lower Yangtze River.

Hunan Market System   Rice merchants in Kiangsu province carefully watched the movement of seasonal rice prices and tried to predict local harvests. With this uncertain information in hand, they dispatched their brokers and boats to Hankow, Hsiang-yin and Hsiang-t'an in Hunan province. In the latter city "shops and stores stretched for ten kilometers, and so closely packed were they as to occupy ninety percent of this area. All kinds of goods were gathered and sold to make it one of the biggest markets in Hunan."[3] To such markets as these came the rice from distant, smaller market towns. An example is Hsing-lu market town, located 30 kilometers west of the county seat of Chih-chiang county:

> It was convenient by water to a government postal office right across the Yangtze River. All the villages had wells and work animals to draw the water. These villages produced rice and millet which were marketed at Hsing-lu market. Buyers in their boats anchored at the nearby river, purchased rice, and left to deliver (in other areas).[4]

The villages and market towns nestled near rivers or on roads in this middle Yangtze region probably resembled those of Chih-chiang county.

These villages produced commodities other than rice, including cotton cloth, tea, metal and bamboo products, noodles, straw braid, fish and assorted oil products. In every village some of the households specialized to produce these different goods upon which daily life depended and then sold them in local markets to brokers who purchased them and sold them in other markets. Each market town and its clustering villages therefore produced enough goods for a small region to be self-sufficient. But good climate and fertile land also allowed households to produce far more rice than these communities could consume. The incentive for households to specialize in producing rice for the market came from the high prices offered in local markets by rice brokers and merchants. The households either grew rice or collected it from their tenant farmers, stored it, and then marketed it when prices rose.

The rice brokers supplied their own copper cash or used cash advanced by their wholesale merchants. As soon as they purchased rice, they shipped it to secondary markets from which it entered Hankow and other large towns. From there rice merchants purchased it and shipped it to the lower Yangtze markets. Meanwhile, in the primary markets of the countryside, as soon as farmers or landlords sold their rice, they purchased assorted goods circulating in the primary markets. Therefore, little cash actually moved into villages; most of the money circulated in market towns. An imbalance of trade very likely existed between the markets in Hankow and its sister cities and the markets in the lower Yangtze that favored the upper Yangtze markets. In other words, a small flow of copper and silver steadily moved from Kiangsu to Hunan to finance the rice trade. In this way commodity specialization was able to continue.

The thousands of rice brokers and merchants that descended upon Hunan's market towns offered prices based upon their shipping and storage costs and a reasonable profit. As merchants had to compete with each other, the final rice price represented the competitive forces of buyer demand and market supply. Individual rice merchants or small groups could not influence price. A description of rice marketing in Hankow for 1913–14 presents a situation no different from that of the eighteenth century:

> Rice exchange in Hankow is no different than in Shanghai, where it is handled through rice brokerage firms. In Hankow the main rice market is in the harbor at Ch'en-chia-tsui. There are 20 rice brokerage firms connected to the same rice merchant guild, which regulates the profits from rice marketing in Hankow. However, there is no case whereby these firms buy large quanitities of rice at a fixed time, or send agents to the rice producing areas to corner the rice supply. Nor are there any examples whereby they resort to cunning means to collude with various shops which buy rice. We can say that these practices simply do not exist on a yearly basis, and for Chinese merchants this is one of their noteworthy characteristics.[5]

On the supply side of the rice market, the tens of thousands of farmers and landlords who stored and sold their rice also competed with each other. They too estimated their production and marketing costs and the expected return for their labor and capital. Suppliers who had invested in storage and could market their rice at the highest seasonal prices earned higher profits. Stable rice shipments from Hunan apparently kept rice prices in southern Kiangsu quite stable during the early eighteenth century. The speculative behavior of rice suppliers contributed toward such stability—as can be seen in the figure 4-1.

Given the inelastic demand DD for rice by buyers in Hunan market towns, if OM quantity was harvested, MN price would prevail in the market. Rice speculators bought RM quantity and stored it so that only OR quantity was sold to nonspeculators at a price of OP. When the rice price threatened to rise, for example, to HF later in the season, speculators sold HQ to the market and thus restricted the price to

OS. Therefore, prices fluctuated only around *OP* and *OS* rather than *HF* and *MN*. The activities of speculators prevented large swings in rice prices that otherwise would have caused consumers great distress. Sometimes, rice prices still rose excessively because of unusual circumstances influencing trade between the central and southeastern provinces:

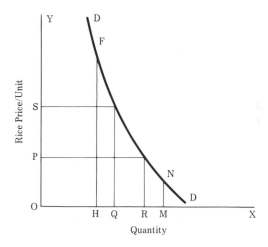

FIGURE 4–1. Inelastic Demand for Grain

In 1724 there was a good harvest in Kiangsi province. But as many ships and their crews had been lost to storms in Kiangsu and Chekiang provinces, rice prices in these provinces did not fall. It was not until 1727 that the food grain crisis in Chekiang and Fukien ended. Until that year rice prices in Kiangsi province had averaged between 5.56 and 6.12 copper cash, and the highest price ever reached had been 7.00 copper cash. But in 1727 an unusually large number of ships and merchants from Kiangsu, Chekiang, and Fukien came to Kiangsi, and the price rose to 9.00 copper cash and even over 1 tael. The people there had never seen the price so high.[6]

Highly competitive economic behavior of buyers and suppliers, well-organized rice markets along rivers and roads, the constant flow of price information to merchants and brokers, and the large numbers of buyers and shippers allowed the central provinces to supply the coastal provinces with rice. The rice export trade of Hunan and other provinces was conducted within community markets that supplied enough rice to meet local needs. Yet the extra income generated through this large, staple trade provided the necessary income and employment for the steadily expanding population of these areas.

Cotton Cloth Industry

By the thirteenth century many farmers had found that the cotton plant yielded far more fiber per unit of land than other fiber plants. More importantly, people preferred cotton cloth because it is easy to wash, durable, comfortable in either warm or cold weather, attractive, and well suited for dyeing. By the mid-fifteenth century, cotton was being grown across much of China, and by the early eighteenth century many regions specialized in its production not only for local use but for export. In the warm, humid areas of southern Kiangsu, for example, rural households planted cotton in sandy soil—alongside rice—and the women and children spun and wove cloth for sale to the market. In many districts, then, specialized spinning and weaving centers developed. Brokers and cotton merchants arranged the import of raw cotton when local supply became scarce, handled the exchange of raw cotton, yarn, and cloth, and supplied the fulling and dyeing industries of larger cities like Soochow with woven cloth for final processing. Many combinations of raw material production, intermediary manufacture, and final processing were carried out within certain districts—depending upon convenience to market, sources of supply, and the availability of labor. In some areas of Fukien, for example, farmers planted sugarcane, used the proceeds from sale of the cane to buy raw cotton, and then spun yarn and wove cloth for sale to the market. By carefully allocating labor between farming and handicraft, households managed to engage part-time in agriculture and part-time in other pursuits.

Technological Improvements   Adjustments in the marketplace and very gradual technological advance either prevented the price of cotton cloth from rising or lowered it relative to other commodity prices. In the Ming period (1368–1643) cotton cultivation rapidly spread throughout the north and central provinces. Farmers improved their soil preparation, planting, and fertilizing so as to raise yields. They developed seeds for better cultivation in poor soils. At the same time a new hand-operated cotton ginning device with rollers became popular and increased the amount of ginned cotton per worker. Then the treadle-driven multispindle spinning wheel became fashionable—especially for women in their homes. Finally, the hand-operated looms that were formerly used for weaving hemp cloth were modified for cotton use. According to Mark Elvin, these gradual adjustments and improvements on the supply side of the market prevented the prices of cotton products at various intermediate stages of production from rising. In fact these improvements very likely discouraged technical change of the labor-saving type. The ever-available supply of cheap labor allowed more households to employ labor in long-standing labor-intensive processes.

Specialization of Labor and the Cotton Market Nearly all of the unfinished cotton cloth was produced in rural households. Brokers and merchants supplied households with raw materials and then purchased the woven cotton cloth back from them. In certain cities and towns the cloth was then calendered, dyed, and finally sold by merchants to other cities or even exported under the famous brand name of "nakeens" on Yankee clipper ships to the United States. The following description of the division of labor at this final production stage in 1898 closely resembled that of some famous centers in Sung-kiang prefecture in southern Kiangsu during the eighteenth century:

> As already mentioned, the white cotton cloth is still an unfin-ished product, and it cannot be sold yet to buyers. It will first pass into the hands of small merchants and then be contracted for processing. The calenders, who are one of these processors, are most numerous. They have a direct relationship with these small merchants. The firms which bleach and dye the cloth are separate from the wholesale merchants. These are the specialized tasks in this industry no matter whether activ-ity is intense or slow.[7]

In numerous sheds clustered in one part of the city, a dozen or so workers would roll a huge stone over white cloth to press the threads closer together. The managers of the calendering operations received contracts from merchants to process cloth in this way, and having no money of their own but possessing experience and skill, they depended on cash advances from merchants to complete the assigned calender-ing work. In similar fashion the cloth would then be bleached and dy-ed—again under contract with agents who organized and managed the operations. Finally, the finished cloth would be packaged and sold elsewhere.

We should note that no single merchant was powerful or wealthy enough to integrate these steps into one operation under a single es-tablishment. Nor was it to his advantage to do so. Contracting each process to the lowest yet most dependable bidder was probably cheaper, and for this reason merchant-capitalists retained their dis-tinctive features of contract work to firms in highly competitive mar-kets.

In villages located near cotton-growing districts or markets, households undertook spinning and weaving for their own needs and sometimes to sell in local markets. Families purchased or constructed their own equipment; they bought raw cotton when they needed it;

they spun yarn and/or wove cloth for sale when they needed cash. Shanghai county of southern Kiangsu in 1750 was a typical rural scene:

> It is not only in the country villages that spinning is to be found, but also in the capital of the *hsien* and in the market towns. In the morning the village women take the thread which they have spun and go to the market, where they exchange it for raw cotton, with which they return. The following morning they again leave home with their thread, never pausing for an instant.[8]

In such districts brokers visited the market towns, purchased the unfinished cloth, and sold it to merchant shops in the cities where intermediate dealers then undertook the processing of the cotton cloth.

The following description sketches out in broad brush strokes the cotton market picture. In and around the economic core areas— especially in the lower Yangtze—households undertook cotton spinning and weaving on a part-time basis. Where specialization of labor, favorable climate, and abundant cotton supply favorably interacted, districts produced more cloth than they could consume. The surplus passed through markets for processing in the cities and then was shipped to other cities. Rural people used the rough, unfinished cotton cloth; the urban wealthy used the dyed and printed cloth. Hundreds of thousands found employment; countless intermediary agents and artisans worked in highly competitive markets; highly labor-intensive practices predominated. Because markets worked so effectively to eliminate scarcity and because competitive forces made it unlikely economic power could be concentrated to establish market control, the inducements for tinkering and introducing inventions were weak. Powerful merchants found that attempts to integrate the different, intermediary stages into or under a single organization were unprofitable. The small amount of "putting-out" work that took place in cities was done solely on a competitive, contractual basis.

Silk Production

By the eighteenth century sericulture was well entrenched in the lower Yangtze, the southeast, and the Lingnan regions. Other regions also contained pockets of silk production, but none as developed as these three areas. Long recognized as a luxury good with many varieties, silk was still widely used by all social classes. Hangchow, one of the main centers for silk, is described by an English traveler in the early 1850s:

> The people of Hangchow dress gaily, and are remarkable among the Chinese for their dandyism. All except the lowest

labourers and coolies strutted about in dresses composed of silk, satin, and crepe. . . . The natives of Hangchow, both rich and poor, were never contented unless gaily dressed in silks and satins.[9]

China began exporting more silk late in the eighteenth century, but the foreign silk market still accounted for only a fraction of domestic production. Like cotton production, sericulture was a part-time activity for villagers. Unlike the situation with cotton, more households devoted their entire resources to producing silk intermediary products because of their profitability.

Some historical sources report that one-sixth of an acre produced 880 kg. of mulberry leaves a year, which fed enough silkworms to produce 4 kg. of silk thread. In 1702 the recorded foreign value of silk, 2.6 taels per kg., meant that a household with only one-sixth of an acre could theoretically earn 10.4 taels a year. By 1760 such a household just held its own. The total cost for production and livelihood for a household of six or eight persons is not known, but some cost accounts for wealthy farm households that owned 2.5 acres in Anhwei province showed total costs during the late 1850s ranging between 25 and 50 taels. When this estimate is adjusted for the price level of the mid-eighteenth century, our hypothetical sericulture household with only one-sixth of an acre was as well off as a well-to-do farm family. The latter probably accounted for only 20 to 30 percent of all village households. Clearly, sericulture provided not only employment but a good family income—especially if the family owned land to produce mulberry leaves. Since many households purchased mulberry leaves in the market, their profits were much less.

Sericulture, of course, provided more employment than for just those households growing mulberry trees. Households that knew how to raise silkworms and spin silk purchased mulberry leaves from brokers and sold their silk to merchant-managed accounting houses (chang-fang) that advanced cash and raw silk to weaving workshops (chi-fang). These shops produced damask, satin, and other silk fabrics, which were then sold to overland merchants and Canton merchants dealing with foreigners. These merchant account houses, located in the large cities, had found that silk fabric production and sale were extremely profitable by the mid-eighteenth century. Many had been induced to reduce their processing costs by organizing the final processing stages of dyeing and weaving on a putting-out basis. Such a system required the merchant to advance cash and raw materials to a master weaver—with the understanding that the merchant would receive silk fabric of desired specifications at a fixed time. The master weaver (chi-fang) used these funds to hire his weavers and pocket his own wage. This is one of the very few instances in handicraft production in which the merchant-capitalist putting-out arrangement can be found in the mid-Ch'ing economic system.

The rest of the silk industry remained nonintegrated with separate specialized stages of production: mulberry growing, silkworm raising, and silk thread spinning. Tens of thousands of households performed these steps, either in single or multiple stages. The highly competitive market structure with brokers and merchants as buyers, and silkworm growers and silk thread spinners as suppliers, operated to produce the results commonly expected from such a market structure. Prices were competitively determined; prices approximated costs of production along with a competitively determined rate of return for merchant and supplier alike. The product was homogeneous; the flow of information abundant and available for all; entry and exit from the market were relatively easy as capital requirements were small, and experience could be learned readily either from parents or on an apprenticeship basis. The skills and techniques accumulated since the Sung and Ming periods merely spread to more centers of supply during the Ch'ing. Intensive labor-using practices also predominated. Therefore, sericulture provided considerable employment and income for the densely populated regions along the coast and in the hinterland as well.

Tea Production

Tea grew primarily in Chekiang, Fukien, and Kwangtung. As early as the seventeenth century these areas exported tea abroad, but customs data—available only from the 1730s—show that tea exports rose to over 50,000 metric tons by 1850. Deep in the interior of China, households cultivated tea on the hillsides. When Robert Fortune visited the green tea-producing districts in Chekiang outside of Ningpo city, he described the farms as follows:

> The farms are small, each consisting of from one to four or five acres; indeed, every cottager has his own little tea garden, the produce of which supplies the wants of his family, and the surplus brings him in a few dollars, which are spent on the other necessaries of life. The same system is practised in everything relating to Chinese agriculture. The cotton, silk, and rice farms are generally all small and managed upon the same plan.[10]

In other words, households not only produced food and fibers for their own needs, but specialized in products to sell for cash that was then spent to buy household necessities. The smaller the household farm, the more specialized it became—with more resources concentrated on producing for the market and supplementing cash profits with wage income. The larger the household farm, the more diversified its use of resources became—in order to strike a balance between efficient use of these products for its own consumption and for sale to the market.

Processing and Marketing Tea   After harvesting the tea, the farmer dried it on pans heated at low temperature, then pressed it against bamboo racks to eliminate moisture, dried the tea again, and finally placed it upon tubs containing charcoal and ashes. When the drying was completed, the tea was picked, sifted, divided into different kinds and qualities, and prepared for packing. Similar production methods characterized the black tea, but preparation of red tea was slightly different and involved drying the leaves out of doors on large screens.

Families then took the tea to the markets and sold it to brokers. Fortune vividly describes the marketing:

> When the teas are ready for sale, the large tea merchants or their servants come out from the principal towns of the district, and take up their quarters in all the little inns or eating houses, which are very numerous in every part of the country. They also bring coolies loaded with copper coin of the country, with which they pay for their purchases. As soon as the merchants are known to have arrived in the district, the tea growers bring their produce for inspection and sale. These little farmers or their labourers may now be seen hastening along the different roads, each with two baskets or chests slung across his shoulder on his bamboo pole. When they arrive at the merchant's abiding place the baskets are opened before him, and the quality of the tea inspected. If he is pleased with its appearance and smell, and the parties agree as to the price, the tea is weighed, the grower gets his strings of copper money slung over his shoulder and returns to his farm. But should the price offered appear too low, the baskets are immediately shouldered with the greatest apparent independence, and carried away to some opposition merchant. It, however, sometimes happens that a merchant makes a contract with some of the tea growers before the season commences, in which case the price is arranged in the usual way, and generally a part paid in advance. This, I understand, is frequently the case at Canton when a foreign resident wishes to secure any particular kind of tea.[11]

Sometimes the farmers brought their tea—still not fully dried—to markets, and merchants who operated tea-drying sheds purchased it, dried it, then packed it for selling in the coastal cities. From these centers the tea was either exported or shipped to other parts of the country by boat and overland.

Supply and Demand The same highly competitive market structure on the supply and demand side characterized tea as it did other basic commodities in the Ch'ing economy. Tens of thousands of farms nestled in hills cultivated tea; thousands of brokers and merchants fanned out into the districts, organized processing, packing and final shipping to large cities. Hundreds of wealthy tea merchants sold tea to foreigners and native buyers through market networks in other provinces. Tea prices, like all commodity prices, slowly rose over the eighteenth century. Production methods remained very labor-intensive; technology remained simple and unchanged. Brokers and merchants had to gather accurate information of their costs and predict fairly accurately their expected demand in order to make normal profits to justify their continuing to do business.[12] In some districts the cash advances by foreign merchants to their Chinese counterparts provided the credit for brokers and tea farmers to organize production, but this was not the typical method of financing production. Usually producers and merchants financed their activities from savings or borrowed from friends.

FACTOR MARKETS

How could these tens of thousands of markets where rice, cotton cloth, silk, tea, and so many other goods were exchanged be linked to each other and successfully operate as they did? An enormous organizational effort by households obviously had to make this possible. This meant that households had to arrange with each other to buy and sell the services of their labor and other resources. Few households, after all, possessed the abundance of resources to be independent and self-sufficient. One farm family sometimes found itself short of labor; another short of land; both might be short of cash at some time. When we multiply this example times other private sector units like artisan households, merchant families, shopkeepers, and transport workers, we can appreciate the complexity involved in having organized production and exchange in such a large, populated economy of only premodern technology. Therefore, households continually had to negotiate with each other to overcome some resource scarcity they faced. And by the very nature of the Chinese market system, household agreements with each other—either in formal markets or conducted informally—were crucial to eliminate some resource scarcity so that this highly competitive, multiple-stage system could work as effectively as it did. In the factor market, then, owners of resources sold their services; buyers of these services bid and eventually purchased them. Let us examine the payments of rent, wages, interest, and profits—the incomes paid for these factor services—to understand how these factor markets actually worked.

Rent Payments and Land Distribution

According to Ch'ing land records between 1661 and 1851 the cultivated area in China rose about 41 percent or from 36.6 to 51.4 million hectares. The clearing and farming of new lands were accomplished by wealthy households and even by poor families who pooled their resources to drain swamps, clear fields, and irrigate dry land. They were obliged by law to obtain permission from officials to do so, pay a land tax, and thereby acquire a title deed to their land. Yet many households settled in this fashion without informing officials or paying taxes, and thus worked and lived beyond the pale of officialdom. The wealthier people usually invited other families to farm their land as tenants, and often these families were kin of the same patrilineal descent line as the landowner. These new arrivals had to rent land or work as day laborers. In the developing areas the percentage of tenants and laboring households were at first a very high proportion of all households. In time, however, many of them had saved enough money to buy land to achieve a full or part owner-tenant status in the community. The following is a section of a typical contract in the eighteenth century between a large landowner and his tenants. Definite incentives in the contract encouraged both landlord and tenants to put the land to its highest economic use:[13]

> A CONTRACT FOR TENANTS TO FARM
> THE LAND OF A LARGE LANDOWNER
> Our village has some barren land located in Chih-pa-li referred to as "Opposite the Ta Lun Barren Peak." My tenants Huang Kai, Ch'en Yen, and Ch'en Shui have already rented small plots of land that can be farmed with a single plough. They have provided the capital to build an irrigation pond, and they have finally succeeded in making the land yield crops. Each year they harvest rice, beans, and various grains. For the farmland they have not irrigated, the rent is on a one-nine-five basis in which the landlord receives 15 percent and tenant 85 percent. The tenants must not alter the amount of actual harvest by selling the grain or secretly shipping it to another village before they pay their rent to the landlord. . . . The annual rent in 8 *shih* of grain or good rice that has been winnowed dry, shipped to our wharf, and then delivered to the granary. . . .
>
> Signed with seal by Landlord Kuo
> *January 31, 1770*

Landlord Kuo lived in Taiwan, which was then being settled by immigrants from Fukien province. Tenants could develop their land and could profit from any rise in productivity. The landlord also had a guarantee of receiving a fixed, annual rent from which he paid his land tax. The contract also reveals the fears of property owners over the theft of harvested grain.

In the north most tenant-landlord contracts lasted no longer than three years. To the south on the more fertile and higher-, stable-yielding lands, these contracts often extended indefinitely. Tenants even transferred their right to rent to their sons or sold it to other buyers. Most contracts were by word of mouth, but written contracts, like Landlord Kuo's, have survived to show that both parties tried to reduce risk and clarify their rights and obligations.

Households with little or no land rented from kin and friends or from strangers—in that order. They also rented land from organizations such as lineages, charitable estates, schools, irrigation associations, and village councils. They paid rent in kind as a percentage of the harvest and sometimes even a fixed amount of the harvest; they also paid in cash according to current crop prices and land productivity. But the share-crop rental system predominated. Thus, different rent arrangements coexisted to allocate land among different users.

Sharecropping Because they could allocate their labor among different activities, those households considering to rent land had to weigh their annual income return for the labor and capital used to farm that land with their alternative income return for the same labor and capital used differently. So too did landowners make a decision of whether the maximum rent they could extract was as much or more than if they used that land differently and, for example, farmed it themselves. Figure 4–2 presents in abstract fashion how the final allocation of land under sharecropping was determined for a single tenant and a landowner.[14] The same analysis could equally be extended to include more tenants.

We must assume that land is privately owned, and that landowners and tenants are competing to obtain the highest rental bid or the lowest rental offer. The MN curve is the typical declining marginal product for the resource of land. As more land is used, the additional product for the last unit of land used declines. Diminishing returns to land occur because the amount of labor and other resources used to work this land is in fixed supply. The QR schedule declines also; it represents the marginal contract share for rent. This expresses the share of output that the tenant and landowner will agree to divide between them. Finally, at OS amount of land, the tenant and landowner agree to the amount of harvest to divide between them—say 60 percent to the tenant and 40 percent to the landowner. If tenants can earn as high as or more than their alternative earnings, they will rent and farm the land. The landowners will agree to this percentage of the harvest as rent only as long as they understand that it is the highest rent the tenants will pay and that any alternative use of the land would cost them more. The tenants will be induced to farm intensively all the land to OS, and they will select a mix of crops or specialize in one crop that they estimate will maximize the return for their labor and capital.

Generally speaking, a landlord collected rent on only one main crop, and a tenant-farmer was free to interplant other crops. This gain to the tenant was understood in the negotiating of the rental contract. To be sure, conditions sometimes existed in which tenants had very few employment opportunities, land was scarce, and tenants numerous. Landlords then had more power to set the share rent higher so that the QR schedule rose. On the other hand, if market prices rose for certain crops or new market and employment opportunities arose, landlords had to compete among themselves for tenants, and the QR schedule could be lowered.

In some areas like southern Kiangsu landlord bursaries, or independent agencies operating on behalf of landowners, collected their rents, demanded unpaid rent, and negotiated new rental terms. Throughout much of south China landowners and tenants had agreed that land provided two kinds of rights: first, for the owners to hold the alleged *surface right* to the land—they collected rent and paid the

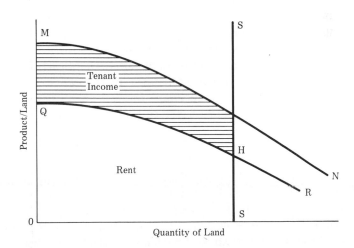

FIGURE 4–2. *Determination of Crop Share Rent*

land tax; second, for the tenants to hold the *subsurface right*—they paid a rent but used the land as they pleased. The tenant generally held this right in perpetuity, and the share rent remained fixed for very long periods—often a decade or more. But when price inflation became severe, as in the very late years of the Ch'ing period, landlords tried to raise the sharecrop rent. Tenants violently resisted because they no longer gained from inflation. Quite often, too, their real rent burden had already increased because they had to exchange more copper cash for silver—the value of silver had risen relative to copper—to pay their rent in money. These tenant rent protest movements occurred principally around large cities on the fertile plain between Nanking and Shanghai where money rentals were prevalent. Further, they originated from factors other than those of the traditional rental contract system itself, namely, unexpected fluctuations in money values.

Redistribution of Estates and Manchu Holdings Another factor influencing regional land tenure patterns was that large estates in the early Ch'ing period were broken up or reduced in size and number. The Ch'ing government had passed new laws in the late seventeenth century that eliminated such privileges as evading corvée and not paying the land tax. Many estate owners found they could no longer manage their estates with the same supply of bonded labor as in the past. Also, many bond servants for the wealthy households fled to other areas to clear and farm land of their own. In Anhwei and Kiangsu provinces some estate owners began giving their land to the servants on a perpetual lease-hold basis in exchange for a sharecrop rent. Still another factor was the gradual transfer of Manchu land—formerly confiscated from the Chinese or set aside for producing crops and revenue for the imperial household—to Chinese merchants and wealthy farmers. Such a transfer did not begin until the 1720s, was later slowed by court actions to help indebted Manchus remortgage their lands, but again accelerated later in the century. By the mid- and late nineteenth century perhaps more than 80 percent of former Manchu landholdings had reverted to Chinese landowners.

Absentee Landownership We have no information of how much rent absentee landlords collected or what share of total rent they received each year. In the early Ch'ing period this group probably was still very small. As more households acquired claims to land, and land values rose, investment in land became increasingly profitable. A study of 127 landlords in Shantung province shows that during the eighteenth and nineteenth centuries half of them had first made their money in urban commerce and industry. They later sold out, bought land, and managed their estates by leasing a part and working the remainder with teams of workers. This shift of urban capital and managerial skill to agriculture might have been more prevalent in the developed economic core areas where the return from agricultural investment often was as high as that of commerce. Buying a rural residence and living the life of country gentlefolk also was a life-style many Chinese aspired to but few attained. We cannot really generalize and say this urban-to-village shift of wealth was widespread. Yet landownership constantly changed, not simply because some had financial success and others failure, but because a dynamic of another kind always operated—that is, household property division.

Household Property Partitioning   A household that had increased its numbers invariably had accumulated some wealth—cash, land, furniture, clothing, or structures. If it had managed its resources well by allocating them to their highest paid use, restricted its consumption and saved its earnings, the household gradually began acquiring more wealth. The more labor it had, the more income it was likely to earn. A time finally came when the household head decided to partition the wealth equally among his male heirs. Many reasons might have dictated this decision, but when made, the decision signaled the end of that household and the beginning of new ones. The wealthy might set aside some land to collect rent for worship of ancestors, for supporting aged parents, or for charity such as schools and relief. The remainder was then divided equally among the male heirs. Even poor households divided their little wealth in this way. The Chinese rigidly conformed to this practice, as surviving contracts for partitioning attest. Therefore, large estates continually were breaking up every other generation; redistribution of accumulated wealth was always taking place. Although some lineages had achieved power and status, this inheritance custom eventually weakened them, too.

Wages

For the Chinese family, having children meant continuing the descent line. A family prized sons above all. A patrilineal society needs sons to carry the family name and, in particular, to guarantee ancestor worship. Each family always singled out certain ancestors for special commemoration, and generally ignored the rest. What distinguished some ancestors to exalted and elevated ranking was their economic and social success—in particular, the amount of wealth they had acquired. As family heads also hoped to be revered and worshiped by their progeny, their best guarantee was to accumulate wealth to dispense as a reminder of their importance to the family. Ambition drove them to work hard and manage the household's resources efficiently, or at least try and do as well as any former, illustrious ancestor. This self-imposed pressure and the fear of not succeeding provided the inner tension to perform and achieve, as demonstrated by all household members in their desire to work hard, to be frugal, and to aspire to be wealthy.

Families arranged early marriages for their children. They regarded these arrangements as extremely important, and considerable thought and planning went into them. A properly arranged marriage was an important strategy by which the household first tried to acquire a daughter-in-law, and failing that, to either purchase a son or young girl to match with whichever child the family had. The aim was to produce children—in particular, male heirs. As soon as children could perform menial tasks, they learned different skills, and their labor became the indispensable key to earn income for the household. They learned the virtue of working hard, of laboring at any task their parents decided, and of becoming frugal. By the mid-teens a youngster was expected to work as an adult; women, too, labored in the fields when work demanded it.

Seasonal Work Demand The clusters of villages dependent upon the small market towns produced nearly all the goods and services demanded, as well as a few for trade elsewhere. The wide range of occupations available in these communities encouraged parents to teach their children these skills or allow the youngster to work for short periods as apprentices. As households farmed only when seasonal demand dictated, the periods of idleness meant that household labor could be allocated to other tasks: to work in the market towns, to perform handicraft work in the home, or to labor for other farmers. During the busy farming season family farms always employed some laborers to work for several weeks or even a month to plant or to harvest. Large, wealthy households might hire several or more laborers to live in, farm the fields, and labor around the farmstead. They paid wages in cash and kind. The local wage rates were competitively determined according to available supply and demand. Therefore, during the busy farm season, day and monthly wages rose but then leveled off or fell during the slack seasons.

Hiring Practices In large and even small communities special streets, corners, and bridges served as points for workers to meet and hire themselves out to the highest bidder. Those people seeking short- or long-term labor could always find likely candidates to bargain for wages and the terms of work. The following description of labor-hiring practices in Soochow city in the early eighteenth century probably was common to all cities:

> The inhabitants of the eastern section of the prefectural city [Soochow] are all textile workers. . . . Each weaver has a special skill, and each has a regular employer, who pays him a daily wage. If anything should happen [to the regular weaver, the employer] will get a worker who is without regular employment to take his place; this is known as "calling a substi-

tute." The weavers without regular employers go to the bridges at dawn each day to await the calls. Satin weavers stand on Flower Bridge, damask weavers on Kuang-hua Temple Bridge, and spinners who make silk yarn at Lin hsi War. They congregate by the score and by the hundred, scanning around expectantly with outstretched necks, resembling groups of famine refugees. They will stay until after the breakfast hour. If work should be curtailed at the silk textile establishments, these workers would be without a living.[15]

As every city and market town contained some kind of formal labor market like those of Soochow, we can begin to understand the labor-surplus character of this economy. With so much labor always seeking employment, the organizers of production and exchange had little or no inducement to find labor-saving methods. The perennial problem was how to find employment for the available supply of labor.

Interest Payments

Households functioned as small, cooperative units to make their decisions on how to allocate resources and distribute and use their income. Considerable group discussion always ensued to decide the allocation of labor, the expenditure of income, and the rate and method of saving. Households always tried to finance their activities from their savings. Rarely did they borrow—except for ceremonies, important social events such as the birth of a male child, a wedding, or a funeral, or out of real desperation. When savings were short, a household first borrowed from kin, then friends, and finally strangers. For a small loan, the borrowers sought funds from kin and friends. For a large loan, a borrower might be compelled to seek out a stranger. Because of the high risk for lenders, a borrower had to pledge some asset as collateral. This practice took two forms. For a small loan the lender might loan against a pledge for a plot of land or a structure. The borrower paid a monthly interest rate usually between 2 and 3 percent and repaid the principal after an agreed-upon period. For a large loan the borrower invariably mortgaged a plot of land (*tien*) or gave other property like a structure to the lender for his use until he could repay the loan. In such a case the borrower did not pay any interest to the lender who used the asset and received the income it earned.

Household Land Mortgages   Such a borrowing arrangement could last as long as sixty years—as the following example, a customary law deed for mortgaging land between two households in Manchuria, shows:[16]

A CONTRACT
FOR MORTGAGING LAND

I, Wang Lien-fu, a Captain in the Plain White Division of the Chinese Banner Troops, have drawn up the following mortgage contract (*tien*). Because I am too poor to make a living and cannot pay my taxes of money and grain, I have decided to mortgage the land attached to my house to Wang Yu-sung for him to develop and farm. I have agreed with all parties concerned that the mortgage price will be exactly 360 strings of cash. I will receive this amount in full without any deficit on the same day this contract is finalized. I fear there is not sufficient proof of our agreement, and I have drawn up this mortgage contract as evidence. . . .

Middleman: Tung Hsiang
Eyewitness: Ts'ui Wan-i
Scribe: Shao Yung-t'ai
June 13, 1771

The last section of this contract describing the location of the land has been omitted. The practice of pledging as collateral and paying interest for small loans or mortgaging property instead of paying interest on a large loan was very widely practiced as lending and borrowing arrangements. After very long periods, the household eventually did repay a large loan and remortgage its land. However, for debtors to give up their remortgage right after a stipulated period and lose ownership was not uncommon. In such cases, that household might even be allowed to farm its former land but then pay rent. The near-money quality of land made it an asset households eagerly tried to buy. These lending arrangements permitted loanable funds to be dispensed and invariably to be used in buying consumer goods rather than resources to produce capital goods.

Wealthy households always loaned some of their savings for secure loans, especially when those agreements were pledged with high-value property as collateral. Two institutions, however, also supplied loanable funds and became more prominent after 1700 than ever before. The first was the pawnshop (*tien-tang*); the second was the financial firm, usually referred to as a bank (*ch'ien-chuang*).

Pawnshop Profits The number of pawnshops rapidly increased after the 1730s. These establishments made loans either of cash or food grain in exchange for a pledge of collateral and a monthly interest payment of usually 1 or 2 percent. Salt and rice merchants first made these kinds of loans. Their rapid trade turnover constantly gave them a supply of funds that easily remained idle if the merchants did not work hard to lend it. Rice merchants, for example, "took 1,000 taels of silver and purchased a lot of rice. They then loaned this to one party and then another, to increase their funds another 700 or 800 taels.

They again bought some rice and repeated the operation to accumulate another 500 or 600 taels. If they repeated this operation many times, the result was their initial cash could be quadrupled."[17] Another source of demand encouraged pawnshop development in the north—particularly around the capital. The Manchu nobility constantly were in debt because of their inability to manage their wealth and bargain as well as the Chinese. They soon became perennial visitors to Chinese *tien-tang* and pledged their household objects and even their land for loans.

Chinese Banks The *ch'ien-chuang,* on the other hand, provided many functions: They accepted deposits from the rich and paid interest for their use, remitted money from one area to another for a client, made loans to merchants until they could sell their goods, or simply loaned to reliable customers. The following description of these financial firms in Ningpo city, a prosperous commercial center in northern Chekiang province, shows the important role of these banks to supply loanable funds:

> The port of Ningpo had long had a reputation for money-lending. . . . This has been true since the time when the wealthy families of Ningpo opened *ch'ien-chuang,* and everyone who had any money wanted to deposit it in these shops, receiving a certain rate of interest on the sum from the manager. In turn, merchants in every line of business have borrowed money from these *ch'ien-chuang,* likewise paying interest on it. They simply record their transactions in a passbook, eliminating the need for an exchange of cash. The people, too, in supplying their daily needs, merely draw a draft on a money house *(ch'ien tien)* for the amount they need and use the draft as payment. . . .[18]

These institutions functioned just as banks. They mobilized the savings of the wealthy households and either made direct loans or issued notes on these deposits they held for any contingency.

In spite of the gradual growth of the supply of funds, either through these institutions or by individual households, the demand for funds also rose. We do not observe any long-term decline in the structure of monthly interest rates. The available supply of such funds merely kept pace with demand so that interest rates did not change.[19]

Profits

Those households organizing production and exchange always hoped to earn an income beyond that of covering their costs to pay for factor services, raw materials, and intermediary products. More importantly, they expected that additional income or profit to be equal to, if not greater than, what could be earned if they organized their activities differently. In other words, they hoped to earn as much as their *opportunity costs*—that is, income foregone when resources had been used in alternative activities. Sometimes, of course, they did earn more—windfall profits—and as unexpected as this money was, such profits could launch the household into great wealth and high social status if the profits were used to buy and sell assets like land.

Business Partnerships   Households sometimes pooled their savings to start a business that they had perceived as potentially profitable. This arrangement included two, three, or more investors pooling their funds, employing a manager and workers, and sharing the profits of the business. Each investor received a share of the profit depending upon the amount he had initially contributed. The following customary law contract for a group of investors who had organized a coal mine in Hopei province in the eighteenth century shows how this arrangement actually worked:[20]

A CONTRACT FOR A BUSINESS PARTNERSHIP

We the undersigned, An Kuo-hsi, An Kuo-ch'ang, and Liu Hsiao-ch'eng have drawn up a partnership agreement. We realize that wealth is derived from joint efforts, and any undertaking largely depends upon human efforts. We three know each other well, and the high moral virtue we possess is so strong it can cut through any metal. Now each of us have advanced some capital to revive the coal mine enterprise called Shang-chen tzu-hai [near Peking]. We have agreed to hire a general manager, paid from our public fund, to operate our coal mine enterprise with determination and hard work. We recognize the outstanding accounts that were incurred before our partnership was formed. Except for that residual coal slag usually reserved for the landlord, the remaining profit will be equally divided between the three of us. Those hired to work outside the mine can be asked to perform services for each of the three families [the two Ans and Liu] on an equivalent basis. From now on we must strive for patience, harmony, and impartiality. We must not act arbitrarily, quarrel with each other, or harbor any selfish desire to profit for ourselves. If any of us commit these evils, the gods in heaven will truly know about it. If one such wrong is discovered, the party in error will be fined ten-fold. This procedure is designed to punish any fraudulent and unbecoming conduct. We will wait until our accounts have been cleared before asking our employees to perform any services. In order to have concrete evidence of this agreement, we draw up four copies of this agreement in the same format. Each party will keep a copy as proof.

Individuals who drew up this partnership agreement: An Kuo-hsi
[signed]
An Kuo-ch' ang
Liu Hsiao-ch' eng
Relatives and Friends Witnessing the Affixing of Signatures:Chao
Wei [cross only]
Liu Yao [cross only]
Yang Chih-mao [cross only]
Landlord: Chiang Kuei
Scribe: Chao Shih-ying
December 13, 1759

Note that the parties strongly emphasized mutual trust and the need to cooperate and to be honest with each other. These important qualities greatly determined the success and durability of such partnerships. All three agreed to share profits equally; all three had invested equivalent sums in the enterprise.

One partner could use a contract to force the others to comply to the original agreement. These customary law contracts served as documentary proof that the investing parties had given their word, and if later broken, the contract could be taken to the official *yamen* and a suit initiated. Of course, this action meant enormous expense, and partners tried to avoid it at all cost. Kinship ties and go-betweens were first used to enforce compliance to these partnership agreements.

How profitable were these partnerships? As this arrangement only served to mobilize capital for large undertakings, profitability still depended upon supply and demand conditions in the market. The historical record about profit is silent. But some twentieth century evidence suggests profits could be great and that losses could bankrupt the partners. A 1937 study of 225 commercial enterprises in Kirin, Yinkow, and Chinchow cities of Manchuria by the Japanese South Manchurian Railway Research Bureau revealed these businesses had invested capital totaling 7,266,846 yuan, and the annual profit received came to 4,062,911 or a 56 percent return on capital invested. Yet, in the depression following the Russo–Japanese War, a partnership bank managed by three brothers of the Huang family in Kiangsi province had over 50,000 taels investment but accumulated liabilities of over 2,447,000 taels, which finally bankrupted the bank.[21]

CONSUMPTION, SAVINGS, AND INVESTMENT

An economy with a per capita income slightly less than 100 U.S. dollars is very poor. China of the eighteenth and early nineteenth century was indeed poor, although some Western travelers during the 1840s did not convey such an impression in their writings about this country. The English tea expert Samuel Ball pointed out in 1848 that the Chinese laborer had a living standard considerably above that of the Indian agriculturalist and not very much lower than the European peasant.[22] By 1900, however, Europeans described China's poverty and backwardness in vivid brushstrokes, strongly emphasizing the huge gap in material living standards between the two worlds.

We know very little about the consumption patterns of the Chinese common people for this time. Surveys of urban and rural household budget sources and outlays during the 1920s and 1930s provide a possible clue for what these patterns might have been in an earlier period, but using these to infer about the past is risky. Let us look at this evidence anyway.

Household Budget Sources and Outlay

First, rural households relied upon product and factor markets to obtain perhaps as much as 30 to 35 percent of their total income in cash. A survey of 681 rural families in northern Manchuria in 1934 showed that 45 percent of total household income was in cash, but 8 percent of this cash came from loans, sale of assets, and loan repayments. If these are excluded, cash income amounted to 37 percent of total household income. Between 1921 and 1925 John L. Buck's rural surveys showed that farm sales exceeded 50 percent of total farm earnings whether the family rented, owned part and rented part, or owned all of the land it cultivated. The late imperial economy still was a highly monetized economy. The very wealthy households undoubtedly had a high cash flow each year.

Second, because per capita income was so low, the average propensity to consume was high. For this reason, most households spent as much as 60 to 80 percent of their expenditures on food alone, the rest for clothing, shelter, and miscellaneous goods and services. The ordinary Chinese dressed simply; his household contained the barest of essentials—a table and some chairs—and roofs were primarily of thatch, except in the towns and cities. Aside from festivals, the daily diet was plain with coarse grains and sweet potato, instead of wheat and rice, as the mainstay.

Upper Class Saving and Spending Habits

Third, as income rose, so too did savings, but only the very wealthy could afford to save. The propensity to save from cash income at the higher income level was probably very high—as twentieth century rural surveys show.[23] Members of the literati or gentry, merchants, and landlords were the principal savers. The gentry constantly acquired cash from the many services they rendered; merchants and landlords always received a large cash flow from sale of goods, rents, or loan repayments. Most of this cash flow at first was hoarded as silver or copper cash, deposited in *ch'ien-chuang,* or later used to buy assets as a financial investment. The Chinese possessed a powerful speculative motive; the wealthy always competed to buy land, structures, precious metals, or stocks of grain in the anticipation that the rise in value of these assets would net a high rate of return.

We are given a fleeting glimpse of the saving and spending habits of the elite from the household account kept by an official in the Board of Works who lived for more than a quarter of a century in Peking.[24] Li Ts'u-ming lived in a fashionable section of Peking, employed three or four servants, and eventually acquired three concubines. Li's mother had sold some land in their hometown of Shaohsing in Chekiang province in order for him to purchase a degree. In 1870 he became a *chü-jen* and later a *chin-shih* with a fifth grade rank. Li kept an annual account between 1836 and 1889, but between 1865 and 1870 he lived in Chekiang. After his return to Peking, Li's total income during the next eighteen years came to 16,863 taels of which 31 percent was in gifts. In only one year, 1887, did expenditures exceed income. His total expenditures came to 8,462 taels of which 10 percent was given in gifts and rewards. Li clearly received more than he gave. All the elite resorted to exchanging gifts in the same way as they spent hugely for feasts and entertainment. Whether one received more than one gave—in proportion to the higher one advanced in officialdom—is unclear, but these spending habits had to be cultivated if one's career was to be successful.

Contrary to the accepted view that officials never lived on their incomes, constantly overspent, and resorted to corruption to make ends meet, Li carefully watched the spending of every copper wen piece and recorded it faithfully. Li certainly lived comfortably, and what he did with the more than 8,000 taels he saved is not mentioned in his financial records or daily diary. Whether he owned property elsewhere or made other investments is unknown. What seems clear in his case is that officials had diverse sources of income. Li lectured, rendered services, received gifts, and, of course, wrote. If Li's case was fairly typical of the nearly fifteen hundred officials in Peking, the elite certainly lived comfortably, saved considerably, and worked hard.

Average Household Saving and Spending Habits

If the masses of people consumed most of what they produced and earned, and thereby saved little, the household, rather than the individual, had to be the major saving unit. As individuals pooled their savings, the household collectively then bought and sold assets but eventually and gradually even accumulated some wealth. They perhaps behaved in the following way: Household members organized their resources as a cooperating unit and allocated their labor and physical resources to the highest bidder—just as in a partnership when its members organized a business enterprise. All earnings, even those received when the household produced and sold goods or services in the marketplace, were pooled. Household consumption was restricted to the tolerable level, and the remainder of the income was then saved. With luck, hard work, and thrift a household might accumulate enough money to produce or buy the capital goods it needed or to purchase assets for speculative purposes. The desire to do one or the other was dictated by the risk attached and the expected rate of return. As one would expect in this labor-abundant, land-scarce economy, the rate of return for buying and using capital goods was low— perhaps not higher than 3 or 4 percent per year or what a household generally earned by investing its capital to farm.

Capital Investments

Practically no information is available on the prevailing rate of return for alternate financial investments in late imperial times. For example, we simply do not know whether a household with one hundred taels of cash savings might prefer to invest in a handicraft business, to buy grain and sell it later, to purchase some land, to loan at the prevailing interest rate, or to spend for a tutor to instruct a clever son to pass the imperial exams. These were some of the short- and long-term possibilities available for households with savings. The low rate of return that could only be realized for the majority of households, namely, for farming, remained low because of the low marginal productivity of farm capital. The small demand for funds to buy and produce capital goods also reflected this low rate of return in farming and handicraft. Technological change simply had not progressed enough to increase the productivity of capital; technological change merely had made land more productive and saved land resources. Had technological change increased capital productivity and enabled the use of more land resources at the same time, the rate of return to capital stock might have been increased as figure 4–3 shows.

Improved technological change would have shifted the marginal productivity schedule for capital from MM to $M'M'$ and thus produced a higher rate of return to capital OR' and reflected capital's higher productivity. But very minor improvements of technology only altered the elasticity of the marginal productivity of capital to schedule $M''M''$ without raising the rate of return OR as the supply of loanable funds gradually increased over time $S'S'$. Therefore, the rate of

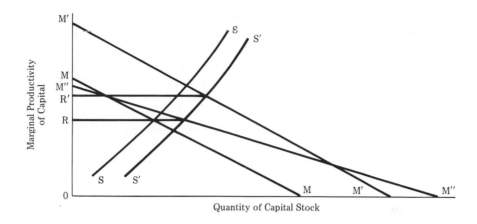

FIGURE 4–3.   The Effect of New Capital Formation on the Productivity of Capital

return to capital stock remained low over time in the vicinity of *OR* or in real terms, probably between 3 and 5 percent.

ECONOMIC DEVELOPMENT BY TECHNOLOGICAL REFINEMENT

The paradox in China was this: In 1313 China already possessed water-powered machines for twisting hemp and silk; Europe also had these. By the nineteenth century, however, China had not been able to take advantage of its former high technological advancement. The Chinese neither developed new sources of energy nor invented machines to increase the productivity of both labor and capital; Europe had done so. Instead, the Chinese had reverted entirely to using labor power to operate multispindle machines for silk spinning and intricate hand weaving looms for making silk and cotton cloth. Refinement of technology rather than technological breakthrough had taken place.[25]

Use of Abundant Labor and Land Productivity

What seems to have occurred was the following: The product and factor markets continually adjusted smoothly to eliminate any threatening commodity and resource scarcities. Therefore, as population steadily expanded, the labor force had to compete even more vigorously to produce enough food, shelter, and clothing just to maintain existing living standards—simple and poor as these were. More people meant using more land resources so that some resources steadily became scarce. Yet with great ingenuity and skill the Chinese devised all kinds of ways to use waste products and substitute more abundant resources to prevent certain land resources from becoming acutely scarce. For example, already by the eighteenth century Chinese farmers transported great quantities of top soil from their fields to nearby piles of waste and then back to the fields to fertilize their land; or they moved great amounts of soil and mud from swamps and rivers to enrich their fields. Concerning the efforts of the Chinese to produce more copper, Wu Chin-yu, governor-general of Yunnan and Kweichow in the early nineteenth century, spoke of the "hundreds of strategems" tried to drain the copper mines, and of the "limitless expense" of the work to dig deeper and find more copper.[26] For producing more salt, workers adopted the slower, more labor-intensive method of evaporating brine through solar energy rather than using fuel to boil the brine in large vats.

Without abundant land resources but possessed with abundant labor, the Chinese might have concentrated on producing capital to offset scarcity of land resources. Instead, technological advance concentrated on how to use labor more intensively and at the same time save land resources. For example, progress in farming technology in late imperial times mainly involved increasing the cropping index or obtaining more crops per year from the same unit of land. Although great efforts were made to reclaim land and expand the land area, in the older economic core areas supporting the highest population density, the efforts continually focused upon improving practices to raise overall yield by cropping the land more intensively. Therefore, the technological improvements that occurred were oriented toward making land more productive but not necessarily toward raising labor or capital productivity. The very low average and marginal productivity of capital simply meant that a low return to capital always existed. Those with savings to invest would not be encouraged to purchase or produce capital goods when alternative investment returns were higher. But this is only part of the explanation for why capital stock did not increase rapidly and why its productivity was so low.

The Role of the Elite   The remaining part of the explanation lies with the attitudes and behavior of the elite, who did most of the saving and were in a position to encourage technological change and more investment in capital stock. Space does not permit a review of Chinese political culture and of the key values and beliefs which the elite held. In essence, the elite were obsessed with how to develop proper moral behavior and how to rule others. Their energy and time were spent chiefly in debating these issues by reference to complex texts, that required many years to master. The cultural ethos necessary to nudge their mental efforts toward mastery of physical phenomenon—either by trying to transform one's environment or developing principles to understand it—did not exist.

The elite used their savings in two ways. First, they spent a large share to maintain a comfortable life-style for ego-satisfying purposes. Part of these expenditures also were income transfers to other elite to ensure their social and political advance. Second, they spent the remainder on projects that in fact created physical capital and, to a lesser extent, even improved human capital. For example, the gentry spent their money to establish irrigation works, bridges, city walls, and roads, but they also founded schools, temples, and famine relief institutions and gave to charity—activities that marginally at least enabled the common people to develop their minds and bodies to labor in this agricultural society. Many examples can by given to show the gentry's role in organizing and financing these projects. For instance, in Cho-hsien of Chihli province, a rural gentry member "took an active part in such matters as bridge and road construction, establishment of shrines and temples, relief work, and charity schools, also promoted an irrigation project for his locality."[27]

For these reasons, then, only a small supply of savings was channeled for the maintenance and augmentation of capital stock. A redistribution of income would not have increased savings or altered this pattern of investment. The prevailing ethos of late imperial China would merely have transmitted the same values and beliefs to a new elite to make for similar spending and saving habits. Meanwhile, successful operation of the highly competitive market economy and the contractual arrangements developed by households to overcome scarcity are two significant factors that account for why units of production and exchange could support such a large and continually growing population. Technological refinements aimed at preventing the decline of land resource productivity and always making lavish use of abundant labor. But these efforts did not raise the productivity of the existing capital stock. This economic system always could expand—except when confronted with the devastating effects of deflation, namely, rising and widespread unemployment. Then the system became increasingly unstable. When unemployment became serious enough to threaten social and political stability—as it did in the 1830s and 1840s—imperial China finally became engulfed by rebellion.

QUESTIONS FOR DISCUSSION

1. What kind of market structure for basic commodities such as rice, silk, and tea characterized the Ch'ing economy? What are the implications for Ch'ing economic development of such a market structure?

2. What role did customary law play in the exchange between households in the factor market?

3. Did any significant long-term change in relative factor prices occur in the late imperial period? What would such a change have signified for this economic system?

4. What factors account for the very low rate of return to investment in capital during the Ch'ing period? What economic conditions probably existed to prevent the rate of return for such investment from becoming higher?

NOTES

1. Quoted from Abe Takeo, "A Study of Rice Supply and Demand," in *Shindaishi no kenkyū* [Studies in Ch'ing History] (Tokyo: Sōbunsha, 1971), p. 495.

2. Ch'uan Han-sheng and Richard A. Kraus, *Mid-Ch'ing Rice Markets and Trade: An Essay in Price History* (Cambridge, Mass.: Harvard University Press, 1975), pp. 70, 72–78.

3. Shigeta Atsushi, *Shindai shakai keizaishi kenkyū* [Studies of Social and Economic History of the Ch'ing Period] (Tokyo: Iwanami shoten, 1975), p. 25.

4. Ibid.

5. Higashi Norimasa, comp., *Chūbu Shina keizai chōsa* [An Economic Survey of Central China] (Tokyo: Fuzambo, 1915), vol. 1, pp. 1 and 361.

6. Abe Takeo, *Shindaishi no kenkyū* [Ch'ing History], pp. 498–99.

7. Yokoyama Suguru, *Chūgoku kindaika no keizai kōzō* [The Modernization of China's Economic Structure] (Tokyo: Akishobo, 1972), p. 63.

8. Mark Elvin, "The High-Level Equilibrium Trap: The Causes of the Decline of Invention in the Traditional Chinese Textile Industries," in W. E. Willmott, ed., *Economic Organization in Chinese Society* (Stanford, Calif.: Stanford University Press, 1972), p. 158.

9. E-Tu Zen Sun, "Sericulture and Silk Textile Production in Ch'ing China," in Willmott, ed., *Economic Organization*, p. 80.

10. Robert Fortune, *Three Years' Wanderings in the Northern Provinces of China* (London: John Murray, 1847), p. 190.

11. Ibid., pp. 207–08.

12. In the parlance of the economist *normal profit* denotes the opportunity costs of using capital in one's selected business. In the long run "normal" profit in purely competitive markets means opportunity costs, and *economic profits* denotes any revenue in excess of covering total costs, which includes opportunity costs.

13. Fu-mei Chang Chen and Ramon H. Myers, "Customary Law and the Economic Growth of China during the Ch'ing Period," pt.1, *Ch'ing-shih wen-t'i* [Problems in Ch'ing History] 3, no. 5 (November 1976): 10–11.

14. This analysis follows the outline in Steven N.S. Cheung, *The Theory of Share Tenancy* (Chicago: University of Chicago Press, 1969), chapter 2, especially p. 17.

15. E-Tu Zen Sun, "Sericulture and Silk," p. 96.

16. Fu-mei Chang Chen and Ramon H. Myers, *Customary Law and Economic Growth*, p. 23.

17. Abe Takeo, *Shindaishi no kenkyū* [Ch'ing History], p. 376.

18. Susan Mann Jones, "Finance in Ningpo: The 'Ch'ien-Chuang,' 1750–1880," in W. E. Willmott, ed., *Economic Organization*, p. 57.

19. In other words, the following shifts in supply of and demand for loanable funds seems to have taken place in late imperial China. The L and L' schedules are the positive sloping loanable funds schedule. The D and D' schedules represent the demand schedule. The equilibrium monthly interest rate of 2 percent occurs for the supplies of OS and OS' funds loaned. The long-term shift in supply and demand schedules merely reproduces the same monthly interest rate but with a larger amount of funds being loaned.

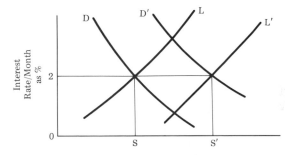

Quantity of Loanable Funds

20. Fu-mei Chang Chen and Ramon H. Myers, "Customary Law and the Economic Growth of China during the Ch'ing Period," pt. II, *Ch'ing-shih wen-t'i* [Problems in Ch'ing History] 3, no. 9 (November 1977).

21. Tōa kenkyūjo, *Shōji ni kansuru kankō chōsa hōkokusho: gōko no kenkyū* [A Survey Report of Customs Concerning Commerce: A Study of Ho-huo Partnerships] (Tokyo: Tōa Kenkyūjo, 1943), pp. 19–20.

22. Samuel Ball, *An Account of the Cultivation and Manufacture of Tea in China* (London: Longman, Brown, Green and Longmans, 1848), pp. 337–40.

23. Ramon H. Myers, "The Commercialization of Agriculture in Modern China," in Willmott, ed., *Economic Organization*, p. 180.

24. Chang Te-ch'ang, *Ch'ing-chi i-ko ching-kuan-te sheng-huo* [The Life of a Capital Official in Late Ch'ing Times] (Hong Kong: Chinese University of Hong Kong, 1970), pp. 70–218, which gives the annual accounts of incomes and outlays. See the excellent review of this work by Thomas A. Metzger, *Journal of Asian Studies* 31, no. 3 (May 1972): 647–50.

25. For examples of different kinds of technological refinements during the late imperial period see Mark Elvin, "Skills and Resources in Late Traditional China," in Dwight H. Perkins, ed., *China's Modern Economy in Historical Perspective* (Stanford, Calif.: Stanford University Press, 1975), pp. 85–113.

26. Ibid., p. 106.

27. Chung-li Chang, *The Chinese Gentry: Studies on Their Role in Nineteenth Century Chinese Society* (Seattle: University of Washington Press, 1955), p. 58.

SELECTED READINGS

1. Susan Mann Jones. "Finance in Ningpo: The 'Ch'ien Chuang,' 1750–1880." In W. E. Willmott, ed., *Economic Organization in Chinese Society.* Stanford, Calif.: Stanford University Press, 1972, pp. 47–78.

2. E-Tu Zen Sun. "Sericulture and Silk Textile Production in Ch'ing China." In Willmott, ed., *Economic Organization,* pp. 79–109.

3. Craig Dietrich. "Cotton Culture and Manufacture in Early Ch'ing China."In Willmott, ed., *Economic Organization,* pp. 109–36.

4. Mark Elvin, "The High-Level Equilibrium Trap: The Causes of the Decline of Invention in the Traditional Chinese Textile Industries." In Willmott, ed., *Economic Organization,* pp. 137–72.

5. Ramon H. Myers. "The Commercialization of Agriculture in Modern China." In Willmott, ed., *Economic Organization,* pp. 173–92.

6. Mark Elvin. "Skills and Resources in Late Traditional China." In Dwight H. Perkins, ed., *China's Modern Economy in Historical Perspective.* Stanford, Calif.: Stanford University Press, 1975, pp. 85–114.

7. ———. "Market Towns and Waterways: The County of Shang-hai from 1840–1910." In G.W. Skinner, ed., *The City in Late Imperial China.* Stanford, Calif.: Stanford University Press, 1977, pp. 441–74.

8. Peter J. Golas. "Early Ch'ing Guilds." In Skinner, ed., *The City,* pp. 555–81.

9. Yoshinobu Shiba. "Ningpo and Its Hinterland." In Skinner, ed., *The City,* pp. 391–440.

10. Ramon H. Myers, "Merchants and Economic Organization during the Ming and Ch'ing Periods." *Ch'ing-shih wen-t'i* [Problems in Ch'ing History] 3, no. 2 (December 1974): 77–97.

11. Fu-mei Chang Chen and Ramon H. Myers. "Customary Law and the Economic Growth of China during the Ch'ing Period." *Ch'ing-shih wen-t'i* [Problems in Ch'ing History] 3, no. 5 (November 1976) and 3, no. 9 (November 1978).

Early Modern
Economic
Development

Part Three

Foreign Economic Impact

5

The Nanking Treaty of 1842 concluded the first British-Chinese conflict known as the Opium War, opened the port cities of Canton, Amoy, Foochow, Ningpo and Shanghai to British trade, and gave the English the right to live and conduct business in these cities. The Tientsin Treaty of 1858 and the Peking Treaty of 1860 further extended foreign influence in the country by opening another fourteen port cities to foreign trade, which will be referred to hereafter as *treaty ports*.[1] However, another thirty-five years had to elapse before vigorous modernization of the economy began. By 1895 very little progress in that direction had occurred. Trade with foreign countries advanced very slowly: between 1871–1884 and 1885–1900 total trade rose only from 208.7 to 253.7 million U.S. dollars. The country had only 1,000 km. of railroads. Modern enterprises using new sources of power and methods were few: by 1894 only 101 foreign and joint Sino–foreign firms operated with not more than 20 million Chinese dollars (yuan).

Why the glacial progress and the long delay before the government truly initiated reforms to launch modern enterprises? When the government did create a few, new industries, why had these "model enterprises" not inspired private investors to follow suit? Foreign trade had stimulated certain industries to supply more for export, and some imports had even undermined local handicraft. Were the gains from foreign trade beneficial enough to modernize handicraft industries without causing massive dislocation and decline in most handicraft industries? By the 1890s the Chinese state began incurring many foreign loans—some for buying military hardware, others for railroads, and still others to pay indemnities. Did this new debt burden seriously impair the state's capacity to encourage modern economic development?

Conditions drastically changed in 1895 after the Treaty of Shimonoseki, which concluded the Sino-Japanese War waged in 1894 and 1895. This treaty permitted foreigners to establish their enterprises and freely invest in China and allowed Chinese business leaders to import foreign machinery without obtaining official permission. During the next two decades total trade rose fivefold to reach 1,092 million U.S. dollars by 1915–1919. Between 1890 and 1920 the country acquired 11,338 km. of railroads to account for nearly half of the country's entire railroad system built by 1948. Between 1895 and 1911 another 649 Chinese firms began using modern machinery with total investment amounting to roughly 120 million Chinese dollars. Then between 1913 and 1920 Chinese business managers established another 1,061 modern factories with capital investment totaling around 170 million Chinese dollars and employing over a quarter million workers. At long last an unprecedented industrial spurt had begun, then accelerated during the World War I period, and still continued during the 1920s but at a slower pace.

This rapid industrial spurt did not penetrate all areas of the economic system. It remained confined to a few specific areas—that is, the port cities and their environs. Had the presence of foreign business operators with superior access to loanable funds, new technology, and foreign markets placed Chinese business people at such a disadvantage as to prevent them from organizing more modern industry than they actually did? Who were the new Chinese business leaders that became aware of the enormous benefits of modern technology and used it to organize production and exchange? Did the state continue to render them assistance or ignore their creative efforts? What were the fundamental characteristics of this new, early modern industry in China?

MODERN ENTERPRISES IN THE TREATY PORTS

The Chinese factor and product markets continually had made adjustments to prevent severe commodity and resource scarcities from emerging. Meanwhile, the state had demanded little from the private sector. This sector had grown to immense size because the organizers of production and exchange had chosen methods that made intensive use of the abundant productive factor—labor—and conserved the scarce production factor—land. Yet this society had failed to create any new technology with enough potential for raising the productivity of land and labor. Crushing the great rebellions of the 1850–1865 period had absorbed all the energies of the Ch'ing state. Chinese officials now focused their efforts to rehabilitate the ravaged economy and with relief looked forward to social stability and peace. They deplored any threats or changes that might create trouble for themselves. Only a handful of officials were really aware of the benefits of modern technology. So, given the psychological temper of the period, most officials viewed modern technology as a threat that most likely would initiate unintended and uncontrolled consequences such as unemployment and the disruption of rural industry.

J. R. Young, the American ambassador to China in the early 1880s, reported to the secretary of state the following information he had received from his deputy consul general in Shanghai:

> The Taotai* says that one half of the population of the provinces of Kiangsu and Chekiang is engaged in farming and the other half in weaving silk. These provinces are among the most populous in the empire. Kiangsu, with a geographical area about the same as Pennsylvania, has a population of over 37,000,000. Chekiang, a province a fraction smaller than Ohio, has over 26,000,000, a density which will be more readily appreciated when we remember that in Kiangsu this gives 850 souls to the square mile, and an average of 671 in Chekiang. The government of a population so vast and so dense, one-half of which depends for bread upon silk weaving, is a task that might perplex any ruler. The Taotai, accordingly, express the fear that "should the foreigners introduce and use machinery for the purpose of weaving silk, the difference between the amount of work done by manual labor and that done by machinery being very great, the latter system, it is feared, would render the Kiangsu and Chekiang people helpless, which would be very detrimental to their interests." The Taotai further points out that as an export the silk trade is of the first importance to the Chinese revenue. Foreigners had never engaged in its manufacture, and for them to do so now would not only "deprive Chinese who depend on silk reeling of their means of support," but divert revenues from the imperial treasury. "Moreover," continues the Taotai, in emphasis of his argument, "the Chinese who depend upon reeling silk and weaving silk goods for their support are countless in number, and they would be in a pitiable plight if they were suddenly deprived of their employments and the question of the support of such large hosts of people, it is feared, under the circumstances, will lead to trouble and complication."[2]

A few officials, of course, recognized that modern machinery for producing modern weaponry had merit, but they agreed with the Kiangsu province's Taotai's remarks that for weaving and tillage the machine endangered the economy. The attitude toward railroads was mixed. Mao Hung-pin, governor of Kwangtung province, argued that animal-driven carts could not compete with railways and many Chi-

---

*The *Taotai* or Intendant was a high-ranking official placed in administrative control over various sections of each provincial government.

nese would be made unemployed. The vicory Chang Chih-tung stressed the military value of railroads, but high-ranking officials like Li Hung-chang and Shen Pao-chen opposed railways on the grounds that foreigners acquired easy entry into the interior, and the country's defenses, already based in part upon natural geographic barriers, would be weakened.

Failure of Industries Sponsored by Officials

The official debate on modernization intensified with each passing year. Some officials with schemes for arsenals, shipbuilding, or coal mines used national defense as the pretext to memorialize and convince the court to grant permission to import machinery. Their initial concern was only to gain imperial permission for their project, for they knew that enough public funds always could be obtained to operate the enterprise. Powerful officials like Li Hung-chang then set up the China Merchants' Steam Navigation Company in 1873, the Kaiping Mines in 1877, and the Shanghai Cotton Company in 1873. Li, and officials like him, also hoped to mobilize merchant savings, but merchants soon recognized that official bribery and managerial ineptness made these ventures too risky to invest their capital. Further, these powerful patrons made grievous managerial errors. Chang Chih-tung located his ironworks too far from iron ore and coal reserves and bought the wrong machinery to process the iron ore of a high phosphorous content into iron and steel, and thus guaranteed high unit costs and virtually no profit margin. Again, these officials insisted upon a measure of enterprise control which rankled merchants and caused them to fear for their investments. For example, a number of merchants quickly lost their high posts in these enterprises.[3]

Chinese merchants readily perceived that investing in the new foreign enterprises instead of in state-sponsored industry could be more profitable and safe. By 1900 they owned some 60 percent of the shares of all foreign-run companies in the treaty ports. Many of these Chinese investors had started their careers as *compradores* or intermediaries by assisting foreign merchants to buy and sell in China. An enterprising young man with good business contacts and passable English might work for a foreign firm to provide information, sell its goods in the interior, and buy raw materials for it from other Chinese merchants. A famous compradore like Tong King-sing received 5,744 taels per annum for expenses in 1865, including 1,500 taels for his own salary.[4] Sunkee, a compradore to the British firm of Russell's at Tientsin from 1862 to 1873, earned 1,200 taels a year along with a house. From earnings like these, compradores started businesses of their own and invested in foreign firms. One estimate placed their total earnings between 1842 and 1894 at 530.8 million taels.[5] A new business class rapidly had emerged in this period, but these new merchants remained very apprehensive of investing in the officially sponsored industrial projects.

The officials promoting the new enterprises were always eager to use public funds and the monies of friends but rarely their own capital. The Mandarin official Sheng Hsüan-huai used the capital of a small group of colleagues in his enterprises—the Imperial Telegraph from the early 1880s, the Hua-sheng Spinning and Weaving Mill, the Hanyang Ironworks, and the Imperial Bank of China in the 1890s. He scarcely invested any of his own money. After China's defeat by the French in 1885 these senior officials redoubled their efforts to promote sponsored projects and relaxed their managerial control in order to attract more merchant capital. But for the same reasons cited above, these attempts ultimately failed—except for the Hua-hsin Spinning and Weaving Mill, which had been set up in 1888 and granted monopoly control in a prime location, Shanghai.

Lack of Court Support   This sorry spectacle of so few officially sponsored projects succeeding or attracting so little merchant capital can be attributed to the following factors: First, the court merely gave permission but not sustained and strong support to officials and their enterprises. The Kiangnan Arsenal between 1867 and 1875 is a good example of this phenomenon. Had the court assisted by underwriting some of the costs of supplying raw materials, parts and machines, and transport facilities for this arsenal, it would not have had to rely on "costly imported materials which raised production costs to prohibitive levels."[6] Even so, by 1875 this enterprise had completed fourteen vessels of Western design—thirteen of which were powered by steam machinery. But then the arsenal switched to producing military ordnance just when the court adopted a new defense policy of emphasizing maritime development. Li Hung-chang had ordered the arsenal to concentrate on ordnance to supply a land military force because he believed that production costs were too high to build ships and ordnance could be produced more cheaply instead. This judgment might have been correct, but the arsenal had to retool and lost a potential customer, the new Chinese navy.

The Noninvesting, Ill-Informed Promoter   Another factor was that official promoters did not take their management seriously because their own capital was not involved. With a private financial interest at stake, an investor-promoter quickly adopts the concerns of the entrepreneur, attempts to manage efficiently and prudently, and becomes very conscious of keeping costs low. Finally, these senior official-promoters had to depend upon the advice—often conflicting—of foreign engineers and business leaders for selecting the location, type of factory design, and kind of machines best suited for the enterprise. These officials simply never comprehended the enormous complexities of staffing, supplying, and operating these enterprises. Further, these enterprises were built in advance of any tangible demand and without any real understanding of the kind of demand and price necessary to cover average unit costs. Numerous initial management errors quickly snowballed and produced high, fixed costs, which were rarely reduced. Therefore, while a few officials grappled with the difficulties of establishing new factories and mines, the foreign business operator was becoming entrenched in the treaty ports, trading with Chinese business people, and helping to organize foreign trade.

The Activities and Influence of the Foreigner

What kind of foreign firms operated in China before 1895? Why did they attract so much Chinese mercantile capital, and why did they not serve as models for Ch'ing officials to learn to create and manage modern enterprises? Between 1840 and 1894, 101 foreign commercial firms were reportedly doing business in China: 70 English companies, 10 American, 9 German, 6 Russian, 4 French, 1 Dutch, and 1 Japanese.[7] Of the 83,000 industrial workers allegedly in modern enterprises—both Chinese and foreign—by 1894, the foreign firms alone employed 34,000 people or close to two-fifths of this work force. Foreign firms invested around 19.7 million yuan, including 4.9 and 4.0 million respectively in ship repair and construction and in tea processing. A rough count of some foreign enterprises places 10 for ship repair and building, perhaps 7 or 8 for tea processing, 6 in silk reeling, 7 in other processing industries like flour and bean oil, 20 in operations such as banking and printing, and 4 in public utilities.

The foreign merchants who came to China after 1840 sought profits from what they could either sell to the Chinese or buy from them to ship to foreign markets—especially in their own countries. The majority engaged in both pursuits and then gradually diversified their activities by entering such industries as tea processing, silk reeling, banking, steamboat shipping, warehousing, and printing. A famous commercial firm like Jardine, Matheson, and Company first made considerable profit in the opium trade between India and China and then branched into other lines. Russian firms like S.W. Litvinoff and Company and Tokmakoff, Molotkoff and Company that located at Hankow in 1863 and 1866 processed tea and shipped it to Russia. In 1878 Russell and Company established the Kee Chong Silk Filature Company in Shanghai. Such enterprises required less capital than did the mining-, metallurgical-, and military arsenal-type enterprises Chinese officials endeavored to create. These foreign firms also produced goods and services for a large market, whereas Chinese officially sponsored enterprises depended upon demand—which rarely materialized—from the public sector. Except for steamboat shipping, these foreign firms served as poor models for Chinese officials to develop their more capital-intensive industries. Nevertheless, their impact upon Chinese business leaders and the economy was considerable.

Profits from Exports   First, the foreigner enabled Chinese business owners to sell to a larger, more profitable market. The foreigner's access to overseas markets encouraged the Chinese to produce and sell more of the staple exports—silk and tea—and to introduce new goods onto the export market—bean oil, wood oil, strawbraid, vegetable tallow, hemp, safflower, hog bristle, medicines, and cotton nankeens. While the quantum growth of exports was only 1.9 percent per year between 1867–1868 and 1894–1895 or a near doubling of trade in 27 years, its profitability was enormous for both the Chinese and the foreigner.

Profitability originated from the large price differential between the prices of goods sold in world markets and the values at which they entered foreign trade. For example, the tea price of Tanshui, which is in Taiwan, then still a prefecture of Fukien province, in the 1860s was roughly 14.7 cents per pound compared to 20 cents per pound in Japan, London, and New York. By the early 1870s foreign tea prices had climbed to between 20.5 and 30.5 cents per pound, while at the same time the Tanshui price had roughly doubled to come more in line with foreign tea prices. As the quantity of tea leaving Taiwan rose fifteen-fold, this rise in price meant huge profits accruing to foreigner and Chinese alike. And what happened for tea applied to silk and other commodities as well shipped from other treaty ports.

Technological Modernization   Second, just as Chinese merchants earned more in an expanding market, so too did they learn and acquire new shipping and producing techniques that gradually modernized domestic transportation and handicraft. This technological transfer not only created a larger demand for goods—especially raw materials—but increased the productivity of labor and made these activities very profitable for entrepreneurs. Steamboat shipping and mechanized silk reeling are noteworthy examples.

An American, Edward Cunningham, a partner in the firm of Russell and Company in Shanghai, managed to induce that firm to set up the Shanghai Steamship Navigation Company in 1862. During the next decade the company eliminated all rivals and achieved an American steamship monopoly in the carrying trade on the Yangtze River and along the coast. Its four ships carried high value goods, such as cotton and woolen piece goods, opium, metals, and sugar, for which safer and speedier transport was preferred. The company could charge high rates because it catered to a low-elastic demand for this type of transportation service; and as the company reduced its costs by reverting to the use of coal, the profit per ton/mile increased greatly.[8]

The Shanghai S.N. Company served a widening circle of Chinese merchants, who shipped more goods from inland ports to Shanghai and ordered more foreign imports from as far north as Tientsin. In the early 1870s the Shanghai-based British firm of Butterfield and Swire mobilized capital in London, acquired several new steamships, and successfully challenged the American steamship monopoly. Then in 1872 Li Hung-chang called for a Chinese government-supported steamship company to be founded. In 1873 the China Merchants' Steam Navigation Company with five steamships began operation. The famous Kwangtung compradore Tong King-sing resigned from Jardine's and became the director of the new Chinese steamship for a brief period. Thus, the advent of the foreign steamship not only made possible the expansion of Chinese merchant trade between the treaty ports but stimulated Chinese enterprise.

After 1873 Chinese business owners began to adopt the steam-powered, silk-reeling filatures that foreign firms had already introduced. First, they used the foot-pedal-operated silk-reeling machines, but later they switched to steam-powered machines during the 1880s. In 1890 only 5 such factories existed in Shanghai, but by 1897 their number had increased to 25 with 7500 reeling machines. The use of silk-reeling machines rapidly spread to other cities near the silk-producing areas as small cottage industry sprang up to adopt them. This development in turn increased the demand for raw silk so that cocoon prices rose greatly. For the next decade the producers of raw materials struggled to supply enough cocoons and raw silk to the steam filature factories. Owners of these factories often had to shut down operations for lack of raw materials. After 1911, however, the domestic silk industry encountered more competition abroad—particularly from Japan and such commodity substitutes as synthetics.

Apprenticeships with Foreign Firms A third favorable influence was the training and salary received by astute Chinese who worked for foreign merchants and later left to organize their own firms. Hsü Jun, born in Macao in 1838, went to work for Dent and Company in Shanghai as a teenage apprentice through the assistance of an uncle. In 1861 he became an agent representing Dent and Company to deal with other Chinese firms—in other words, a compradore. From his large commissions he began to set up—on his own—establishments in the tea trade, insurance, and shipping, and he even served a brief stint as general manager of the China Merchants' Steam Navigation Company until 1884. Later Hsü Jun invested heavily in Shanghai real estate, but in 1883 he found himself financially overextended, and thus one of the city's wealthiest business leaders suffered huge financial losses.

The foreign influence during these decades was favorable for Chinese business people. As the treaty ports grew in size and complexity, so did trade between the interior and the outside world. The technological transfer from foreigner to Chinese and the new, lucrative export trades made possible the creation of new Chinese firms and their investing large sums in foreign firms. The impact of these activities upon the hinterland also was far reaching.

RESPONSE OF THE HINTERLAND ECONOMY

We have already observed that the cotton textile industry produced two types of cotton cloth: coarse cloth woven and used by villagers themselves, and fine cloth fulled and dyed in the cities but consumed by the wealthy. Expanding foreign trade after 1867 created new production possibilities in hand spinning and weaving and brought about a structural and locational transformation of the cotton textile industry.[9] In foreign trade, machine-spun yarn imports rose sharply until 1900 and then leveled off to decline during World War I. Cotton cloth imports increased slowly, tapered off after 1890 and then declined after the mid-1920s. Until 1900, then, yarn imports increased fortyfold while cloth rose only twofold. What did this imply for the domestic cotton textile handicraft industry?

Foreign cotton cloth imports did not circulate widely because they were expensive and preferred only by the wealthy who could afford to buy them. The average Chinese preferred the cheaper, durable, coarse native cloth. Cotton yarn was another matter.

The Putting-Out System

First, the price of imported yarn steadily declined and its quality improved. At the same time raw cotton exports from China began to increase because of rising world market prices. As domestic supply failed to keep pace with demand, local yarn prices rose so that foreign yarn became increasingly competitive and attractive for hand spinners to use. As a result, workers in the economic core areas of Kiangsu, Fukien, Kwangtung, and even in the middle and upper Yangtze areas rapidly began to substitute foreign yarn as the warp used along with the handspun weft yarn to make a cloth far superior to the simple native variety. From 1870 onward households began to scrap spinning and concentrate more on weaving. Merchants, moneylenders, and even officials supplied working capital and organized cloth production on a new cottage industry basis. Managers were employed to supply foreign yarn and cash to groups of weavers in one establishment in exchange for their cloth. Spinning in the household declined greatly but did not disappear completely, and weaving of native cloth, referred to as *t'u-pu*, in a single firm under the putting-out system organized by a merchant capitalist increased. Many areas that formerly produced for local consumption began to produce for distant markets, and some areas that had once flourished went into decline.

Bruce Reynolds has estimated that in 1875 the manufactured yarn imports only accounted for 2 percent of the total yarn supply to produce handicraft cloth. By 1905, however, this share had risen to 49 percent and by 1931 to 76 percent. Perhaps as many as 2 million full-day spinning jobs were displaced by 1905 as a result. And what of handspun yarn? In 1875 handicraft accounted for perhaps 98 percent of the total supply of yarn, but by 1905 only 50 percent. Thus, a very large displacement of hand spinners occurred as this cotton handicraft industry adopted a new technology and organizational form, namely, the putting-out system.

Meanwhile, the improved *t'u-pu* competed very well against both imported cloth and the machine-made cloth manufactured by new textile mills established in the country around the turn of the century. In 1875 handicraft produced an estimated 78 percent of the total supply of cotton cloth; only 22 percent came from imports. Even by 1905 the handicraft sector still supplied this same share, and by 1931 its vitality was such that it still supplied 61 percent of the total cloth supply of the country. As hand spinning became depressed, hand weaving flourished on the new basis. It is impossible to gauge whether the workers eliminated from hand spinning found employment in the new hand-weaving or other processing industries that began developing in response to both foreign demand and new demand from the maritime port centers in China. This reallocation of resources—especially labor—proved painful for many communities. As the Chinese economy in the late nineteen century was probably producing quite close to its production frontier, such restructuring of handicraft was bound to create temporary unemployment, which hypothetically would place the economy further back from its production frontier. But the redeployment of these resources to new putting-out systems stimulated by foreign trade and port-city demand could very well have kept the economy close to its production frontier over this quarter century.[10]

Increased Labor and Product Specialization

Other handicraft or agricultural processing industries also expanded their supply in response to the widening of the domestic market brought about by increased demand from the new city-ports and their links to world markets. Instead of adopting any new technology, the organizers of these industries, such as tea processing, simply employed more resources and encouraged greater resource specialization in tea planting. The structure of the tea industry, with its simple, labor-intensive methods, did not require any new technology. In Hunan, for example, tenant farmers substituted more tea shrubs for other crops they grew. The landowners decided to grow more tea and hired more workers to this end. In other words households merely increased their specialization in tea production by working harder and longer hours when seasonal demand dictated. More merchants entered the market to finance the building of more tea-drying establishments. The large price differential between tea expressed in Chinese prices and the prices paid in foreign markets meant windfall profits to the industry. But meanwhile, Japan, Ceylon, and India constructed tea plantations with new tea plants. The plantation not only produced a lower unit cost quantity of tea but a superior brand to that of Chinese tea brands. An expanding world market allowed Chinese and foreign suppliers to benefit from rising tea prices, but after World War I the contraction in world trade brought depression to the tea-producing districts throughout the Far East.

THE MODERN SECTOR
IN ITS FORMATIVE STAGE

The Growth of Industrial Enterprises

A major indicator of an emerging modern sector is industrial production. New organizations that harness modern technology to manufacture new commodities cannot flourish unless their environment also changes. And so, many associated developments such as a growing skilled work force, more banks, and railroads make their appearance under the rubric of a modern sector. John K. Chang has constructed the first reliable index to measure industrial production between 1911 and 1949.[11]

This index covered 15 commodities representing 40 percent of total industrial product value. It embraces a large enough sample to show the rate of growth of all industrial enterprises. Chang used unit prices and the *value-added* date of 1933—that is, the production value the firm adds to the materials that it buys from other suppliers—as price weights by which to value the output quantities of these 15 goods. From 1911 until 1936, both the gross and net value production index moved alike. They show a very rapid annual growth rate of around 9.4 percent to give an eightfold expansion of industrial output. This growth rate is higher than that of the United Kingdom (1820–

1870, 3.0 percent), the United States (1860–1914, 5.9 percent), and Japan (1906–1935, 6.4 percent), and it is almost the same growth rate of 10 percent achieved between 1952 and 1978 in China by the present socialist government.

To be sure, the rapid creation of modern enterprises where none exist and where industrial production is already nil is bound to lead to a very rapid growth in the formative period. Yet, such growth requires that considerable resources be diverted from producing goods and services from current consumption, and this imposes a severe strain on a traditional economy of great backwardness. Unless considerable resources that are already unemployed can be deployed to these new activities, resources must be bid away from alternative uses, and this means producing fewer consumer goods and services than otherwise would be the case.

In China, however, most of the modern enterprises created were for the production of consumer goods and services, and this meant enormous competition with the various handicraft industries. Virtually all of these industrial firms, naturally, remained confined to the city-ports opened to foreigners through various international treaties. The reasons for this will be explained below. Further, except for very brief periods, the state was powerless to assist this industrial transformation.

The State and Modern Industry

Prior to 1894–95 the Ch'ing court had established only two new offices: the Tsung-li Yamen to deal with foreign affairs and the Imperial Maritime Customs Service to collect customs revenue. The Ch'ing state had resisted other overtures to reform and restructure its offices. These two new offices actually had little power; the court felt very uneasy with them yet used them out of necessity, and both the court and officialdom regarded them as abnormal and outside the permanent structure of government. Many in the court probably felt that ultimately the two offices could be phased out after serving their purpose. This state of affairs reflected the court's attitude that modern technology and organization were unnecessary for China. Meanwhile the less skeptical provincial and lower-echelon officials lacked the authority to do anything without permission from Peking.

Government Reforms The Treaty of Shimonoseki in 1895 and the Allied Expeditionary Force's pillaging of Peking in 1900 in the wake of the Boxer Rebellion sounded the alarm for state action. "Almost overnight Chinese—imperial government, reformers, and revolutionaries—accepted the challenge."[12] This challenge was to somehow modernize the country, reclaim those many rights transferred to foreigners, and oppose foreign imperialism. Henceforth China would be in a turmoil, but during the next decade the reforms came thick and fast.

In 1901 the Ministry of Foreign Affairs (Wai-wu pu) replaced the old Tsung-li Yamen. In 1903 the Shang-pu or Ministry of Commerce was established. In 1905 the government abolished the age-old imperial examination system. In that same year the government tried to recover national control over railroads that had slipped under foreign control, and a powerful movement spread among the provinces whereby associations emerged to press for a constitutional monarchy. These and other dramatic steps reflect the avalanche of reforms to roll back foreign imperialism and launch China on the road to modernization.

But reform of the Ch'ing bureaucracy that might initiate rapid modernization proved transparent. Let us examine the case of the Shang-pu. Considerable disagreement among officials marked the creation of this new ministry. Some saw it as a powerful vehicle to launch new commercial industries. Others saw it as a threat to long-standing agencies like the Board of Works or Board of Revenue. Soon the Shang-pu became bogged in conflicting claims of jurisdiction, and it lacked the funds to finance its ambitious schemes.[13] Its department of auditing, for example, overlapped certain duties with the Board of Revenue. Likewise the Shang-pu tried to control salt and customs, which brought it into conflict with the Salt and Imperial Maritime Customs offices.

As a result of these and other difficulties, the Shang-pu merely initiated commercial surveys, drew up plans, and recommended new commercial laws for business. With the creation of the new Ministry of Posts and Communications (Yu-ch'uan-pu) in 1906, which came under the control of Yuan Shih-k'ai, and the reorganization of the Shang-pu to merge with the Ministry of Works to become the new Ministry of Agriculture, Industry, and Commerce (Nung-kung-shang-pu), the stage was quickly set for even more rivalry within the bureaucracy. The new ministry did poorly. It continued to be inadequately funded and its activities greatly circumscribed.

Inadequate Tax Support   Although the state became committed to modernization, it failed to reform the tax system so that more revenue could be generated to finance the many projected reforms. This is not to say it did not try. Officials consolidated salt taxes for the first time into a single, national account to be used for constructing railways, building new schools, developing a modern military, and promoting industry.

But rather than rationalize the land tax system to give incentives to owners to improve their land and still increase the land tax, the state merely levied surcharges on the land tax and introduced new taxes on commerce like the *likin* or a duty on the value of goods in transit from one point to another. An even more prevalent practice was for the state to impose assigned tax quotas (*t'an-k'uan*) to each province and leave it to the officials to determine how to make good the quota. This procedure was used when the court urgently needed funds—as when it had to pay the Boxer indemnity, which averaged 25 million taels each year or about 10 percent of the country's tax revenue.

The state had increased taxes only slightly between 1880 and 1895, mainly through the *likin* and customs duties. Between 1895 and 1909 total taxes doubled, yet more tax revenue merely whetted the state's appetite for obtaining more in the same way. Basic tax reform did not follow. Then when the 1911 revolution ended the Ch'ing government, tax receipts quickly began to decline as did state expenditures. Between 1913 and 1916 forecasted revenue fell from 38.6 to 27.3 million yuan, and expenditures likewise dropped from 59.3 to 18.8 million yuan.[14] The new state of political anarchy that had rapidly engulfed China quickly dried up normal revenue sources.

Until April 1927 when a new political power, the Kuomintang party, installed itself in Nanking, the Republican government remained too weak to influence economic affairs favorably for achieving modernization. Province after province fell under the control of military elites. Some provincial assemblies tried to achieve greater fiscal independence from Peking, but warlord fiscal rule became the norm rather than the exception. These warlords simply imposed more surcharges on land taxes, taxed more commodities sold in markets, and demanded that county administrations pay the extraordinary levy (*t'an-k'uan*) by whatever means they wanted to use. Meanwhile, more state expenditures flowed to support the military, to bolster up provincial, municipal, and county police, and to support the administration. After 1911 the state became virtually powerless to use the budget for promoting modern growth. For all practical purposes a central state had disappeared.

The Mini–Hong Kong Phenomenon

Since 1945 the British crown colony of Hong Kong has been characterized by the following economic features: First, controls over prices and incomes did not exist. These two indexes fluctuated according to the forces of supply and demand. Second, foreign capital moved freely in and out of the colony. Third, the municipal government provided neither protection nor subsidy to industry. Finally, the Hong Kong government supplied valuable services such as law and order, and utilities such as water, power, and waste disposal. All this was

achieved within a balanced budget that actually produced annual surpluses. The free market system of Hong Kong, then, produced the dynamic economic growth that made possible an affluent middle class
and wiped out so much poverty.

Free, Unregulated Market   By 1913 forty-eight city-ports shared
characteristics similar to post-1945 Hong Kong. First, virtually free
trade existed. The Nanking Treaty of 1842 limited import tariffs to a
maximum rate of 5 percent ad valorem, and the most-favored-nation
clause in the Treaty of Shimonoseki in 1895 extended this rate to all
foreign imports. No export tariffs existed. Imported goods also were
exempted from internal transit taxes, but in reality they were taxed
by *likin* once they entered local markets.

   Second, the municipal governments of these city-ports did not attempt to control prices and incomes. The free market system flourished. Prices were influenced as much by forces in the world market as
in the domestic economy. Incomes in the city-ports rose more rapidly
for property owners and wage earners than anywhere else in the domestic economy. In response to rising income and improved urban
welfare, a substantial migration from villages and market towns into
the mini–Hong Kong cities took place. By the early 1930s the Chinese
population in these city-ports reached more than ten million—compared to only around one million at the turn of the century.

Enlightened City Government   These same city-port municipal governments initiated urban improvements, which made living and
working conditions more desirable than anywhere in the country. In
response to the way the foreigners had established their
minimunicipal governments to manage their concession areas—that
is, districts within the city-ports where Chinese law and authority did
not penetrate—the Chinese organized city councils to manage urban
affairs. Between 1905 and 1914 the Shanghai city council, established
by leading Chinese civic leaders, collected taxes, managed a police
force, and provided services such as cleaning and lighting of streets.
During this decade the council spent more than half a million yuan or
the equivalent of 60,000 pounds sterling on roads, bridges, sewers, and
wharves.[15] It also ensured public health, safety, and the movement of
human traffic and goods. By 1923 the council had installed a central
sewage system that eliminated an enormous sale of human waste and
garbage by contractors to farmers outside the city. It had built the
Shanghai Power Company, which accounted for an average of 83 percent of the total sales of electric power in the city between 1925 and
1934 of which 78 percent went to industrial users such as cotton mills.
   These city-ports or mini–Hong Kongs with their free markets
and enlightened city governments provided the freedom, security, and

monetary incentives for the Chinese to develop modern industry. The modern sector really emerged only in these cities and their environ communities within a radius of fifty miles or so.

Establishment of New Factories

Modern enterprises rapidly increased in number. Between 1895 and 1913 business leaders built 590 new factories to employ 186,000 workers. Between 1913 and 1920—the golden age of industrial growth—business people founded 1,061 more factories. By 1933 over 3,100 factories employed over a half million workers. This number is not impressive for a country of over 500 million people, but such development had been achieved by private business owners alone, without any assistance by the state. Further, this progress had occurred during a period of acute political anarchy and civil war when business conditions were extremely uncertain.

Production of Consumer Goods   Of course these new factories produced mainly consumer goods, many of which competed with and were supplied to the handicraft sector. Iron and steel, chemical, and machine tool industries were virtually nonexistent. But the new factories for consumer products relied upon new machines, employed much skilled labor, and demanded new procedures for their successful operation. The cotton textile industry, one of the largest segments, accounted for 22 percent of all modern factories and sold much of its machine-spun yarn to handicraft centers producing native cloth.

Even so, these same factories also upgraded their plant facilities and their equipment over time and became multiproduct firms. Prior to 1911 cotton textile engineering design and plant equipment were entirely borrowed or adapted from England. These mills could not even use Chinese cotton, and they manufactured only the coarse 10–14 count yarn to be sold to handicraft weavers. After World War I textile equipment from the United States became widely used. Textile engineering greatly improved, and more mills began producing finer 20–40 and 60–80 count yarn suitable for machine weaving of cloth. Thereafter, more machine weaving became prevalent; mill design improved; and labor productivity increased.

Production of Capital Goods   Even though the capital-goods-producing component of this modern sector remained small, certain enterprises began making capital goods after 1920 and became the critical foundation for expanding such equipment after 1949. The case of electrical equipment illustrates this point. The pioneer firm was the Wahson Electrical Manufacturing Company formed in 1917 to manufacture current limiters, feeder panels, and power switches. In 1922 the Chinese National Electrical and Potter Company was founded, and three technicians trained at Westinghouse Electric in the United States became the driving force for this firm's growth. It manufactured equipment that could handle as many as 33,000 volts. Similar firms sprang up thereafter to produce wires, cables, batteries, and various insulation materials. By 1935, of the 2,000 principal towns in China, more than 400 had electric-light and power plants. In certain southern cities an extensive electrical equipment industry had emerged.

Financing a Factory　The majority of investors and owners of new factories probably got their start in commerce and banking. But how did they actually establish a new factory? Several business people might perceive that manufacture of flour or yarn had suddenly become very profitable. Perhaps they had observed that the importation of these goods had boomed, or that local prices had risen whereas new materials had become cheaper so that a profit margin could yield a capital return as attractive as the return from real estate investment, moneylending, or commerce. Although these business investors knew nothing about the technical side of the industry they wanted to launch, they were shrewd enough to approach a foreign firm and obtain from its technical staff a preliminary estimate of the total costs on which they would have to base their financial arrangements. The following sequence then perhaps unfolded:

> They may find they can get a promise of sufficient capital among themselves to pay for the imported machinery, buildings and land will be partly financed by shares, and local banks will supply at exorbitant rates of interest the necessary finance for the purchase of raw material and carrying of stocks. The shareholders are well aware of the lack of experience of the promoters, and are correspondingly distrustful. They will advance as little cash as possible at the outset and they like to have proof from actual operation that profits can be made before they will act up to all their promises. . . . The whole of the capital required is rarely provided at once, nor can a promise to take up shares be enforced. Even public utility companies are rarely founded on share capital or the security of a particular town, but on money borrowed from banks at rates varying from 12 to 20 percent, which has to be repaid at every Chinese New Year, the Chinese settling day. The result is that while Chinese industrialists are fully aware of the relative merits of different types of plant and machinery, the question of a low first cost is of paramount importance to them in order to reduce the heavy interest charges, a fact which Brit-

ish manufacturers are sometimes slow to appreciate when their terms are underquoted, as they frequently are, as much as 20 or 25 percent.[16]

The Chinese firm then purchased machinery from England or the United States, and usually a foreign merchant granted a loan with payment being deferred from one to ten years, at a rate of interest usually 1 percent higher than the bank rate. The risk for the foreign creditor was great. Rarely could creditors either enforce payment, take over the firm if the loan were not repaid on time, rely upon Chinese officials for assistance, or easily find another buyer for the machinery.

Because of the uncertainty and risk associated with investing in manufacturing, investors rarely advanced more than their initial share capital. The promoters and their managers had to rely upon banks for working capital—especially when raw material prices rose or demand slumped. For this reason, most factory owners were perennially in debt to the banks. A 1930s survey revealed that roughly two-thirds of the capital for modern enterprises came from loans, and the remainder was supplied by share capital and retained earnings.[17] Business entrepreneurs were acutely sensitive to changing costs and prices. The highly competitive market often produced volatile price movements that greatly affected profitability and investment return. One Western observer remarked that China was "so overwhelmingly a price market that, speaking by and large, hardly any other factor in merchandising is of outstanding importance. Low price is so essentially the factor that attracts them that if it is within their means nearly anything will sell to the Chinese, if it is not, nothing will."[18]

The free market of these city-ports encouraged investment spurts in factory building and industrial growth. When prices of raw materials lagged behind those of finished goods, an investment boom began. The capital outlays were financed in part from savings and in part from bank credit—especially Western bank loans. Chinese firms increased their orders for equipment to set up their factories or increase production. These orders were supplied from abroad so that imports of machinery, fuel, and construction materials increased. After a time interval of a year or so, these factories began manufacturing products to sell to urban consumers, handicraft centers in the interior, and export markets. But increased competition for raw materials by foreign and Chinese firms would then bid up their prices, and sometimes disruption in the hinterland also sent raw material prices soaring. Wheat, for example, could be imported more cheaply, and domestic raw material shortages were overcome through imports. Eventually, raw material prices began to converge with the prices of finished goods and squeeze profit margins, and thus forced firms to cut back production. Inventories began to grow; idle capacity developed; and an industrial recession commenced. This process is confirmed by foreign trade trends and commodity price movements. Let us consider the business slump of 1923 through 1926 and the boom of 1927 through 1931. From 1924–25 prices of cotton yarn and raw cotton converged but then diverged after that. Imports of textile machinery and aniline dyes fell sharply during the 1923–1925 recession, increased in the late 1920s boom, and rose sharply until 1931 as firms ordered new equipment and built new factories.

Chinese Entrepreneurs in Public Enterprises   Who were the Chinese entrepreneurs? In the last decade of the Ch'ing, from 1900 until 1911, many of China's business organizers were still prominent officials who began to invest their own funds instead of using government monies. In 1906 an official named Chou Hsüeh-hsi (1866–1947) established the Lanchow Official Mining Company and the Chee Hsin Cement Company.[19] Chou had begun his official career under Yuan Shih-k'ai and became judicial commissioner of Chihli province in 1907. He also supervised industrial development and went on to found the first water works company in Peking and banking, glass works, and textile firms during the teens. These enterprises prospered—especially the Chee Hsin Cement Company, which eventually became the country's largest producer.

Chinese Entrepreneurs in Private Enterprises   Private entrepreneurs who had done well in commerce and overseas trade flourished as well. The Chien brothers, Chao-nan and Yu-chien, were overseas Chinese in the import-export business between Hong Kong, Japan, and Siam.[20] In 1904–05 they pooled their savings with funds borrowed from relatives, and with a Japanese technician friend that was formerly employed in a Japanese cigarette factory, they launched a cigarette business. The British-American Tobacco Company (BAT) in Hong Kong immediately pressured the colonial administration to have their competitor's products destroyed because the wrappings looked like the BAT's products. The company folded in 1908. But in 1909 it reorganized, and this time the Nanyang Brothers' Tobacco Company became a huge success. The company's profits rapidly grew through the teens and the 1920s.

Two factors loomed large to explain the new cigarette enterprise's success. First, the market increased enormously because the fad of cigarette smoking spread like wildfire. Second, the Nanyang brothers introduced advertising to spread their brand name to nearly every household of the country. The company donated funds to flood relief, to educational institutions and to subsidize newspapers, and each time displayed its brand name conspicuously for all to see. The company built up strong goodwill with the public in this way. The strong floodtide of nationalism at this time sparked Chinese consumer preference toward Nanyang products and away from foreign cigarettes—especially those distributed by BAT. The successful example of the Nanyang Brothers' Tobacco Company attests to the entrepreneurial abilities of Chinese businessmen to compete with powerful foreign firms and still capture a substantial share of the domestic market. After 1927, however, the company encountered new difficulties that began to confront every private concern during the next two decades. The fate of the Nanyang brothers' company will be discussed in chapter six.

AGRICULTURE AND THE MODERN SECTOR

What was the impact of the new city-ports upon agriculture? From the 1880s onward, China began importing food grains in modest amounts but a trend upward is unmistakable. After World War I food grain imports soared and did not level off and decline until the 1930s. During the 1880s the grain tribute traffic on the old Grand Canal was phased out, and the new city-ports became more dependent upon cheap food grain from abroad. Meanwhile, railroad development in north China commenced during the 1890s and early 1900s, and very quickly new cities emerged on the north China plain.

Distribution Network

Dwight Perkins has already pointed out this railroad development and growth of northern cities altered the distribution of food grain shipments between provinces. Prior to the 1880s Peking received its food grain via the Grand Canal from sources in the southern provinces, and the cities of Canton, Hankow, Foochow, Soochow, and Hangchow obtained their food grain from the hinterland provinces. In the next two decades the Ch'ing interprovincial food grain distribution network began to change.

First, the population greatly increased in the new cities—mostly in the new city-ports. Between 1900–1910 and 1938, the cities in Manchuria, north China, and Shanghai increased their population from 4,580,000 to 13,030,000, a threefold increase—compared to an urban population expansion in the Yangtze valley, the southeast, and the southwest of only 10,060,000 to 11,530,000.[21] The growth of railroad lines in the northeast and the north greatly encouraged urban population expansion. These new railroads shipped grain from Szechwan, Hunan and Hupeh to these northern cities. When rail shipments were interdicted or when insufficient grain was shipped on this network, food grain imports to Tientsin, Tsingtao and Shanghai greatly increased.

After 1900, cities across the north China plain like Chi-nan in Shantung province, Shih-chia-chuang, Pao-ting, and T'ang-shan in Hopei province, T'ai-yuan in Shansi, Sian in Shensi, and Cheng-chow in Honan became important grain-collecting centers. As these cities grew in size, surrounding communities began specializing in vegetables. Other districts turned to fibers and oilseed-bearing crops. Finally, some regions specialized more in food grains. In other words the new transport network and urban demand patterns encouraged considerable new crop specialization throughout the northern provinces and increased the volume of marketed surplus from the villages. More households entered into this new crop specialization and exchange so that land productivity increased but without any decline in labor productivity.[22] A reason for this was that labor obtained higher production returns from intensive crop specialization, yet at the same time very little technological growth accompanied this move toward specialization. Meanwhile, the new specialization and market dependency, which definitely favored the very small farms of one or two acres, were also associated with factor dislocation and painful adjustment for certain districts. Markets formerly dependent upon the old Grand Canal went into decline. Centers once relying upon inland waterway networks found themselves bypassed by the railroads. Handicraft centers not favored by the new railway network found their markets drying up.

Although the city-port and railway development greatly encouraged commercialization, it did not bring technological change to the farming communities. Farmers still depended on selecting the better seeds from their harvested crops. Farmers still learned about the best farming practices through contact with the market towns. Therefore, the trial and error method and the gradual diffusion of best traditional farming technology continued to be important forces for agricultural output growth through the early modern period.[23] To be sure, after 1895 the Ch'ing state did try to establish new agricultural colleges and some experimental stations—even agricultural associations in some provinces—but these activities remained underfunded, small-scale, and separated from the local administration links that might have channeled new seeds and farming techniques to large farming districts.

FOREIGN ECONOMIC IMPERIALISM

Three dimensions of foreign economic influence in China deserve clear discussion: foreign economic gain from Chinese military defeats, foreign loans to China—principally for railroads—and direct foreign investments in China. The controversy that has raged over the costs and benefits of foreign economic imperialism in China has not distinguished between these three dimensions carefully. Further, the issue of foreign economic influence upon domestic politics and military activities remains to be treated. The economic motives of the foreigner— either business owner, bureaucrat, or soldier—were inextricably mixed with the strategic concerns of a political-military nature, but these latter concerns usually loomed larger and served as the motor force for foreign interests in China. What of the strict economic influences of foreign activities in China? Did these influences create impediments for modernizing the Chinese economy? Were the consequences of foreign activities in economic matters paralyzing and burdensome both for Chinese business operators and for the state?

Military Debts to Foreigners

Let us ignore for the moment the numerous military loans borrowed by the Ch'ing government. The first major payment stemming from the military defeat went to Japan. China paid 250 million Kuping taels between 1895 and 1898: 200 million as indemnity for defeat and 50 million for the expense of the Japanese garrison at Wei-hai-wei and the retrocession of the Liaotung peninsula.[24] The Chinese government had to borrow three loans totaling 47.8 million pounds sterling for meeting this payment. Next, the Boxer uprising in 1900 forced China to pay 450 million Haikwan taels—the equivalent of 334 million U.S. dollars. China paid installments of silver for the first three years, but as the foreign powers demanded payment in gold, the Chinese had to pay another 8 million taels in 1904 to make up for "loss on exchange" that resulted from the decline in price of silver in terms of gold. During World War I the allied powers agreed to defer indemnity payments for five years. Later, some countries suspended and even canceled payments.

The Chinese government had to make these huge payments just when it became committed to modernizing the country and urgently needed funds. Transferring such large sums abroad meant relinquishing claim to domestic resources that would otherwise have contributed to producing more national income. Because little of these transfers abroad were respent on Chinese goods and services, export industries failed to derive any potential benefit. These transfers represented a very large share of the budget—10 percent in the case of the annual Boxer indemnity payment in the early 1900s. Therefore, indemnity payments to foreigners from military defeat constituted a major burden on the Chinese economy.

Foreign Loans to China

Between 1851 and 1937 China incurred 257 million pounds sterling in loans at current prices of 274.8 million in 1913 prices. Roughly two-thirds of these loans were for military and indemnity expenses and for railroads. By 1914, estimates show that even excluding the Boxer indemnity, the total payment on account for foreign debts—that is, interest plus amortization—would have amounted to 25.2 percent of the budgetary revenue in 1914 and 36.3 percent of actual revenue in 1931.[25] The actual payment on debt in 1925 came to 20.8 percent of the revenue. How did the government get itself into such a financial mess? Weakness, poor judgment, and lack of foresight undoubtedly account for why China went so deeply into debt—particularly during the 1894–1926 period when 82 percent of all loans were incurred. How much foreign political-military pressure weighed in the decisions of China's political leaders to continue to borrow is very difficult to say. Needless to say, many of these loans produced no direct economic benefit for the economy. The constant transfers abroad out of the budget represented a large burden on the economy. Loan mismanagement, then, proved to be a powerful destabilizing factor in politics and military affairs. Chinese growing foreign debt became the source for much passion and resentment, which in turn made it even more difficult for leaders to unite the country and deal with the basic economic issues at hand.

Railroad Construction   By 1911 Chinese railway loans alone totaled 330.5 million Kuping taels—almost 28 percent of China's total foreign loans.[26] Until 1895 the Ch'ing court had refused to authorize railroad construction because it feared the baleful effects at home and the advantages the railway would give foreigners. The court reversed itself in late 1897 when foreign powers began seizing territory and demanding concessions in China and the right to build railroads inland. In November of that year Germany used the killing of two German missionaries in southwest Shantung as the pretext to demand and seize Chiao-chou Bay at Tsingtao in order to establish a naval base.[27] The Tsung-li Yamen agreed to Germany's new privileges and also granted railway rights in the interior of Shantung. This action opened the floodgates for other foreign powers to make similar demands. For the next three years Peking vainly tried to balance off one power against the other. But in each case a foreign power obtained some territorial concession with rights to construct railways and to have access to minerals within a ten mile zone on either side of the railway.

The court responded to this kind of foreign aggression by trying to build railroads itself. But shortage of capital compelled the Chinese to borrow from foreign banks and even from the capital funds market in London. Various foreign powers quickly observed that the power balance in east Asia might shift unless steps were taken to loan funds to China and even build railroads themselves. For example, the British feared that unless the Chinese-sponsored Peking-Mukden railway was completed, nothing stood in the way of a union of the Russian railway in Manchuria and the Franco–Belgian consortium-controlled Peking-Hankow railway. In such a case British interests in the Yangtze valley would be threatened. Therefore, the British began negotiations with Russia and authorized a loan agreement with China for completing the Peking–Mukden line.[28] China borrowed heavily for railway construction of her own during the next three years. By 1902 nationalist feeling began to mount to finance the private construction of railways and to purchase outright from the foreign powers certain railway lines already constructed and in operation. China's railway recovery movement had begun.

By 1908 the Chinese had redeemed the Peking-Hankow railway with the assistance of an Anglo–French loan secured by provincial taxes. The new Ministry of Posts and Communications now fully controlled that railway and all its profits. Yet in spite of this and other successes, the Ch'ing government did not have the financial capability to redeem all railroads under foreign control, and foreign loans still were increasing. The period 1895–1911 saw China placed on the defensive and made to choose among alternatives that would not have existed a decade or so before. Would China have built the same kind of railroad system, or would the Ch'ing government have integrated fewer railroads with more roads and waterways? Could not the tax revenues earmarked for payment of railway loans have produced higher economic benefits if used instead for improving agricultural research, education, and public health? We still have no study that clearly measures the benefits and social costs of the railroads. Therefore, the benefit of these railway loans for the Chinese economy still remains most problematic.

Direct Foreign Investments

Estimates vary on the amount of foreign investment in China and its effects. Two scholars, Remer and Wu Cheng-ming, estimate that in 1902 foreign investment totaled 503 and 507 million U.S. dollars respectively; by 1914 these had risen to 1,067 and 1,090 million respectively. In 1930 they estimate 2,483 and 2,347 million U.S. dollars respectively. A more recent estimate for 1936 places direct foreign investment at a lower figure of 1,149 million U.S. dollars.[29] Of this latter amount about 149 million U.S. dollars or 13 percent of total investment went to factory manufacturing. Apparently the bulk of the 1936 total went to finance foreign trade—30 percent—and to support banking and insurance—25 percent. The largest share, then, financed Chinese imports or helped Chinese business firms through extension of credit.

Whatever the true investment figure, foreign business people played an important role in developing China's modern economic sector. First, foreigners occupied a large role in that sector but not by virtue of their monopoly power. By 1933 foreign-owned firms produced 35 percent of the total value of production by manufacturing industries, but this share had been greater in the 1910–1920 period when 75 to 90 percent of modern coal mining and nearly 50 percent of the cotton textile industry remained in foreign hands. Chinese business organizers steadily expanded their market share by learning and doing. And the foreign business manager was the unwitting agent.

Foreigners supplied the credit, the new technology, and the information for overseas markets. Nevertheless, the unregulated economy of the port cities made for a highly competitive market, which compelled foreigner and Chinese to compete vigorously to survive. Unlike the colonies of advanced countries where foreign business leaders held special privileges giving them the economic power to extract minerals cheaply or to obtain tropical products through special pricing procedures, the foreigner in China either manufacturing goods or selling and buying merchandise had to compete with thousands of Chinese business owners doing the very same thing.

Foreign business operators at first held certain advantages of technical know-how and working capital, but Chinese business people possessed information about the domestic market that gave them considerable advantage over the foreigner. As soon as the Chinese had selected and copied techniques used by the foreigner in factory operations, the gap between the two groups narrowed. Depending upon the state of the market and the entrepreneurial response to it, the advantage could tip toward either the foreigner or the Chinese.

Finally, foreigners appear to have reinvested much of their profits in China. One study concluded that nearly 57 percent of the foreign firms reinvested 30 percent or more of their profits while 45 percent of the foreign firms reinvested 40 percent or more of their profits.[30]

Foreign economic imperialism adversely affected the Chinese economy between 1895 and 1907. During that critical period large indemnity payments and poor loan management forced the government to allocate a portion of its budget for payments to foreigners—an enormous burden for this poor economy to bear. Bearing this burden at a time when the state had finally committed itself to modernizing the economy was unfortunate, and from the Chinese point of view unjustified.

Yet foreign business operators' direct investments and economic activities in the new city-ports bestowed considerable benefits on the

Chinese economy in terms of initiating technological transfer, providing valuable information, and supplying loanable funds. After 1860 these city-ports became the motor force for widening the market, encouraging producers to specialize for the market, transferring modern technology to handicraft, and finally establishing a new mode of production—that is, factories and their machines. These city-ports produced only modest economic growth-spread effects, however, because these centers largely depended upon foreign trade and they had to compete with an entrenched, large, and well-developed traditional sector.

SUMMARY: THE MODERN SECTOR
AND INHIBITED ECONOMIC GROWTH

As long as China exported agricultural and mineral products and these production activities did "not rely to any appreciable extent on the product of other sectors and [were] used extensively as inputs in other sectors," foreign demand would not stimulate the development of manufacturing to produce capital goods.[31] China mainly imported consumer goods that satisfied only final demand and "served neither as inputs in China's production nor as capital goods to increase China's productive capacity."[32] In other words weak backward-and-forward linkage features of foreign trade partially explain why manufacturing remained small and confined mainly to the production of consumer goods and services.

Imbalance of Trade

Between 1896 and 1940 China imported a larger value of goods than it exported and thereby ran a trade imbalance. This trade imbalance was highest between 1921 and 1925 when it averaged 184.8 million U.S. dollars. This trade balance was paid mainly through foreign investments, overseas Chinese remittances, and foreign payments for the use of garrisons and naval vessels in Chinese territory and rivers.

Local Competition

The other factor that inhibited the growth of the modern sector was competition from the tens of thousands of local markets. First, the pattern of domestic demand from these markets favored consumption of low-cost food and items produced through labor-intensive techniques used by farmer and artisan. Household budget studies for the 1920s and 1930s show that between 60 and 80 percent of expenditures went for food. In other words the mass market did not have the purchasing power to buy the high-quality, high-priced manufactured goods flowing out of the foreign and Chinese firms in the city-ports. Only a small urban market catered to these goods. A study of 1,270 students at Yenching University in Peking during the early 1920s showed their families spent only 28 percent of expenditures on food.[33] Only these households could afford to educate their children in the new schools and universities and also buy goods from the modern sector.

Second, producers outside the city-ports used labor-intensive methods to sell their low-cost items to the market towns and villages. Some producers also used machine-spun yarn from the city-port factories, but the majority supplied to the mass market what people could afford to buy. Manufacturers of consumer goods and services in the city-ports could not compete with them. These producers confined their sales to the cities, a few surrounding communities, and markets abroad.

Prerevolutionary Conditions

China's lack of tariff protection is alleged to have prevented the emergence of new, infant industries and put Chinese firms at the mercy of foreign importers and manufacturers. To be sure, Chinese business owners were left to their own devices, but the free, unregulated market of the city-ports gradually enabled a new generation of Chinese investors and promoters to learn new techniques, borrow funds, and copy from the foreigner. These mini–Hong Kong city-ports enabled business operators to make a profit as long as they organized, managed, and distributed their products efficiently. The state might have transferred modern technology to the hinterland markets if the country had remained politically unified after 1911 and if officials had actually promoted such steps. Even the creation of modern enterprises to produce capital goods for the domestic market might have gradually taken place had law and order prevailed in China. But China had entered a revolutionary phase. By the end of World War I serious difficulties had also developed in agriculture. Between 1927 and 1937 the state tried to extrude into the private sector in ways that proved more harmful than beneficial. And after 1937 war and civil war engulfed the country.

QUESTIONS FOR DISCUSSION

1. How could China have a trade imbalance for over a half century and still develop a small modern economic sector?

2. What factors account for the lack of success of the Ch'ing government to develop modern industry in the late nineteenth century? How would you measure and interpret successful development of modern industry as initiated by the state?

3. In what ways was foreign economic imperialism harmful for Chinese economic development? Did these harmful effects occur throughout all of the nineteenth and early twentieth centuries?

4. What is the economic process by which a free market economy accumulates capital and expands the production of goods and services?

5. What was the economic relationship between the modern economic sector of the city-ports and the traditional economic sector of the small cities, market towns, and villages of the hinterland? What were the implications of this relationship for the modern economic growth of China?

NOTES

1. By 1900 another eighteen port cities were trading with foreigners, and in 1913 an additional eleven brought the total to forty-eight.

2. Quoted in the exemplary study of official attitudes toward modernization of the economy by Hatano Yoshihiro, "The Response of the Chinese Bureaucracy to Modern Machinery," *Acta Asiatica* 12 (1967): 18–19.

3. Wellington K.K. Chan, "Bureaucratic Capital and Chou Hsüeh-hsi in Late Ch'ing China," *Modern Asian Studies* 2, no. 3 (1977): 430.

4. Yen-p'ing Hao, *The Comprador in Nineteenth Century China: Bridge between East and West* (Cambridge, Mass.: Harvard University Press, 1970), p. 90.

5. Ibid., p. 109.

6. Thomas Kennedy, "Industrial Metamorphosis in the Self-Strengthening Movement: Li Hung-chang and the Kiangnan Shipbuilding Program," *The Journal of the Institute of Chinese Studies of the Chinese University of Hong Kong* 4, no. 1 (September 1971): 225.

7. The information cited in this paragraph comes from Sun Yu-t'ang, *Chung-Jih ya-pien chien-cheng ch'ien wai-kuo tzu-pen tsai Chung-kuo ching-ying ti chin-tai kung-yeh* [Foreign Investment in China's Management of Modern Industry prior to the Sino–Japanese War] (Shanghai: Shang-hai jen-min ch'u-pan-she, 1955).

8. An excellent study of this is Kwang-ching Liu, *Anglo American Steamship Rivalry in China: 1862–1874* (Cambridge, Mass.: Harvard University Press, 1962), pp. 85, 93, and especially p. 96. Given the high inelastic range of demand for certain Yangtze transportation services, this company could maintain a high rate structure and still earn the maximum revenue possible. The following figure depicts this phenomenon. Given the shipping rate of price/ton on the OX axis and quantity transported on the OY axis, the DD demand schedule for Yangtze shipping was inelastic at

the upper range and more elastic at the lower range. By charging prices *OP* and *OQ* the Shanghai S.N. Co. earned maximum revenue—as opposed to lower earnings if it had charged any shipping prices below *OP* for *ON* tons hauled.

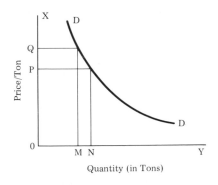

9. This discussion is based upon Ramon H. Myers, "Cotton Textile Handicraft and the Development of the Cotton Textile Industry in Modern China," *Economic History Review* 18, no. 3 (1965): 614–32; and Bruce L. Reynolds, "Weft: The Technological Sanctuary of Chinese Handspun Yarn," *Ch'ing-shih wen-t'i* [*Problems in Ch'ing History*] 3, no. 2 (December 1974).

10. The diagram depicts this hypothetical production frontier situation show-

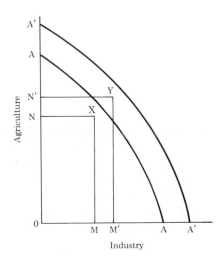

ing alternative industries of agriculture and industry (handicraft). The *AA* curve represents the production possibility frontier for the Chinese economy in 1870. Point *X*, located slightly inward from the frontier, indicates some resources that are idle but produce an output for handicraft of *OM* and for agriculture of *ON*. By 1900 the frontier has moved to *A'A'* because of the expansion of land and labor, and new technological change through the foreigner. The new output at point *Y* indicates successful redeployment of resources. If this transfer had not been possible, resources would be still employed to produce a combined output at point *X*.

11. John K. Chang, *Industrial Development in Pre-Communist China* (Chicago: Aldine, 1969), pp. 60–61.

12. Mary Claubaugh Wright, *China in Revolution: The First Phase, 1900– 1913* (New Haven and London: Yale University Press, 1969), p. 1.

13. These comments are based upon Wellington K. K. Chan, *Merchants, Mandarins and Modern Enterprise in Late Ch'ing China* (Cambridge, Mass.: Harvard University Press, 1977), chapter 8.

14. Yang Hsien-mai, *Min-kuo tsai-cheng-shih* [A History of Republican Period Finance] (Shanghai: Shang-wu yin-shu-kuan, 1917 and 1924), vol. I, p. 134.

15. Mark Elvin and G. William Skinner, eds., *The Chinese City between Two Worlds* (Stanford, Calif.: Stanford University Press, 1974), p. 260.

16. A. H. George, *Report on the Commercial, Industrial and Economic Situation in China to 30th June, 1926* (London: His Majesty's Stationery Office, 1926), p. 21.

17. Ch'en Chen, ed., *Chung-kuo chin-tai kung-yeh-shih tzu-liao* [Materials on China's Modern Industrial History] (Peking: San-lien shu-tien, 1961), vol. 5, pt. 1, p. 71.

18. Charles K. Moser, *Where China Buys and Sells* (Washington, D.C.: U.S. Government Printing Office, 1935), p. 43.

19. The information cited comes from Wellington K. K. Chan, "Bureaucratic Capital and Chou Hsüeh-hsi in Late Ch'ing China," *Modern Asian Studies* 11, no. 3 (1977): 435–38.

20. For a good account of the growth of this enterprise see Y. C. Wang, "Free Enterprise in China: The Case of a Cigarette Concern, 1905–1953," *Pacific Historical Review* 29, no. 4 (November 1960) : 395–414.

21. Dwight H. Perkins, *Agricultural Development in China, 1368–1968* (Chicago: Aldine, 1969), p. 155.

22. Ramon H. Myers, *The Chinese Peasant Economy* (Cambridge, Mass.: Harvard University Press, 1970), p. 524.

23. Modest improvements of traditional technology such as adoption of best traditional practices for fertilizing the soil and selecting better seeds can shift a leg of the production possibility curve for family farms and increase the output of certain crops. In the diagram family farms produce a product mix of subsistence goods *(S)* and industrial cash crops *(X)*. The production possibility curve *AB* shows the amounts of *OM* and *OP* of food and industrial crops initially cultivated. Improved techniques transferred

from one area to another shift the lower part of the curve to *AD* to permit more cash crops *(OP')* to be produced with the same output of food crops *(OM)*. This process occurred during the Ch'ing era and throughout the Republican period.

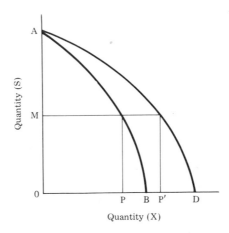

24. This discussion is based on Chi-ming Hou, *Foreign Investment and Economic Development in China: 1840–1937* (Cambridge, Mass.: Harvard University Press, 1965), pp. 24–26.

25. Ibid., pp. 43–44.

26. Lee En-han, *China's Quest for Railway Autonomy, 1904–1911* (Singapore: Singapore University Press, 1977), pp. 17–19.

27. John E. Schrecker, *Imperialism and Chinese Nationalism: Germany in Shantung* (Cambridge, Mass.: Harvard University Press, 1971), chapter 1.

28. Arthur Lewis Rosenbaum, "Chinese Railway Policy and the Response to Imperialism: The Peking-Mukden," *Ch'ing-shih wen-t'i* [Problems in Ch'ing History] 2, no. 1 (October 1969): 56–59.

29. Fujiwara Sada, "Kindai Chūgoku ni okeru gaikoku toshi zandaka no suikei" [An Estimate of Net Foreign Investment in Modern China], *Tōa keizai kenkyū* [Studies on the East Asian Economy] 45, no. 4 (November 1976): 15–55.

30. Chi-ming Hou, *Foreign Investment,* p. 103.

31. Robert F. Dernberger, "The Role of the Foreigner in China's Economic Development, 1840–1949," in Dwight H. Perkins, ed., *China's Modern Economy in Historical Perspective* (Stanford, Calif.: Stanford University Press, 1975), p. 34.

32. Ibid, p. 34.

33. Ava B. Milam, "Standards of Living among Intermediate Income Groups in China," *Journal of Home Economies* 19, no. 8 (August 1927): 427–38.

SELECTED READINGS

1. Wellington K. K. Chan. *Merchants, Mandarins and Modern Enterprise in Late Ch'ing China*. Cambridge, Mass.: Harvard University Press, 1977.

2. Albert Feuerwerker. *The Foreign Establishment in China in the Early Twentieth Century,* Michigan Papers in Chinese Studies No. 29. Ann Arbor: Center for Chinese Studies, University of Michigan, 1976.

3. ———. *China's Early Industrialization: Sheng Hsuan-huai (1844–1916) and Mandarin Enterprise*. Cambridge, Mass.: Harvard University Press, 1958.

4. ———. "China's Nineteenth Century Industrialization: The Case of the Hanyehping Coal and Iron Company Limited." In C. D. Cowan, ed., *The Economic Development of China and Japan*. London: George Allen & Unwin, 1964.

5. K. H. Kim. *Japanese Perspectives on China's Early Modernization: A Bibliographical Survey,* Michigan Papers in Chinese Studies. Ann Arbor: Center for Chinese Studies, University of Michigan, 1974.

6. Shih Min-hsiung. *The Silk Industry in Ch'ing China,* Michigan Papers in Chinese Studies. Trans. by E-tu Zen Sun. Ann Arbor: Center for Chinese Studies, University of Michigan, 1976.

7. Chi-ming Hou. *Foreign Investment and Economic Development in China 1840–1937*. Cambridge, Mass.: Harvard University Press, 1965.

8. Y.C. Wang. "Free Enterprise in China: The Case of a Cigarette Concern, 1905–1953." *Pacific Historical Review* 29, no. 4 (November 1960): 395–414.

9. Yu-kwei Cheng. *Foreign Trade and Industrial Development of China*. Washington, D.C.: University Press, 1956.

10. Ramon H. Myers. *The Chinese Peasant Economy*. Cambridge, Mass.: Harvard University Press, 1970.

11. Bruce L. Reynolds. "Weft: The Technological Sanctuary of Chinese Hand-spun Yarn." *Ch'ing-shih wen-t'i* [Problems in Ching History] 3, no. 2 (December 1974): 1–19.

12. John K. Chang. *Industrial Development in Pre-Communist China: A Quantitative Analysis*. Chicago: Aldine, 1969.

13. Ramon H. Myers. "Cotton Textile Handicraft and the Development of the Cotton Textile Industry in Modern China." *Economic History Review* 18, no. 3 (August 1965): 614–32.

14. Rhoads Murphy. "The Treaty Ports and China's Modernization." In Mark Elvin and G. William Skinner, eds., *The Chinese City between Two Worlds*. Stanford, Calif.: Stanford University Press, 1974, pp. 17–72.

Economic Growth and Crisis

The rapid adoption of machinery with modern sources of energy after 1895 in the new city-ports signaled China's entry into a new epoch. The old epoch, which lasted more than a millennium, had been the period of intensive cultivation of land by labor-intensive methods and land-saving practices to produce a constant per capita availability of food and fibers over time. The harnessing of modern technology made possible a new epoch of rising income per capita on a sustained basis. China irrevocably staked its future upon the ultimate mastery of the machine. The key problem was how to take advantage of the new technology.

New technology in the form of the machine spread rapidly at first, then gradually slowed after 1920 as political, military, and even economic upheavals periodically swept China. The trend of industrial production shows this deceleration. Between 1912–13 and 1920–21 industrial production grew at the very swift pace of 14.7 percent per year, slackened to 6.9 percent between 1920–21 and 1927–28, and further slowed to 5.4 percent between 1927–28 and 1935–36.[1] The Japanese invasion, World War II and its civil war aftermath brought further decline, and industrial production fell between 1935–36 and 1948–49 at the rate of −2.3 percent. Modern economic growth had quickly spread through the principal city-ports and beyond to certain large, inland cities but failed to penetrate the countryside. With modern economic growth and its retardation came new crises. What were they?

First, the central government virtually disappeared after 1914 when warlords began competing for control over key provinces. Although little fighting between warlord armies ever occurred, these military leaders and their minions introduced new taxes and imposed heavy levies to mobilize resources to support their armies. These armies lived off the land like locusts combing the landscape of all vegetation, so that the private sector paid a high price for this breakdown in law and order. As natural disasters continued to befall this huge country, local officials received little or no assistance from the central government; the private sector bore the full costs of rehabilitation. As civil war also raged throughout this period, considerable resources were diverted from normal economic activities to nonproductive, military conflict. Added to this was foreign aggression by Japan. First the Japanese seized Manchuria in 1931 and then in the summer of 1937 they invaded north China and ports further south. Upon conclusion of this war followed civil war between the Communist armies and those of the Kuomintang government. The full effect of these upheavals was a substantial rise in the unemployment of labor, entrepreneurship, and capital, and a decline in Gross National Product.

Yet the Chinese economy remained a paradox throughout this period. Through this turbulence modern economic growth still became a reality in some parts of this great economic system. Private business operators invested to buy machines so that the stock of physical capital increased. Although this capital often went unutilized when market demand weakened or when the monetary crisis occurred in 1934 and 1935, the production of basic industrial goods like coal, iron, cotton yarn and cloth, cement, and machine tools steadily increased. City-ports and cities in the interior like Tsinan in Shantung province also underwent modernization, gradually acquiring banks, factories, and access to railroads and telecommunications. Finally, provinces such as Kiangsu and Chekiang even expanded their modern infrastructure of roads, railroads, schools, government office buildings, and research institutes. An enfeebled state, trying to extend its authority over this vast country, contributed in no small part to this paradox of gradual modernization with crises.

THE STATE AND THE ECONOMY

Growth-Promoting Strategies for the Private Sector

In a poor, backward economy with considerable resources already unemployed, the state can pursue three strategies to promote modern economic growth. The first strategy provides maximum scope for the private sector to organize production on a new basis. This approach characterized the early phases of the industrial revolution in Great Britain and the United States. The state uses the resources at its command to encourage the private sector to pursue profits. The state creates those external economies of scale such as roads and telecommunications to enable entrepreneurs to reduce their costs. The state also initiates legal reforms that favorably influence the structure of property rights so as to give organizers of production the incentive to specialize and supply more to the market. The state further establishes a modern education system with research institutes to make available to entrepreneurs an expanded supply of skilled workers and professionals, as well as to disseminate modern technological know-how.

Direct Economic Assistance   Second, the state intervenes in the private sector to channel more resources to privileged organizers of production in the private sector. The state founds new banks to assist certain firms to finance their investment in modern capital and technology. The state even subsidizes some of those firms to establish a new industry. The state also builds industries with its resources—as Meiji Japan did in the 1870s—and later turns these over to private companies to operate at very low cost. Finally, the state confers monopoly rights to certain private producers and provides lucrative contracts to ensure sufficient profits until they can compete on their own in the marketplace. Japan and Germany used a combination of these policies in the late nineteenth century to strengthen their military power and catch up with the advanced industrialized countries of the day.

Planned Economy   Finally, the state gradually extends its control over the private sector by actually determining the amount of investment and the quantities and kinds of goods and services to be produced. A planned economy based upon administered controls over prices and incomes becomes necessary. The state budget and banking system directs the required volume of saving to investment. State ministries and their subordinate organizations of production and exchange fix prices to balance the supplies of resources available for their demand in production and to ensure that goods and services are cleared in the marketplace. Socialist economic systems like the Soviet Union resort to these controls to mobilize resources and organize production rather than allowing private individuals to make these decisions.

  These strategies are simply a caricature of how state and economy have interacted in the historical experience of countries that began their modern economic growth in this century or the last. A variety of policies under each of these strategies have at one time or another guided a country's passage into the epoch of modern economic growth. A necessary but insufficient condition for these strategies to have borne fruit was a long period of peace matched by law and order. As already mentioned, this condition did not exist after 1911 in China, and the moderate advance toward modern economic growth scored until 1949 must be evaluated against the acute disorder that prevailed from time to time.

Problems in Implementing Modern Growth Strategies

The successful implementation of the above strategies requires that the state have the necessary fiscal and organizational capacities to carry out specific policies. If the state tries to extract more tax revenue from the private sector but discourages private investment and invites popular protest by its new tax-garnering efforts, production and exchange are disrupted, and little economic development occurs. The state must somehow extract more tax revenues but not discourage producers at the same time from investing money or supplying more goods to the market. The competition for scarce resources becomes very intense when the state seeks ways to increase its tax revenues. Unless ways can be found to reduce such competition and dispel the apprehensions and fears of the business people who privately organize production, state organizations quickly become overextended and operate with diminishing efficiency.

Another difficulty for the state is to create new organizations within its bureaucracy to assign tasks to make these strategies workable. The creation of any new agency, such as a bureau for promoting enterprise or a land reform institute, is quickly viewed with suspicion by existing state agencies as a potential competitor for budget funds and an encroacher upon their authority. Rivalry between state agencies for budget funds or for administrative power to enforce, regulate, or initiate laws and policies becomes more intense. Unless such tensions between new and old state organizations are quickly resolved, considerable delay, misunderstanding, and confusion spread through administrative channels with harmful, paralyzing effects for policy making and for groups within the private sector.

These two sets of broad problems characterized late Ch'ing efforts to launch modern economic growth after 1895 and the state building efforts of the Kuomintang government that made its capital at Nanking in 1927. Unless we understand the enormity of these problems faced by the state, the achievements and failures of these governments will be misunderstood.

THE FISCAL SYSTEM

By the late nineteenth century the Ch'ing state's power to increase taxes had shrunk considerably. Not only had the most important source of revenue—the land tax—in real terms declined, but the state did not have an accurate record of who owned what amounts of land to reassess land values and increase the land tax. The land tax accounted for around 90 percent of total tax revenue for the county (*hsien*) government.[2] The Ch'ing state included about 1,300 *hsien* —

each with a population probably between 150,000 to 250,000 people. The county magistrate relied on an average of five officials—not including secretaries—and 160-odd clerks and runners to carry out county administration including collecting of taxes. The actual supervising of land and tax records and the collecting of taxes were done by individuals of a semi-official status on a tax-farming basis. We know very little about how the actual tax-farming system worked.

Tax-Farming System

In north China these semi-official individuals were referred to as *she-shu* or *li-shu;* in Kiangsu and Chekiang they were called *chuang-shou* and *chuang-shu* respectively. They received payment in grain as "thank-you" money from the households that paid land tax. Apparently this semi-official responsibility was retained by the household and transferred to future generations on a hereditary basis. In some instances the magistrate knew these households by name and authorized them to collect the tax from those household groups such as *pao* and *chia* or *lin* and *lu* under the traditional *pao-chia* system. In other instances they served without the magistrate's knowledge and transferred the land taxes to a clerk or runner. Just how corrupt this tax-farming system became is not clear. The internalized values that governed the behavior of these hereditary tax farmers has never been specified. Very possibly they operated with considerable honesty and fairness under analogous norms characterized by the *probationary ethic* of Ch'ing officials.[3] In other words, these tax-farming households perhaps realized the obligation of their community to pay taxes of a certain amount, made every effort to obtain their collection, and experienced a sense of moral failure or a sense of guilt if they had not performed their duties properly.

This system had worked reasonably well during the Ch'ing period to give the state the revenue it needed. But it is not surprising that between 1770 and 1870 the land tax per unit of land declined in real terms perhaps by as much as 27 percent for the entire country according to a recent study by Hou and Li.[4] By 1900 the land tax amounted to only 2 percent of the value of what the land produced. The reason for this is that land productivity had increased over time and prices had risen, but the land had not been revalued accordingly nor the rate of land tax increased. In Taiwan after the Japanese land survey and land tax reform between 1897 and 1904 the actual land area farmed was found to be around 777,000 hectares instead of 361,000 and the new land tax collected came to 2.9 million yen instead .9 million yen.[5] This new land tax amounted to 5 or 6 percent of the value of what the land produced. The late Ch'ing farming area was greatly undertaxed. In spite of local official efforts to levy surcharges on the fixed land tax rate of the early eighteenth century, the increased land tax revenue still fell far below the potential revenue that could be collected had officials been able to launch a land survey and fix new land tax schedules.

But we should realize the enormous difficulties and costs for the state to do this. The Japanese colonial government in 1897 had sufficient military power and control over the small island of Taiwan to carry out such reform. Even so, the Japanese encountered fierce local resistance in the form of guerrilla activities, which did not cease until around 1904. By the same token, the Meiji government encountered widespread farmer opposition in the 1870s when officials surveyed the land in Japan and revised the land tax. Any government contemplating such a survey and tax reform first requires trained specialists in land cadastre work, officials and police to defuse community opposition, and new state institutions of record keeping, tax computation, and property litigation. The Ch'ing administration simply did not have the trained manpower for such an undertaking. And neither did the feeble Kuomintang (KMT) government in Nanking.

The land tax reforms in Meiji Japan and Taiwan not only had enabled the state to collect more tax revenue for its spending programs to modernize, but had stimulated the private sector to mobilize its resources, allocate them to their highest paid use, and work harder. First, the land survey conferred legal ownership to households that actually farmed the land. This important fact has been lightly dismissed because of ignorance of how property rights had been distributed under the ancien régime. In Taiwan, for example, the so-called ta-tsu or great rent households had long claimed the topsoil right, had always paid a land tax, but had leased their land to tenants to farm on a hereditary basis. The land survey and land tax reform eliminated the ta-tsu by denying them land ownership and conferring that right to those actually farming the land, and thereby granted the bona fide farming class full scope to use its entrepreneurial abilities. The Japanese were careful to compensate the ta-tsu so as to avoid trouble from them, and this transfer payment of income encouraged some of the ta-tsu to take up productive pursuits, such as banking and trade. This first phase of property rights distribution enabled the state—if it chose—to initiate land reform later between the new landowners and their tenants. The Japanese never undertook such far-reaching reform while managing Taiwan, but the KMT between 1950 and 1953 introduced a major land tenure reform that further extended property rights to full- and part-time tenants.

Second, the land tax reform called for new land tax schedules based upon a new assessment of the land's worth.[6] Landowners understood the market value of their land. They quickly recognized that by supplying more to the market and improving their land, they greatly gained because the new land tax schedules were fixed. They were encouraged to allocate their land to the highest economic use, to invest more to improve its productivity, and to work harder in management of their property. The result was that greater specialization began to take place. Production increased more rapidly than before, and the powerful impulse of commercialization—whereby owners supplied more to the market—increased exchange between town and countryside. Thus, the land survey and land tax reform generated more tax revenue to the state for modernizing markets and creating new infrastructure. They also greatly encouraged owners of resources to work harder and produce more for the market, and thereby speed up the rate of farm production.

Failure of Kuomintang Land Tax Reform

The KMT party had only de facto control over Anhwei, Kiangsu, and Chekiang provinces. Let us review what the KMT attempted in Chekiang, a province of 22 million people, to reform the land tax system. Land taxes made up 60 percent of all tax revenue, but the province like all others was greatly undertaxed.[7] In 1927 officials estimated that 20 percent and 15 percent of the assessed taxes in Fuyang and Sung-yang counties respectively were not paid by taxpayers. Officials first resorted to asking landowners to report voluntarily their size and value of land, and surprisingly, a number of people came forward in some counties to do this. At the same time land survey teams were sent to certain counties to make cadastral surveys. But the costs proved extremely high. A single year's survey cost for Chu county, a mountainous and poor area, came to 18,000 Chinese dollars, which exceeded the additional 8,000 dollars revenue generated by the revised land tax records. Many officials complained the survey costs were too prohibitive to complete properly. A third approach was to select a model *hsien,* P'ing-hu, which contained many large estate landlords, to register land and revise the land tax assessment, but the Japanese invasion cut short this effort. By 1936 provincial officials could report that only half of the cultivated land actually produced land tax. Governor Huang Shao-hung later wrote in his memoirs:

> At that time we should have rationalized the fiscal system, and of course, developed new sources of revenue which could have been depended upon. The most fundamental way to have achieved that would have been to press for an increase in the land tax and wipe out all existing debts. The land records still had not been revised, and those registers were held by the *chuang-shu.* Chekiang already had spent considerable funds and labor time to carry out the registration of land, but the

results of those efforts could not be used. The reason was that the land survey teams had neither training nor experience. Most landowners refused to report their landholdings or had supplied misleading information. Therefore, even though the government had vigorously tried to increase taxes, it could not mobilize any additional tax revenue.[8]

This example of Chekiang shows that KMT attempts to reform the land tax failed. The KMT government merely took over a ramshackled administration of the Ch'ing without sufficient staff to make a land survey. Furthermore, Nanking already had committed its military power to extend its rule over other provinces instead of consolidating its power in a single base area and developing several model provinces with substantial popular support. When we perceive the 1927–1937 Nanking period in this perspective, we can see that the government clearly made a tactical mistake in spreading state power to control other provinces instead of reforming the institutions and local administration within the few provinces it controlled fairly well. By carrying out socioeconomic reforms, generating more tax revenue while increasing production, and concurrently introducing an ambitious modernization program, the KMT might have been able to turn Chekiang and Kiangsu into modern, model provinces as it would do in Taiwan beginning in the early 1950s. But the KMT failed to recognize that introducing modernization required more resources than the state could muster by relying upon the taxing methods and administration of its predecessor, the Ch'ing. In order to introduce a land tax reform, the state needed both power and considerable finesse so as not to disrupt production in the private sector, but instead to increase it even more rapidly.

Property-Rights Pyramiding

The redistribution of rural property rights that occurred from Taiwan's land tax reform has profound implications for our understanding of how the KMT tried to introduce land tenure reform in Chekiang around 1927 but completely failed to carry through. Had the KMT at least carried out the first phase of property rights distribution, such as the elimination of the *ta-tsu* in Taiwan, this accomplishment alone might have given the KMT party broad popular rural support. The KMT land reform in Taiwan during the early 1950s clearly indicates that the government obtained popular backing for its general policies of modernization. In Chekiang the lower-ranking KMT rank and file were poorly informed about rural customs and the distribution of property rights. Had these city-bred intellectuals understood rural customary law, they probably would not have urged at the outset such a policy as lowering tenant rents. Upon pressure from

these KMT party members to introduce a rent reduction policy between 1927 and 1929, rural Chekiang was quickly thrown into pande-
monium. Enormous confusion and fear spread throughout villages;
litigation greatly increased to the distress of local officials; and ru-
mors abounded as to what rent reduction really was all about.[9] The
authorities in Nanking quickly realized that all discussion of a rent
reduction policy would have to cease if order was to be restored, and
local party officials were ordered to shelve rent reduction for the time
being. After 1929 no further attempts were made to introduce institutional reforms on property rights. Instead, the provincial government
spent heavily to build roads, railroads, schools, and research institutes. The KMT has been severely criticized for its failure to modernize the few provinces it did control.

From the few sources about Chekiang's land system, something
like a Japanese property rights redistribution in Taiwan clearly
might have been a first step for the KMT to have made Chekiang into
a model province. The rebellions of the 1850s had laid waste much of
Chekiang and had created vast tracts of wasteland from which former
owners had either fled or disappeared forever. Peace brought families
of all types to open these lands to the plough; some reclaimed their
former lands; others established riparian rights. Within a few years
the old property rights system of two owners for one plot of land (*i-t'ien
liang-chu*) again was operative. This extraordinary system allowed a
number of households to lay claim to land and derive a stream of income from it. With their appreciation for contractual agreement and
their keen awareness of how a scarce resource can be shared in ways
beneficial to several parties, the Chinese had devised a property rights
system for land that made possible the pyramiding of household
claims to income from a single unit of land.

In its simplest form the system operated as follows: Households
with prior claim to the land, either through registration or by
purchase, might lease it permanently to another household. The original owner (*ta-tsu-hu*) or large rent-collecting household claimed the
subsurface right to the land (*t'ien-ti*) and paid the land tax to the state
if the land was registered. The leasing household (*hsiao-tsu-hu*) or
small rent-paying household claimed the surface right to the land
(*t'ien-mien* in north or west Chekiang or *shang-pi-ch'uan* in south
Chekiang) and paid a rent— typically in kind—once a year as a fixed
proportion of the harvest.[10] Tenants could transfer parcels of this land
to their heirs; they could sublet portions to other households and collect rent; they could pledge part of it as collateral for loans; they could
mortgage it to other tenants for a large loan in which they gave up use
of it but could reclaim it when they repaid the loan without interest;
or they could sell their hereditary tenancy right to another household.
As all of these transactions applied to plots of varying size; in short

order, an outsider would have no inkling of how extensively claims had accumulated to a single plot of land.

Other variations also existed. Associations such as lineages, charitable estates, schools, irrigation societies, or village councils also claimed lands. These groups leased their land to other households or to an intermediary who in turn sublet plots to other households. Finally, bursaries (*tsu-chan*) or brokerage organizations handled the leasing of land for private owners in turn for a fee. These bursaries saw to the collection of rent and payment of land tax for landowners. Similar-type liens upon land held by these owners could be established for various households in the manner described for *ta-tsu-hu* and *hsiao-tsu-hu* household relationships.

The state naturally had little information on how complex property-rights pyramiding had evolved in this province or any other for that matter. The few records in official possession covered less than half of the province's cultivated land, and most of these were probably in error. Therefore, the land tenure surveys of the early 1930s, which reported that 48 percent of the population were tenants, 31 percent part-owners, and 21 percent owners, merely mislead and fail to clarify precisely the actual property right of the households. For example, a so-called tenant probably included the *hsiao-tsu-hu* with hereditary rights to farm the land. The high percentage of tenants recorded for central and south China by these surveys actually include a large number of hereditary tenant households that were real owner-proprietors from the standpoint of customary law. The shifting of these households from the tenant to the owner and part-owner categories quite possibly meant that the distribution of tenants and owners in the south did not differ very greatly from that of the north.

As Chekiang officials never completed a careful landownership survey, they never distinguished households with subsurface rights from those with topsoil rights nor identified other households with various rights to the topsoil. As all households organized their resources to acquire property and receive income, they endorsed the customary law practices, which made this property-rights system work. This is not to say that for many households—like the hereditary tenant households—property rights could not have been improved. Let us suppose that the hereditary tenant households had acquired de jure rights to their land and did not pay rent to the subsoil-owning household but did pay the land tax to the state. This arrangement would have given these hereditary tenant households enormous incentive to improve their land and produce for the market. They would not have to incur the transaction costs of dealing with the rent-collecting households, and their transaction costs with other households also would be greatly reduced by not requiring approval from the rentier households. This reform of property rights undoubtedly would have been very popular in the villages as long as the rentier households could have been recompensed to remain silent. The next reform measure to logically follow was to formalize rent and lease rights between the new landowners and their tenants and thus to give tenants the possibility of obtaining property of their own.

As Chekiang officials had proposed to reduce tenant rents and freeze them, this program really threatened most of these hereditary tenants, as well as the rentier households. By not conferring legal ownership to the large class of hereditary tenants in exchange for allowing the state to collect a land tax on the reassessed value of their land, the state not only alienated most of the rural people but never obtained that great revenue potential to modernize Chekiang in a more dramatic and effective manner than was already the case.

BUREAUCRATIC CAPITALISTS AND ENTREPRENEURIAL BUREAUCRATS

If the state initiates modern economic growth, the new organizations created for this purpose must fulfill their assigned tasks instead of becoming tools of political factions bent only upon acquiring political power. If the legitimacy of the state weakens, political factions struggle for political power instead of effectively performing their economic or administrative roles. Several things then happen.

First, individuals in government enrich themselves and squander public monies by their inept and oftentimes illegal management of the enterprises they are charged to lead. Second, these individuals misallocate or waste scarce resources by imprudent choice of projects that have little benefit for the private sector. Third, the new organizations managed by these individuals exert a stultifying effect upon the private sector, limit its investment, and discourage entrepreneurship. We call these officials *bureaucratic capitalists*. Politically appointed and vested with state power, they use their economic organizations for seeking political power or influencing how political power can be used. The more widespread such behavior, the less likelihood the government they serve will weather a serious crisis.

When officials manage their organizations for the purpose of improving production and distribution of the private sector and devise imaginative means for their organizations to perform more effectively than originally conceived or expected, we refer to such individuals as *entrepreneurial bureaucrats*. These individuals might initiate fiscal reforms, use state power to subsidize an industry that will be turned over to private enterprise, or undertake a project that will provide external economies of scale to private firms so as to lower their unit costs. Where the state has successfully legitimized its power and such official behavior becomes widespread, the private sector can be induced to save, invest in capital formation, and adopt modern technology.

A Model Bureaucratic Capitalist

The warlord period, 1916–1928, saw many political factions scheme and struggle to consolidate their political control at Peking and the rest of the country. Within this context, bureaucratic capitalism flourished. Take the example of Ts'ao Ju-lin who led the New Communications Clique between 1916 and 1919.[11] Ts'ao briefly attended the Hupeh Railway School at age twenty, then spent six years in Japan to earn a law degree from Chūo University. In 1906 he returned to China to rise in the Board of Foreign Affairs and to align with the Yuan Shih-k'ai faction, a group close to Viceroy Yuan who governed Chihli province. Ts'ao became director-general of the Bank of Communications in late 1916. This bank, created in 1907 with 10 million taels—of which 40 and 60 percent respectively represented state and merchant capital shares—handled the revenues from railways, postal, and telecommunications. It served the Ministry of Communications and acquired more financial leverage in the economy than even the Ministry of Finance.

When Ts'ao assumed control over this bank, he immediately concluded the ongoing negotiation of loans with the Japanese and used half of these funds to support the Tuan Ch'i-jui faction, which was trying to seize power in north China, and used the remainder of the Japanese loan to reorganize the Bank of Communications and thus increase its economic power. Ts'ao next negotiated the infamous Nishihara loans, which permitted his associates to continue their support of Tuan's faction and also establish the Exchange Bank of China under Sino–Japanese control. Thereafter, Ts'ao used bank assets, as well as his own funds, for investing in coal mines, real estate, and small banks. While some of these investments undoubtedly did stimulate output growth, Ts'ao's manipulation of bank wealth for political purposes exemplified the bureaucratic capitalist behavior of this period.

An Entrepreneurial Bureaucrat

With Kuomintang power established in Nanking in 1928, the situation changed. Many officials, trained abroad and given new responsibilities, began performing as entrepreneurial bureaucrats. One such famous example was Sung Tzu-wen (T.V. Soong), the brilliant prime mover who modernized the government's financial system.[12] Born in

1894, Sung received his education at Harvard, returned to China in 1917 to work in the Han-Yeh-P'ing Iron-Steel Works, and in April 1927 when Chiang K'ai-shek located in Nanking, he began masterminding financial strategy for the new government.

The Kuomintang inherited a financial mess. Monthly expenditures ran at 11 million Chinese dollars with revenues only 3 million dollars. The national debt probably was around 2.25 billion Chinese dollars. Foreign pressure to repay long-standing debts remained strong. Sung proved a brilliant, courageous, tough, and entrepreneurial minded official. As the new minister of finance, he abolished the hated *likin* tax on inland traffic of goods. By 1930 he had concluded tariff autonomy treaties with major powers and secured for China control over its customs duties with the right to set tariff schedules freely. By 1932 he had managed to refinance the foreign debt on a new basis with favorable prospects for China to acquire international loans. He terminated costly bond financing for balancing the budget, abolished the former currency unit, the tael, in 1932, and instituted the new Chinese dollar based upon the silver standard unit. He created a new central bank to assist the government in its financing. These and other activities earned him some enmity from his opponents but awesome respect and praise from people who supported the nationalist government's efforts to modernize China.

Perhaps more important, he had vigorously opposed Chiang's demands for more funds for military operations, and the prospects in late 1933 appeared bright for balancing the budget soon. But Sung's resignation in that year was sparked by his very failure to curb Chiang's spending mania for the military. Thereafter, Chiang's strategy to unify the country at any price was never so strongly contested, and he still received whatever amount of funds he demanded.

Although Sung later returned to government service, he must have realized the eventual fate that would befall the Nationalist government. Not surprisingly then, Sung—like so many other prominent officials at that time—reverted to bureaucratic capitalist behavior to amass a personal fortune from private business activities outside of his office. For example, in March 1937 Sung obtained financial control of the Nanyang Brothers' Tobacco Company. His business acumen for profit making can be seen from the following recommendation he proposed the company's board adopt on 13 May 1940 for future production and pricing:

> Although cigarette prices will rise much faster in the future, they will not rise as fast as the price of foreign exchange, and in due course this gap will become even larger. Even if we try to re-estimate production costs, there is no certainty we can

show a profit. We should neither alter our brand nor terminate production. In my opinion we first should estimate a profit margin and adjust output accordingly to realize that profit. After a few months of carrying out such restrictive production, we can then save our existing raw materials and wait until prices rise later.[13]

Sung's resolution to restrict supply was adopted by the board. Sung went on to become one of the wealthiest individuals in China, and his family was referred to as one of the four wealthiest families of Nationalist China.

TWO ASSESSMENTS OF THE ECONOMY UNDER NANKING RULE: 1928–1937

A Period of Stagnation

Critics of the Nanking government argue that even if Japan had not invaded China in 1937, the Nationalist government would never have unified and modernized the country because it had not created the preconditions for economic development in the provinces under its control. Douglass S. Paauw points out that economic stagnation prevailed throughout the decade. Agricultural production barely rose; capital formation remained unchanged. The government failed to initiate reforms that might have increased savings in order to increase investment in capital formation. Rather than try to redistribute income and tax the wealthy who could afford to pay, the government relied upon a regressive tax system that bore most heavily upon the lower-income classes. Its only success was to mobilize the banking sector to finance Nanking's insatiable demand for more funds. By 1937 the government controlled only a small, powerful apex of society, but without any firm, supporting foundations.[14]

Lloyd Eastman's assessment of Nationalist policies during this period endorses the same view. He cites the many land tax surcharges and commodity taxes Nanking imposed upon the rural order to extract more tax revenue without providing compensating services to increase production and welfare. The government was even more successful in extorting large sums from prominent business organizers in the cities and levying new taxes on them. The economy slipped deeply into depression from 1933 through 1935, and while some recovery occurred by early 1937 no new economic foundations appeared to suggest that economic development might begin to accelerate.[15]

A Period of Growing, Modern Infrastructure

Defenders of the regime list a series of important economic policies ranging from banking and currency reforms to measures to complete new projects—in water control, transportation, and research and extension services for agriculture—that comprised a significant infrastructure development basic for modern economic growth.

Arthur N. Young contends that the currency reform of 3 November 1935 nationalized silver and made the notes issued by the Central Bank, Bank of China, and Bank of Communications full legal tender.[16] The stage was set for a single currency—managed by a centralized banking system—to serve as the new unit of account, store of value, and medium of exchange in China. The Central Bank was to be converted into a federal reserve bank, and China for the first time had a unified banking structure.

The Nationalist government had to create a system of budgets, accounts, and fiscal controls from scratch. Military and debt payments absorbed 84 percent of total expenditures in 1928–1929 and between 1929 and 1937 never fell much below 66 percent. The remainder of budget expenditures went to education and culture, economic construction, and administration. The new government had been compelled to raise new taxes and borrow; borrowing roughly covered 20 percent of total spending during the decade. Defenders of the government's programs argue that in spite of supporting large military spending, Nanking managed to pay its foreign debts and still spend considerably for modernization. And these expenditures promoted the growth of a modern infrastructure that in time would have enabled the private sector to acquire more technology and produce more efficiently for the market.

Examples of this are the following.[17] Educational research and instruction, particularly in agriculture, improved. New farmer organizations such as cooperative marketing societies in Anhwei at Wu-kiang, provincial agricultural banks, and cotton, rice, and wheat research institutes were created. Under the Natural Resource Commission the government financed the construction of a new steel mill, a machine-manufacturing plant, a vegetable-oil-processing firm, an alcohol plant, and a newspaper plant. Further, new railroad lines were built and trunk lines like the one between Canton and Hankow completed. Many thousands of miles of new highways were constructed in Kiangsu, Chekiang, and other provinces.

We can sum up these views by noting that the critics of the Nanking government stress that (1) the economy merely stagnated during this decade; (2) resources had been diverted from the private to public sector and squandered; and (3) aside from several new banks, the government had not created new institutions to mobilize saving and increase investment for rapid economic development. Therefore, even without war in 1937, we have no assurance this government could have unified the country and modernized the economy.

Defenders of the Nanking government argue that basic financial reforms, the creation of a central banking system, and the building of a small, improved, modern infrastructure gave the new government sufficient means to continue to unify the country and modernize the economy had the war not intervened.

Additional Factors for Evaluating Nanking

Both schools ignore two important questions which ought to be posed and pondered before an assessment of Nanking government policies and achievements can be made. First, what were the likely future costs to unify the country and extend modernization had war not intervened? How long would military activities have continued, and could the Kuomintang have continued to mobilize resources for its armies without creating new difficulties for organizers of production and exchange? Second, did the Nanking government possess the institutional means to mobilize resources sufficiently to meet these costs, so that the private sector could have continued to improve production and increase supply? In other words, could the government have elicited popular support for its activities merely by providing the private sector with a modern infrastructure?

Possibly, the long-term costs to unify the country and restore peace would have remained very high for many decades so that the vitality of the Nanking government steadily might have weakened. On the other hand, the private sector might have been able to take advantage of the newly created infrastructure to expand output rapidly and thereby allow the state to extract more tax revenue to improve that infrastructure still further. The Nanking government had struggled under extreme adversity to balance (1) military unification of the nation with (2) economic construction. Territorial losses to Japan, natural disasters, severe deflation, and an agricultural crisis had caused extreme difficulties for this regime in allocating resources between these two competing ends and yet scoring substantial gains on both fronts. The Nanking government probably could have succeeded in its twin tasks by concentrating first upon developing several model provinces and then transferring these tried and tested techniques to the newly won territories in order to ultimately unify the country. But the task proved more arduous and final success more problematic by adopting the strategy of trying to balance national unification with gradual modernization of a few provinces from the top to the bottom of society. Historically, this latter strategy does not seem to have ever succeeded in any country that has achieved modern economic growth.

THE AGRARIAN CRISIS

By the turn of this century the agrarian system still remained in the grip of the weather cycle with good and poor harvests determining the welfare of the countryside and cities alike. The available scraps of evidence do not convey any hint of pending rural crisis in which unprecedented output decline and unemployment might occur to drive the rural people to violence. The following excerpt from a British Legation official's report of his wanderings in eastern Shantung in late 1906 describes what the countryside in much of China was like at this time:

> The villages all look very poor, though they are frequently well built, and the houses constructed of stone and mud bricks, and the whole village surrounded by a wall. Nearly everyone owns a little land, which he cultivates, and the produce of which he lives on, taking the surplus to the local market for sale. Though the people are so poor, yet beggars are rarely seen. . . . The bad wheat crop this year has raised the price of food some 30 percent, but though it is likely to cause distress, it is not thought that troubles will ensue, partly because in Eastern Shantung the bean crop (the great food of the people) has been exceptionally good, and the people also eat kauliang, which was good this year; down in the chiningchow (southern Shantung) the export of wheat from the province has been forbidden. The chief food of the people is millet, kauliang, beans, sweet potatoes, and vegetables—rarely meat. Little, or practically no rice is procurable in Eastern Shantung, but the nearer one approaches the rice-growing province of Kiangsu, the more easily it can be obtained.[18]

When taken together, the writings of foreign observers and even native experts on rural conditions in the final years of the Ch'ing dynasty convey neither a sense of production decline, a singular state of food grain or fiber shortage, or a deterioration of rural welfare. The Chinese farmer still remained a victim of the weather, and he was still very poor.

The rural economy certainly did not possess any features which prevented the increase of output through the improvement of technology and organization. Rural markets were highly competitive; producers were highly sensitive to price change and adjusted their supply accordingly. Farmers were very skilled in their farming arts, worked hard, and carefully saved. While land tenure studies of the 1920s and 1930s show different results, the general findings indicate that a little over half of all households owned their land, another 20 to 25 percent were part-owners, and the remainder included landlords, tenants, and laborers. As these farm surveys included hereditary tenants in central and southern China as either part-owners or tenant households, the findings underreport the true proportion of households that enjoyed the de facto, and by customary law, the de jure right to farm their land. Even so, the fact that less than 20 percent of rural households had precarious claim to land and its income still indicates this huge rural economy had not created secure property rights for all households. Yet, if the tenancy problem was exaggerated and this private sector functioned capably until World War I, what went wrong later?

For indeed, after 1920, something went seriously wrong in Chinese agriculture that is worthy of being called a *severe agrarian crisis*. This crisis can be defined as a set of new market conditions in which (1) the prices received by rural households for their goods and services did not cover their costs of production, and (2) fewer household resources were demanded to produce an output of goods and services, which fluctuated in the 1920s, stagnated during the 1930s, and declined in the 1940s. The effects of these new market conditions were to (1) impoverish an increasing proportion of rural households, (2) redistribute income and assets more unequally among rural households during some periods— particularly 1929 through 1935—and (3) create more unemployment of labor and withdraw land from production. From 1920 onward the organizers of production in the rural sector produced an output of goods and services increasingly below what the sector actually could produce.

Sharp Decline in Demand

The following panels of supply and demand shown in figure 6–1 depict different market conditions that began to characterize different sections of the country during this period. The supply schedule SS denotes the output of farm products and/or handicraft goods supplied by rural households. The demand schedule DD depicts the market demand at the small market towns where these goods are traded. Let us take Part A to show various examples of the new market conditions that became prevalent after 1920.

Equilibrium farm and handicraft prices exist at P_0 and Q_0 where they are supplied, demanded, and cleared from the market. A sharp decline or shift leftward in the demand curve $D'D'$ for farm products and/or handicraft goods—given the current supply commitment—results in a lower market price P_1 with a smaller amount Q_1 transacted. Households receive less income to cover their costs of production. The persistence of the new demand conditions quickly creates some unemployment of resources. Even if producers try to increase supply so that $S'S'$ shifts and a new quantity Q_2 is transacted, price P_1 declines and if demand is inelastic over this range—as is likely the case—income for producers might further fall. The following are examples of such market conditions.

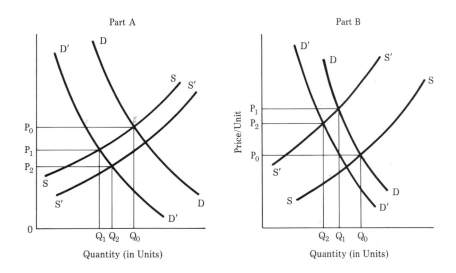

FIGURE 6–1. *Rural Market Conditions between 1920 and 1949*

The seven major handicraft products exported from China declined in quantity and value after 1924, and another six showed stagnation. As a result industries like tea processing, sericulture, carpet making, straw braiding, oil pressing, paper making, and sugar refining declined or stagnated. In the world fiber market, synthetic fibers began replacing Chinese silk in the early 1920s. Between 1923 and 1930 Chinese silk prices in New York declined by 6 percent. The following evaluation of the demand pattern for sericulture products at this time describes the trends:

> There are three kinds of articles in the American market that have used silk: first, cloth satins and velvets; second, embroidered materials, handkerchiefs, and fine undergarments worn by women; third, gauze, and embroidered curtains and drapes. The latter use a great deal of silk ... and handkerchiefs require much of the kind of silk produced in Kwangtung. Al-

ready, synthetic fibers are replacing the silk formerly used in these various products. The greatest decline had been for fine silk handkerchiefs, and for much of the embroidered apparel, which also required finely spun Chinese silk. Both are now being replaced by synthetic fiber. Embroidered items in which 80 to 90 percent used consist of Chinese silk now only require half that amount.[19]

In the early 1920s foreign cotton cloth again began circulating in local markets to compete with handicraft cloth (t'u-pu). Japanese and even Chinese textile mills began producing more cloth from their mechanized looms to make such competition more intense. Demand contracted; price fell; and producers supplied less to the market and thereby earned less and rendered considerable resources to unemployment.

The loss of Manchuria meant a sharp contraction of demand for farm and handicraft products sold to that region. After 1931 handicraft industries in rural markets, such as in Ting county south of Peking, which had long depended upon the demand from Manchuria as a major source of income went into decline. The severe deflation the befell China beginning in 1933 reduced prices significantly so that producers went into debt, sold assets such as land, and suffered great hardship. The following report of the impact of declining demand on the tea industry shows this clearly:

> Since the world depression, imperialism has been stricken by overproduction, and the collapse of markets has dealt the Chinese peasants' subsidiary industries—silk and tea—a severe blow. Prior to 1929, the crop area for tea in China was 5,353,355 mow and production amounted to 5,915,574 piculs. Of late, 1932, the crop area has declined to 4,475,928 mow and production had fallen to 4,449,445. The farmers in Anhwei, Kiangsi, Chekiang, and Fukien greatly depend upon tea cultivation as their main industry. The collapse of this industry now makes it very difficult for the peasantry to support themselves.[20]

The great outflow of silver that first commenced in 1932 and then cascaded forth in 1934 further depressed market demand by causing an acute liquidity shortage for merchants and brokers. A 1933 banking study cited the difficulties rural producers suddenly encountered:

> Because of the decline in crop area, the fall in farm prices, and the decline in farm revenue, peasants have not been able to buy daily necessities from the market without incurring debt. The wealthy farming families now flee to the cities because of banditry, hard times, and the collapse of farm production. They do not reinvest in the land. Those with savings move to

the larger cities. As a result of a deficit balance of payments, a steady outflow of money has taken place from villages to market towns to large cities, and from the latter to the great commercial city-ports. Take the example of Shanghai. In 1932 the flow of money from the interior to Shanghai averaged 6 million *yuan* each month. For the year alone, the inflow of silver dollars to Shanghai came to more than 89 million *yuan*. [21]

As these new market conditions generally lasted several years and the contraction of world trade affecting exports continued even longer, great sections of the countryside found that production costs were not covered by prices. Even by supplying more to the market, farmers soon realized that their farm income still declined. They then tried to curtail production, but the result was to create more unemployment as demand for rural workers declined.

Sharp Decline in Supply

The market conditions depicted in Part B of figure 6–1 created quite different supply and demand shifts. The abrupt shift of the supply schedule leftward to $S'S'$, which depicts a reduction in supply commitment to the market, initially produces a new market equilibrium of a higher price, P_1, for a reduced quantity, Q_1, transacted. These conditions might persist for a time or alter if demand also contracts to $D'D'$, in which case the quantity now supplied further falls to Q_2 but clears from the market at a lower price. What factors might produce these new market conditions?

Breakdown of Law and Order Two factors frequently reduced the supply of goods to market towns. During the 1920s warlord armies increased their demand for resources used by farmers for production. They confiscated livestock, carts, and grain supplies and mobilized farm labor for military activities or corvée labor without compensation or at prices far below current market values. If warlord armies were not responsible, then the attacking bandits were. Conditions in north China became so lawless that hundreds of thousands of people migrated to Manchuria each year. These grim conditions are described by a Japanese journalist:

> Not only have arson, theft, and rape occurred everywhere, as if wild beasts were on the prowl, but murders and kidnappings are performed in broad daylight. Further, after the food mobilized for the military has been seized by bandit groups, more food is forcibly taken by various warlord armies. In this fashion the peasants in the same locale are pillaged two and three times by outsiders. Bandits and warlord factions abscond with their chickens and dogs. The people are without houses, with-

out food, and their plight has become extremely miserable. They now are abandoning their villages. The old, the young, and the women flee to Manchuria and the south. These waves of migrations are like an endless tide. No matter how much time elapses, these same conditions persist.[22]

By 1927 and 1928 nearly a million Chinese each year left Hopei and Shantung for Manchuria to flee the ravages of war and banditry.

New Taxes and Levies The imposition of land tax surcharges or levies that communities had to provide on their own also proved to be an odious burden that adversely affected the capabilities of households to organize production—as in the recent past—and continue to supply the same output to the market. The following account of the various taxes and levies imposed on rural Kwangtung by different military factions in the mid-1920s describes conditions throughout China at this time:

> We peasant cultivators [of Kwangtung] now use our labor to farm our land when before we were simply tenants and laborers. But aside from paying the land tax each year, we now have to pay extra tax surcharges. For example, in the Hsiangshan area there were at least 30 different kinds of levies. These were earmarked for the costs of Kwangtung University, the military and their campaigns against the northern warlords, self-government, the peace preservation corps, a lunatic asylum, refugees, famine relief, the people's defense league, the peace preservation league, the self-production office, the self-defense agency, not to mention the surtaxes on fowl, fruit, lumber, paddy land, etc. In addition to these various kinds of imposts, there were all kinds of markups *(likin)* added.[23]

Natural Disasters The second factor was the disruption of farm production caused by floods, drought, and famine, which forced farmers to market less, reduced their seed for the next harvest, and drove many to seek work elsewhere. In 1918 a great drought swept the 6 northern provinces. It persisted for several years and eventually claimed a half million lives and severely injured crops in 317 counties. In February of 1918 a great earthquake ripped Shensi and Kansu. In 1921, 6 provinces suffered great floods. In the following year a typhoon struck Swatow, and in the next year 12 provinces experienced both drought and floods. By 1924 and 1925 the scope and impact of such natural disasters worsened because so much labor had been diverted to warfare and could not be mobilized to provide proper relief. Yunnan suffered a tremendous earthquake and then great floods. Six more provinces were beset by crop pests, and floods churned the Yellow River region. The province of Hunan in 1924 virtually became an armed camp as military troops operated to prevent the smuggling of rice out of the province because grain had become so scarce. Hunan, one of the country's major rice bowls, actually ceased shipping grain to the lower Yangtze because of continual flooding and natural disturbances between 1921 and 1924. Local governments now functioned far less efficiently than in the past. The recovery costs for communities to revive production were more difficult to meet. As a result the marketed surplus declined and agricultural prices rose sharply.

It is little wonder that China's net grain imports, which were zero between 1916 and 1920, suddenly jumped to 807,340 metric tons, 938,830 metric tons and over 2.0 million metric tons for the 1921–1925, 1926–1930, and 1931–1935 year periods respectively. Between 1886 and 1910 these imports had only ranged between 250,000 and 300,000 metric tons on a five-year basis. These massive grain imports fed the city-ports because far less grain was shipped to them from the interior as a result of the decline in marketed surplus. Farm production violently fluctuated during the 1920s, and the huge errors and omissions in crop statistics make describing the trend in grain production impossible. Grain supply per capita probably declined slightly if production merely fluctuated and the city-ports became more dependent upon foreign sources. Between 1930 and 1937 crop statistical reporting greatly improved, yet the food grain production trend showed neither rise nor fall, so that the supply of grain per capita definitely declined slightly.

Between 1937 and 1949 war and civil war disrupted production, and after 1943–44 food grain and fiber production did decline. Therefore, from 1937 onward, massive disruption to rural markets and mounting inflation shifted the terms of exchange against the organizers of rural production. The prices of goods and services they purchased rose more rapidly than the prices paid for the godds they supplied to markets. For this reason, as supply contracted so too did demand, and a new equilibrium price was associated with a smaller quantity supplied to the market. Throughout the 1940s, then, the marketed surplus steadily declined, and cities suffered severe shortages of food grains and fibers.

The new market instability that became more widespread after 1920 originated from forces beyond the control of the rural people and outside their sphere of production and exchange. The decline in market demand for handicraft products was caused by substitute goods supplied to world markets and industrial growth at home in the city-ports. The decline in marketed surplus of agricultural and handicraft goods was caused by disruptions to the supply side and new financial burdens imposed upon organizers of production. The increased unemployment in villages, the influx of refugees to the city-ports, and growing rural poverty led many observers to believe that China had incurred an agrarian crisis of unprecedented severity. R. H. Tawney wrote in his famous *Land and Labor in China* that "the revolution of 1911 was a bourgeois affair. The revolution of the peasants has still to come." What explanations were advanced by contemporaries for this agrarian crisis?

Two Explanations and Two Cures for Crisis

There were two principal schools of thought. One school asserted that once law and order prevailed, farmers and tenants merely needed access to modern inputs to improve their land and labor productivity. For adopting new seeds and fertilizers the rural sector also required state assistance through flood control projects and improved markets. The application of modern science to farming would immediately increase farm production because farming practices, although traditional, were already well advanced. This school did not view the tenancy problem as serious, and contended that the property rights issue in agriculture could be resolved by modest legal reforms to ensure the protection of tenant rights and access to acquiring land of his own.

The second school—more diverse in nature—believed that the very unequal distribution of income and wealth, which in turn originated from the distribution pattern of property rights, was at the root of the agrarian problem. First, this distribution pattern had progressively become more unequal since the nineteenth century, and many people were unable to even farm land of their own. Second, the removal of so many people from farming stemmed from very exploitative practices in markets where landlords, moneylenders, and merchants exacted high rents, interest rates, and exorbitant prices from farmers and tenants, and thus squeezed them financially, drove many farmers into debt, and forced them to sell their land. Third, these powerful exploitative groups did not use their earnings for productive investment in agriculture but instead spent their income on unproductive activities ranging from conspicuous consumption to the hiring of local "toughs" to render protection and assist them in their extortionist practices. Finally, agriculture had developed a market dependency, especially in world markets, which made the organizers of production very vulnerable to price fluctuations and new demand patterns. The combination of this new market dependency with the activities of exploitative groups forced more and more households to sell their land so that the concentration of property and wealth into fewer hands increased.

The policy implications of these two schools of thought are readily clear. The former school stressed that only minor reform of property rights, the creation of a modern infrastructure of roads and water control, and the establishment of an agricultural research and extension system were necessary for the modernization of agriculture. The latter school contended that only by drastic restructuring of property rights and the creation of new organizations to influence decision making and reward in agriculture could farm production be rapidly developed. In fact, both schools have proven to be correct in their policy prescriptions and results. The examples of Japanese success in Taiwan and the Liaotung peninsula confirm the validity of the former school's policies, and the changes in China after 1949 attest to the validity of the latter school's policies. Yet controversy continues on which school offered the best explanation of why agriculture developed difficulties after 1920.

Both in the Liaotung and in Taiwan Chinese farmers organized agricultural production and exchange as in other parts of China. Japan ruled Taiwan from 1895 to 1945 and the Liaotung peninsula from 1907 to 1945. In both regions agricultural output growth began to exceed population growth on a sustained basis, and rural living standards greatly improved. In the Liaotung between 1910–1912 and 1920–1921 population expanded annually at 2.7 percent—compared to the growth of food and oilseeds crops at 3.5 percent per year. Again, between 1920–1921 and 1935–1937 population grew at the rate of 5.7 percent per year, largely because of immigration from north China, but grain production expanded at the annual rate of 6.2 percent.[24] In Taiwan, on the other hand, between 1910 and 1926 and between 1921 and 1937 population grew at the annual growth rates of 1.0 and 2.3 percent respectively, but total farm production expanded at 1.6 and 4.4 percent.[25] In two Chinese regions controlled by a foreign power, per capita grain availability increased whereas elsewhere in China over this same period it either declined or stagnated.

Even though the Japanese colonial administration enforced discriminatory economic policies which favored Japanese business owners but worked to the great disadvantage of the wealthy Chinese, their policies bore remarkable fruit. The Japanese did not meddle in the countryside except in the following ways: First, they conferred property rights on those who actually farmed the land—be they hereditary tenants or simple owner-operators. Second, they simplified the levying and collecting of the land tax through a land survey, the valuing of land, and the applying of a fixed land tax according to the quality of land. Third, they improved transportation, marketing, irrigation, and public health for urban and rural people alike. Finally, they made available to farmers modern technology such as high-yield seeds and new fertilizers. As the Japanese brought peace and order and increased the supply of modern services, the Chinese worked harder, delivered more to the market, and prospered.

The agrarian crisis that gripped China between 1920 and 1949 seems to have arisen mainly from the breakdown of domestic law and order, Japanese aggression, and shifts in world trade. Rural markets and communities no sooner had recovered from one shock, and they were jolted by another. Therefore, as the rural sector became poorer and supplied less to the nonagricultural sector, unemployment and hardship became more serious and widespread. The unemployed tried to find a livelihood within the ranks of the new military armies of this era, or they migrated to cities and distant regions like Manchuria. Those either living in or visiting China during this period could easily believe that China always had been plagued by such difficulties.

WAR, REVOLUTION, AND INFLATION

The 1935 currency reform gave China a managed currency system that was pegged to neither silver nor gold, but to bank notes issued by the Central Bank of China and three other banks. Between November 1935 and June 1937 bank notes in circulation rose from 435.0 to 1,477.2 million. In spite of more than a threefold increase in money supply, wholesale prices as registered in Shanghai rose only 24 percent. Because of widespread unemployment of resources—especially labor—and considerable business uncertainty at the time, much of this increased note issued was held as *idle cash balances*—that is, little money was spent to bid up the prices of raw materials, labor, and goods and services. The second Sino–Japanese War from 1937 to 1945 and the civil war that followed from 1946 until 1949 plunged China into a twelve-year period of production stagnation and decline.

By late 1938 the Japanese military virtually controlled all Chinese city-ports with their links to foreign markets. The Nanking government had lost the modern sector. It hastily moved offices and staff, entire factories and their workers, and troops to Hunan, Szechwan, and the southwest provinces of Kweichow and Yunnan to continue the war against Japan. Food and other imports ceased until late 1945, and only a trickle of goods entered China through India and Burma. The Chungking wartime government, as it was called, also entered upon an alliance with the Chinese Communists who were then based in their capital at Yenan in the northwest province of Shensi. Both parties agreed to cease fighting each other and strive to defeat their common enemy, Japan.

Foreign Currencies Issued in China

China became ruled by three governments, which varied in their spheres of influence and issued their own currencies. Until very late 1948, the Nationalists issued their notes, the Chinese national currency (CNC). Until late 1945 the Japanese used both a script called "military yen" and notes issued by their banks in occupied territories. Until late 1948 the Communists issued around thirty local currencies and ten different paper currencies in their various areas of control. The stock of money in each sphere rapidly rose—more so in the Nationalist areas— and the supply of raw materials and finished goods, particularly in cities, became increasingly scarce.

The great inflation that began to overtake China after 1941 has been referred to as a classic example of rampant note issue, which can lead to hyperinflation and thereby cause economic collapse and reversion to barter of goods. Hyperinflation yes, but the Chinese economy did not totally collapse nor did barter ever entirely replace the use of currency.

Increased Supply and Velocity of Money

What fueled the inflation? The Nationalist government lost its customs revenue and business taxes when Japanese troops seized the city-ports. After relocating to the interior, the Nationalists began using the land tax and introduced new direct and indirect taxes, but its budget deficit still rose from 2.0 to 8.6 million CNC dollars between 1939 and 1941. In 1941 the tax revenue collected by the government amounted only to 13 percent of total expenditures, but by 1944 this source had increased to 22 percent of total expenditures because of successful extraction of more resources from the agricultural sector. Meanwhile, the government financed its deficit by creating new notes and making loans, which in essence meant creating bank deposits for loan recipients to draw upon. This latter financing step proved equally inflationary, because these deposits rapidly converted to notes in circulation. Both sources of financing government deficit rapidly fed the inflationary forces at work—as table 6–1 clearly shows. Note in table 6–1 the rapidity of the deficit rise, and the sustained growth of note issue and bank deposits.

But the rise in the money supply alone did not cause prices to spiral upward as table 6–1 indicates. In 1938 and 1939 prices rose faster than the quantity of money because the velocity of money jumped to a higher level.[26] But from 1937 and 1938 prices had risen less rapidly than the money. The reason for this increase in velocity by 1938 is that people must have realized that prices would rise continuously. They began holding smaller cash balances, so that the circulation or velocity of money rose sharply. Velocity continued to rise thereafter, but for a different reason. Table 6–1 shows that between 1938 and 1944 and in 1947 wholesale prices rose more rapidly than the money supply. The rate of money circulation must have increased because holding money became more costly. If people expect prices to rise at a constant rate and their expectations prove correct, the cost of holding money tends to be constant. But in wartime China, people expected prices to rise faster and faster, and as this became the case, the cost of holding money steadily increased. As a result, people tried to hold less currency, so that money velocity became still more rapid. Therefore, the expectation of rising prices and the increased costs of holding cash balances combined to increase the velocity of money.

Finally, the supply of goods and services—except for certain industrial products—did not rise over this period but remained constant in some years and fell in others. Perhaps more than 10 million long-distance refugees fled the advancing war, and as many as 2 million moved and settled in Szechwan alone. The near cessation of foreign trade and the frequent interdiction of rail and water transport created shortages harmful for production. The massive mobilization of farmers for military labor diverted needed hands during the busy seasonal work period so as to prevent those people left behind from producing the same harvest as when labor had not been conscripted. By 1944 the acreages of Anhwei, Kiangsu, and Chekiang provinces were reported to have fallen some 30 percent below their pre-1937 area, and food grain and fiber output declined as much as 20 percent.[27]

Mild Redistributive Effects The Nationalist government eventually abandoned all attempts to control prices except to freeze real estate prices in major cities. By collecting the land tax in kind and periodically forcing grain dealers to sell at fixed prices, it managed to obtain enough grain to supply government employees and military personnel with rations to supplement money wages. These money wages were computed by multiplying 1937 wage rates by a cost-of-living index that usually lagged only a few days behind market prices. As persons on fixed nominal incomes were extremely rare, money incomes for all groups, except perhaps city landlords and military personnel, rose at the same rate and in constant relationship to each other. Certain individuals with political power and access to information about foreign exchange control policy naturally profited from the war, but the redistributive effects of this hyperinflation were far less severe than those that normally occur under more moderate inflation. Free market adjustments and the indexing of money wages to the 1937 cost of living base greatly offset such redistributive effects. This is not to say that living standards did not decline; indeed, they did. But great, relative deprivation of certain social classes does not seem to have taken place.

As notes were issued in ever larger denominations and prices rose astronomically, business firms and individuals became more accustomed to referring to U.S. currency as both a unit of account and a store of value. Yet, the official currency continued to be used as a medium of exchange. Only by 1947 and 1948 in some rural areas had barter of goods evolved—chiefly because of the collapse in distribution

TABLE 6-1. The Supply of Money, Wholesale Prices, Government Deficit, and Bank Deposits in Nationalist China, 1937–1948

Year	Money Supply		Wholesale Prices		Note Issue		Government Deficit		Bank Deposits	
	Billions of CNC Dollars	% Increase	Index	% Increase	Billions of CNC Dollars	% Increase	Billions of CNC Dollars	% Increase	Billions of CNC Dollars	% Increase
1937	3.6	—	100	—	1.7	—	1.2	—	2.2	—
1938	5.0	39	127	27	2.3	35	.8	33	.7	−68
1939	7.4	48	214	68	4.2	83	2.0	150	1.6	128
1940	13.5	82	498	133	7.8	86	3.9	95	1.3	−18
1941	25.0	85	1,258	153	15.1	93	8.6	120	4.9	277
1942	52.0	108	3,785	201	34.4	128	18.8	118	8.8	79
1943	104.0	100	12,556	232	75.4	119	38.4	104	11.2	27
1944	270.0	159	41,927	234	189.5	151	133.1	247	64.4	475
1945	1,472.0	445	158,362	277	1,031.9	444	1,106.6	731	431.6	570
1946	8,532.0	479	367,406	132	2,694.2	161	4,697.8	414	4,893.9	1033
1947	55,000.0	544	2,617,781	612	29,462.4	993	29,329.5	524	20,413.9	317
1948	—	—	—	—	163,332.8	454	434,565.5	1381	11,101.8	89

Source: Data for money supply and price increase compiled from Colin D. Campbell and Gordon C. Tullock, "Hyperinflation in China, 1937–1949" Journal of Political Economy 62, no. 3 (June 1954): p. 237. © 1954 by the University of Chicago Press. Data for the other variables compiled and reprinted by permission from Chang Kia-ngau, The Inflationary Spiral: The Experience in China, 1939–1950 (Cambridge, Mass.: MIT Press, 1958), chapters 1–4.

and local producers forced to revert to producing for subsistence. Meanwhile, in the cities the inflated CNC notes, both in number and denomination, served as the medium of exchange. Interest rates, of course, skyrocketed. Following World War II interest rates on bank deposits in Tientsin were 2 percent a day compounded daily. In spite of such a high return for holding bank deposits, few persons kept their money recorded in banks, as most Chinese expected the Nationalist government to collapse soon.

Even in areas controlled by the Communists, inflation quickly became rampant. In the base area of Shensi, Kansu, and Ninghsia provinces with a population of 1.5 million people, the Communist party had to issue notes to finance its economic and military activities. The party tried to collect taxes in kind and tax the rich more heavily than the poor, but this region was exceedingly poor and there were few rich households to tax. The party reported success in balancing tax revenues and expenditures between 1938 and 1940, but in this period the Communists received some external support from the Nationalists and merely consolidated their forces. Between 1940 and 1943 they bore the brunt of the vicious Japanese extermination campaigns, and government deficits quickly shot upward. The party financed these through note issue. The relationship between note issue and price increase in this base area can be observed in table 6–2. In 1942 and 1943 price increase exceeded the expansion of note issue. The velocity of money must have shifted. More people recognized that further price increase would occur, and the costs of holding cash balances increased. The bountiful harvest in 1944 and the respite from fighting probably alleviated shortages greatly, and material living standards are said to have returned to their 1938 to 1939 levels. Price increase was less severe even though note issue continued to expand. Severe inflation continued during the civil war period, and prices did not stabilize until peace was restored in 1949 and 1950, and economic recovery rapidly resumed.

In late 1937 the Japanese North China Area Army created a provisional Government of the Republic of China to maintain order and develop the economic potential of north China. The Japanese army also established a Peace Preservation Committee (*pao-an-hui*) led by prominent local Chinese leaders who had agreed to cooperate with the Japanese. These were later replaced by provisional councils as instruments of local authority for the Japanese. The Japanese transferred funds, capital, and technicians from Manchukuo and Japan to organize companies in mining, textile production, and food processing. They envisaged North China supplying raw and processed materials for Manchukuo and Japan. By 1941 they abandoned this hope when they had to contend with the spread of armed resistance throughout north China.

TABLE 6–2. Note Issue and Wholesale Price Increase in the Shensi, Kansu, and Ninghsia Communist Base Area, 1938–1944

Year	Note Issue		Wholesale Prices	
	Millions of Yuan	% Increase	Index	% Increase
1940 (Dec.)	3.5	–	100	–
1941 (Dec.)	25.0	614	614	514
1942 (May)	52.0	108	1,409	129
1943 (Dec.)	350.0	573	47,978	3305
1944 (May)	1,600.0	357	77,587	145

Source: Reprinted from Guerrilla Economy: The Development of the Shensi-Kansu-Ninghsia Border Region, 1937–1945, p. 199, by Peter Schran by permission of the State University of New York Press.© 1976 by the State University of New York Press.

To counter mounting Chinese guerrilla activity—much of which was organized by the Communists—the Japanese army launched campaigns to surround areas where alleged guerrilla units operated and then exterminated all life within the designated zones. The guerrillas retaliated by interdicting railroad lines between the Japanese-occupied cities and the countryside. The extermination campaigns failed to contain guerrilla fighting for long. By 1944 and 1945 Japanese troops had been reduced by deployment to other war theatres, and the northern Japanese field army retreated to protect railroad lines and major cities from direct Chinese assaults. Meanwhile, inflation became more serious as food and material shortages increased and the Chinese puppet government and Japanese military resorted to expanding note issue.

War and inflation after 1937 brought modern economic growth to a standstill. Although industrial output in parts of Szechwan and Manchuria continued to increase during the war years, production and exchange elsewhere ceased to expand, merely fluctuated around a stagnating trend, and after 1944 steadily declined until the Chinese Communist armies united the country in 1950. From that year dates a new epoch of economic development.

QUESTIONS FOR DISCUSSION

1. Given the options for the state to promote modern economic growth, how would you evaluate the Nanking government economic policies between 1927 and 1937? Assuming that war had not intervened, what then?

2. How might the Nationalist government have mobilized more resources from the agricultural sector to carry out its economic programs? What fac-

tors account for government's failure to obtain greater tax revenue from agriculture?

3. What are the different explanations for China's agrarian problem between the two world wars? In what ways did the agrarian problem hinder the spread of modern economic growth at this time? What are the policy implications resulting from the different interpretations of what caused China's agrarian problem for the modernization of agriculture?

4. In what way was the Chinese hyperinflationary experience (1941–1949) different from other hyperinflations, for example, the German economic situation after World War I?

5. Compare and contrast the management of the economy during wartime in the three regimes of Nationalist-, Communist-, and Japanese-occupied China?

6. What impact did inflation have upon China in the 1940's?

7. Would you expect to observe the characteristics of either bureaucratic capitalist or entrepreneurial bureaucratic behavior in a socialist economic system? If not, why not?

NOTES

1. I have computed these growth rates from the estimated production index based upon 1933 yuan prices in John K. Chang, *Industrial Development in Pre-Communist China: A Quantitative Analysis* (Chicago: Aldine, 1969), p. 131.

2. This discussion on the land tax is based upon Chi-ming Hou and Kuo-chi Li, "Local Government Finance in the Late Ch'ing Period," Conference on Modern Chinese Economic History, Taipei, 26–29 August 1977, pp. 559–88; David Faure, "Land Tax Collection in Kiangsu Province in the Late Ch'ing Period," *Ch'ing-shih wen-t'i* 3, no. 6 (December 1976): 49–75; Yeh Chien Wang, *Land Taxation in Imperial China, 1750–1911* (Cambridge, Mass.: Harvard University Press, 1973), pp. 41–48; and Ramon H. Myers, *The Chinese Peasant Economy* (Cambridge, Mass.: Harvard University Press, 1970), pp. 268–71.

3. This *probationary ethic* describes the internalized norms and values of officials who had studied the Chinese Neo-Confucian classics and developed a strong sense of moral purity. Thomas A. Metzger first introduced this concept in his study of Ch'ing bureaucracy to denote the sense of shame and guilt that officials felt in not doing their utmost to carry out their official duties and comply to the law. See Metzger, *The Internal Organization of Ch'ing Bureaucracy* (Cambridge, Mass.: Harvard University Press, 1973), p. 265.

4. Chi-ming Hou and Kuo-chi Li, "Local Government Finance in the Late Ch'ing Period," in *Conference on Modern Chinese Economic History, 26–29*

August 1977 (Taiwan: Institute of Economics, Academia Sinica, 1978), p. 544.

5. Ramon H. Myers, "Taiwan's Agrarian Economy under Japanese Rule," *Journal of the Institute of Chinese Studies of the Chinese University of Hong Kong* 7, no. 2 (1974): 456.

6. Land values were computed by estimating the net income to owners and a fair or normal rate of return to their capital investment. By using a formula to estimate the present value based upon the discounted rate of return of future income yielded by that land asset, the present, capitalized value of the land was obtained. This formula is $A = P/(1+i)^n$, where A is the present capitalized value of the asset, P denotes the net annual return of the asset, and i is the rate of return or the discounted rate to equalize future earnings with the present value of the asset; n is the number of years. In order to estimate on the basis of perpetuity, drop n from the equation.

7. This discussion of Chekiang's land tax reform efforts is based upon Noel Ray Miner, "Chekiang: The Nationalists' Effort in Agrarian Reform and Construction, 1927–1937," unpublished dissertation, Department of History, Stanford University, Stanford, Calif., 1973, pp. 161–86.

8. Huang Shao-hung, *Wu-shih hui-i* [Recollections at the Age of Fifty] (Hong Kong, 1969), p. 296.

9. See Noel Ray Miner, "Chekiang," chapter 3.

10. This discussion is based upon D.K. Lieu, "Land Tenure Systems in China," *Chinese Economic Journal* 2, no. 6 (June 1928): 457–74; "Tenancy and Land Ownership in Chekiang," *Chinese Economic Monthly* 3, no. 10 (October 1926): 432–38; Li Wen-chih, ed., *Chung-kuo chin-tai nung-yeh-shih tzu-liao* [Historical Materials on Modern China's Agriculture], 3 vols. (Peking: San-lien shu-tien, 1957), vol. I, pp. 162–250.

11. My discussion of Ts'ao is based on Madeleine Chi, "Bureaucratic Capitalists in Operation: Ts'ao Ju-lin and His New Communications Clique, 1916–1919," *Journal of Asian Studies* 34, no. 3 (May 1975): 675–88.

12. The account of Sung's remarkable activities is drawn from Howard L. Boorman and Richard C. Howard, *Biographical Dictionary of Republican China* (New York: Columbia University Press, 1970), vol. III, pp. 149–53; and Arthur N. Young, *China's Nation-Building Effort, 1927–1937: The Financial and Economic Record* (Stanford, Calif.: Hoover Institution Press, 1971), chapter 4.

13. Chung-kuo k'o-hsueh-yuan Shang-hai ching-chi yen-chiu-suo, *Nan-yang hsiung-ti yen-ts'ao kung-ssu shih-liao* [Materials on the History of the Nanyang Brothers' Cigarette Company] (Shanghai: Shang-hai jen-min ch'u-pan-she, 1960), p. 619.

14. See Douglass S. Paauw, "The Kuomintang and Economic Stagnation, 1928–1937," in Albert Feuerwerker, ed., *Modern China* (Englewood Cliffs, N.J.: Prentice-Hall, 1964), pp. 126–35. A similar argument but one based upon political considerations can be found in Hung-mao Tien, *Government*

and Politics in Kuomintang China 1927–1937 (Stanford, Calif.: Stanford University Press, 1972), pp. 177–82.

15. Lloyd E. Eastman, *The Abortive Revolution: China under Nationalist Rule, 1927–1937* (Cambridge, Mass.: Harvard University Press, 1974), chapter 5.

16. Arthur N. Young, *China's Nation-Building Effort,* p. 279.

17. Many such examples can be found in Paul K. T. Sih, ed., *The Strenuous Decade: China's Nation-Building Efforts, 1927–1937* (New York: St. John's University Press, 1970), pp. 83–124; 255–84; 237–49.

18. W. J. Garnett and A. Rose, "Reports of Journeys in the Provinces of Shantung and Kiangsu," *Confidential Prints (8903)* (British Foreign Office, March 1907), p. 7.

19. P'eng Tse-i, comp., *Chung-kuo chin-tai shou-kung-yeh shih tzu-liao* [Materials on the History of Handicraft Industries for Modern China] (Peking: San-lien shu-tien, 1957), vol. III, p. 6.

20. Chang Yu-i, ed., *Chung-kuo chin-tai nung-yeh-shih tzu-liao* [Modern China's Agriculture], vol. III, pp. 629–30.

21. Ibid., p. 678.

22. Kozawa Shigeichi, *Shina no dōran to Santō nōson* [Shantung Villages and the Upheaval in China] (n.p., 1930), p. 3.

23. Chang Yu-i, ed., *Chung-kuo chin-tai nung-yeh-shih tzu-liao* [Modern China's Agriculture], vol. III, p. 568.

24. Ramon H. Myers and Thomas R. Ulie, "Foreign Influence and Agricultural Development in Northeast China: A Case Study of the Liaotung Peninsula, 1907–45," *Journal of Asian Studies* 31, no. 2 (February 1972): 340.

25. Ramon H. Myers, "The Economic Development of Taiwan," in Hungdah Chiu, ed., *China and the Question of Taiwan: Documents and Analysis* (New York: Praeger, 1973), p. 38.

26. This discussion is based on the analysis of China's hyperinflation by Colin D. Campbell and Gordon C. Tullock, "Hyperinflation in China, 1937–49," *Journal of Political Economy* 62, no. 3 (June 1954): 237–38.

27. Chung-yang tien-hsin-she, comp., *Chung-kuo chien-shih ching-chi chih t'ao-lun* [An Inquiry on the Chinese Wartime Economy] (Nanking: Chung-yang tien-hsin-she, 1944), p. 9.

SELECTED READINGS

1. Hung-mao Tien. *Government and Politics in Kuomintang China, 1927–1937.* Stanford, Calif.: Stanford University Press, 1972, chapters 4 and 9.

2. Hsi-sheng Ch'i. *Warlord Politics in China, 1916–1928.* Stanford, Calif.: Stanford University Press, 1976, chapter 7.

3. Lloyd E. Eastman. *The Abortive Revolution: China under Nationalist Rule, 1927–1937.* Cambridge, Mass.: Harvard University Press, 1974, chapter 5.

4. Paul K. T. Sih, ed. *The Strenuous Decade: China's Nation-Building Efforts, 1927–1937.* New York: St. John's University Press, 1970.

5. Chang Kia-ngau. *The Inflationary Spiral: The Experience in China, 1939–1950.* New York: Technology Press of M.I.T. and John Wiley & Sons, 1958.

6. Colin D. Campbell and Gordon C. Tullock. "Hyperinflation in China, 1937–1949." *Journal of Political Economy* 62, no. 3 (June 1954): 236–45.

7. Scott R. Dittrich and Ramon H. Myers. "Resource Allocation in Traditional Agriculture: Republican China, 1937–1940." *Journal of Political Economy* 79, no. 4 (July/August 1971): 887–97.

8. Hsiao-tung Fei and Chih-i Chang. *Earthbound China: A Study of Rural Economy in Yunnan.* Chicago: University of Chicago Press, 1945.

9. Graham Peck. *Two Kinds of Time: Life in Provincial China during the Crucial Years 1940–1941.* Boston: Houghton Mifflin, 1967.

10. Robert A. Kapp. "Chungking as a Center of Warlord Power, 1926–1937." In Mark Elvin and G. William Skinner, eds., *The Chinese City between Two Worlds.* Stanford, Calif.: Stanford University Press, 1974, pp. 143–71.

11. David D. Buck. *Urban Change in China: Politics and Development in Tsinan, Shantung, 1890–1949.* Madison: University of Wisconsin Press, 1978.

12. Mark Selden. *The Yenan Way in Revolutionary China.* Cambridge, Mass.: Harvard University Press, 1971.

13. Peter Schran. *Guerrilla Economy: The Development of the Shensi-Kansu-Ninghsia Border Region, 1937–1945.* Albany: State University of New York Press, 1976.

Modern Economic Growth

Part Four

The Development of the Socialist Economy

7

The unification of China under the Communist party on 1 October 1949 signaled a new era—the development of a socialist economy. Under the Ch'ing state a huge private sector had expanded by households cooperating and competing in the marketplace. Te state had progressively withdrawn from the economy until it merely regulated the money supply, monitored the harvest cycle to provide famine relief, and very lightly taxed the private sector.

The late Ch'ing government had tried to modernize the economy; to finance the projects that allegedly would promote modernization, it imposed new taxes on the private sector. After the collapse of the Ch'ing government in 1911 a near half-century of political and military turmoil ensued, in which the private sector slowly experienced modest modern economic growth in the new city-ports and their market environs. This small subsector also acquired a modest-sized modern infrastructure of railroads, communications, educational facilities, and various research institutes.

Meanwhile, the organizers of agriculture and handicraft suffered a series of disturbances so disrupting as to produce widespread unemployment of land and labor in some regions and gradual, overall decline in output and income. By the late 1940s economic decline in the countryside had spread to the minuscule modern city-port subsector to disrupt economic activities there as well. The Communist party rapidly reversed these conditions and radically altered the relationship between state and private sector. By 1954—a mere five years after unifying the country under its control—this party had created the foundations for organizing the economy on a socialist basis. The state had extruded deeply into the private economic sector, and its new organizations had begun to mobilize land and labor on an unprecedented basis for the purpose of accumulating modern capital. The extraordinary rate of capital accumulation that followed—much of which embodied modern technology—enabled this socialist economy to achieve very high growth rates of industrial and agricultural production. How could this new state increase the employment of land and labor and yet encourage men and women to work harder and for longer hours at only very modest income rewards? How did the state manage to discourage its people from spending this income and to increase savings to finance the huge accumulation of capital underway? The party had to create new economic organizations, develop extensive controls, and resort to various price incentives for these purposes. This chapter first examines how the state quickly and effectively established its control over the private sector and then describes the means by which modern capital expanded in such plenitude. Finally, it analyzes the economic organizations responsible for the sustained, high rate of capital accumulation in this socialist economy.

THE STATE AND THE PRIVATE SECTOR

In its wartime base areas the Communist party leadership always had concentrated on building a strong, unified party administration and an effective military organization. The party's top leader, Mao Tse-tung, quite early had advanced an important principle by which one party activity would nurture another. This principle, tersely translated as "crack troops and simplified administration" (*ching-ping chien-cheng*), argued for two complementary activities.[1] The party must organize highly effective guerrilla troops that could win enough victories to maintain public morale and preserve the safety of the people living in the base areas. Second, the party must establish an efficient, simple, and incorruptible administration to manage its base areas. The latter meant party officials had to work for little or no reward and keep administrative costs as low as possible.

At the same time the public and private sectors were to assist each other (*kung-ssu chien-ku*), and the military and citizenry were to cooperate and help each other (*chün-min chien-ku*). In the first case the party ordered public industries to supply goods and services to private industry and agriculture whenever possible. In the second instance troops helped farmers plant and harvest their crops, and villagers supplied grain, material, and manpower to the guerrillas. Mao Tse-tung and other party leaders believed that by (1) carefully balancing successful military operations with low-cost, efficient administration, (2) similarly coordinating the use of military labor with the resources of the private sector, and (3) encouraging the public sector to help the private sector, the supply of goods and services could be greatly increased; a fairly equitable distribution between laboring groups could be achieved; and severe scarcities could thereby be avoided.

To maintain these balances and coordinate different sector activities, the party had to create organizations at the village level that it could depend upon. This intense concern of how to build new organizations in villages and expand upon them was precisely the element that distinguished Communist party activities from those of its rival, the Nationalist party. The latter sought to penetrate society and economy from the commanding heights but still leave considerable scope for the private sector to organize its activities. The former first built organizations in the villages to achieve total control over all households and then linked these organizations to higher party units of power.

If the party could control the village, it could then unleash large "campaigns" *(yun-tung)* to mobilize the population for various tasks. The "campaigns" later became a frequently used tactic to create new organizations for the party, as well as muster greater effort and sacrifice from the populace. Paying strict attention to expanding the role of party and military, building new organizations of control at the village level, and relying upon mass "campaigns" became the principal means by which the Communist party established great control over Chinese society and economy and even penetrated to the smallest organization of each. Let us now trace how the party did this in both the countryside and town between 1947 and 1954.

Land Reform

Land reform became the single, most important policy for the Communist party to gain control over the villages. By *land reform* we mean those party policies that greatly influenced the ownership and use of land, as well as the distribution of income earned from land. The party carried out its land reform policies in two stages and modified these according to local conditions. The first stage covered the period from late 1947 until very early 1950 and applied throughout the north of China. The final stage lasted until the end of 1952 and applied to the rest of the country.

Prior to 1945 the party did not meddle with private property relationships but confined its efforts to limiting debt charges for farmers, reducing rents, organizing teams to farm the land, and encouraging households to increase their production by appeals to their patriotism. In the northern base areas these rural policies proved to be very successful for increasing farm production. By 1945 small teams in nearly every base area village engaged in soil preparation and harvesting; members shared the proceeds of the harvest; and many households even increased their supply of farm tools and labor animals from these windfall earnings. But in the late fall of 1947 the party decided on war with the landlord class.[2] Trained party personnel or cadres were ordered to carry out land reform in all base areas and even in villages just liberated by the People's Liberation Army (PLA). The party classified landlords as any households owning land but either not farming it, hiring others to farm it, or deriving rent from it. The process of land reform worked in the following way.

Seizure and Distribution of Large Landholdings On 14 August 1945 the Communist Eighth Route Army liberated Long Bow village in Lu-cheng county of Shansi province.[3] Shortly thereafter, Communist militia assembled the villagers to identify and ferret out all local collaborators of the Japanese and confiscate their property and any of their stolen goods. After dispensing with these collaborators, several Communist cadres organized village meetings to create a Peasants' Association for the purpose of attacking the landlords, confiscating their property, and distributing it to those villagers with very little or no land. The association convened many meetings to muster evidence and mobilize the villagers against each of Long Bow's landlords. After judging each landlord, the association took the landlord's household property and land and then divided it among the village poor. By the end of January 1946 Communist cadres reported that "feudal landholding and feudal political power had been effectively destroyed" in Long Bow and the surrounding districts.

Party Control over Villages The events of Long Bow were repeated throughout north China, often with violence and bloodshed. The peasants' associations that initiated land reform became the party's instrument for controlling village affairs. The association leaders appointed committees to organize the village women and set up mutual aid teams. They selected village representatives to go to the county and participate at meetings convened by the party cadres to integrate all villages under a single county administration. Meanwhile, party cadres selected friendly villagers to fill key association jobs and introduced them to party ideology and work tasks. Gradually, the new Peasants' Association leadership became a blend of outside party cadres and new party adherents with bona fide village roots. The party had built new village organizations managed by trusted party cadres and their sympathizers, which in turn had delegated representatives to new county-level organizations.

Liu Shao-ch'i, the party's top organizer, pointed out in early 1948 the linkage between land reform and the establishment of party control over villages in a report of how this process was carried out in the base areas of rural P'ing-shan county of Hopei on the border of Shansi province:

> In P'ing-shan county the land reform and building the party amongst the people were closely linked together. Much later, we gained valuable experience from the land reform move-

ment to equalize land distribution. The most important form which the linking of land reform with building our party took was the establishment of the party cell. We developed the party from the support of the broad masses. Party meetings and those of the masses were combined to meet together. From villages to the county seat we set up a system of People's Congresses and gave all power to them. At first, the party cells strictly regulated entry into the party. They carefully checked on class background, attitude toward work, and avoidance of taking an extreme position. Although such meetings were held seven or even eight times, there still might not be any definite results. Later, the party cell admitted members. At first, it would admit a poor peasant, then even some middle peasants. The party members attending such meetings usually numbered 20 or 30 while the non-party members numbered between 70 or 80. By these means we eventually altered the aura of mystery which had seemed to prevail at these village cell meetings. At last we had broken down the barriers created by certain 'bad elements' who had prevented the masses and our party from uniting with each other. We had submitted each party's cadres' class thinking, work attitude, and behavior to the judgements of the masses. We had elicited from the masses their opinions and criticisms of party cadres.[4]

The same careful screening of party cadres and new party members took place in Long Bow after land reform. As a result, party influence and control over Long Bow, as in other villages after land reform, rapidly expanded to penetrate all committees and organizations within the village community.

Reclassification of Households The second stage of land reform began in mid-1950 with the issue of a document listing new procedures for land reform. This Agrarian Reform Law contained forty articles outlining in detail the type of land to be confiscated, how to distribute such land, and how to deal with special lands and their joint ownership. Article Six, in particular, protected those farmers euphemistically referred to as "rich peasants" from losing their land except if they leased out more land than they farmed themselves. In the south many households who worked very small farms of scattered plots fell into this category. The party cadres first ordered that rent deposits be refunded to tenants and rents be reduced and refunded if already paid.[5] Next, they organized peasants' associations and singled out individuals known for exploiting or bullying their neighbors. Village meetings were organized to denounce these individuals, seize their wealth, and redistribute it among the poor. The cadres then classified all households according to party class terms: landlords, rich peasants, middle peasants, and agricultural laborers. Landlords, of course, lost their land; the remaining households retained their land, and some even received redistributed land. By late 1952 the entire country had experienced land reform. The former village elite who had owned land had been destroyed. The party had created a new village organization to manage village affairs: the Peasants' Association. The Communist party controlled the peasants' associations. Meanwhile, all households in villages had been classified according to party-defined class lines.

Control of Urban Businesses

The Communist army's takeover of cities paved the way for the party to extend its control over all business organizations—especially the factories. In early 1951 party cadres organized mass meetings in companies and factories to attack counterrevolutionaries and the Chiang K'ai-shek regime.[6] From these gatherings cadres collected information about "bad elements" in these organizations. In the fall of 1951 the party launched the san-fan campaign, a three-part opposition movement, aimed at graft, waste, and bureaucratism in the urban private sector. The campaign began in the northeast, rapidly spread throughout the country, and ended in mid-1952. In this campaign, party cadres ordered meetings to "struggle" against the "bad elements" responsible for sabotaging industry. The natural targets for these attacks were managers, business leaders, and factory owners. Many were imprisoned, fined, or lost their jobs. The result was that the party soon established full control over urban enterprises by delegating new managers to run these businesses and instructing the labor unions to concentrate upon reviving production and abstain from pressing for wage increases. Just as land reform eliminated the rural elite who dominated the countryside, so did the san-fan campaign destroy the urban-business-class elite who controlled commerce and industry. The Communist party had organizational control over economic activities in both cities and villages, and its organizations penetrated throughout the entire private sector.

Campaigns

The final tactic frequently used during these same years was the drive or "campaign" (yun-tung). The Communist party candidly admitted through its leader Mao on 23 October 1951 that "the three great movements which were developed in our country during the past year—resistance to American aggression and aid to Korea, land reform, and suppression of counterrevolutionaries—have achieved great victories. ... As a result of the victories already achieved by these great movements ... our country has attained a unification that is unprecedented."[7] The party relied upon these campaigns to eliminate individuals and their organizations that might obstruct its attempts to control and reorganize communities.

By 1953 the party had achieved more than military and political unification of the country. It had systematically destroyed those groups and organizations that had greatly influenced village and urban economic activities. Furthermore, it had replaced these groups with organizations of its own creation and staffed them with dedicated, loyal party cadres and supporters. The state had successfully extended its control over the entire private sector—only households and small-scale organizations with some private property still remained untouched. But by 1956 the state would control these as well, and all households would be receiving only wage income. The stage was set for rapid capital accumulation.

CAPITAL ACCUMULATION

Modern economic growth begins by the widespread use of new capital goods that embody or use a new technology in production. By *capital goods* we mean the commodities used for nondefense structures—that is, the equipment, machines, and tools that produce goods for final consumption—and the inventories or stockpiles of unfinished goods. An economic system only can increase its supply of capital goods by allocating more resources of land and labor to their production rather than for final consumption goods. To divert more resources for capital formation, then, organizers of production—whether private or public—must have the funds to purchase the necessary resources for capital goods' production. A socialist economy with broad control over society mobilizes these funds through its budget and state-managed organizations and enterprises. The state channels these savings to purchase resources for the production of capital goods and by direct purchase through foreign trade. The state naturally must rely upon extensive economic controls and plans either to limit the supply of consumer goods produced in order to deploy more resources to capital formation or to allow the supply of consumer goods to grow slowly at the expense of a slower growth of capital goods' stock. Figure 7–1 outlines where the Chinese socialist economy obtained funds for expanding the stock of new capital after 1949, how funds were allocated to produce more capital, and the relative share of capital goods to consumer goods produced over the period.

Between 1949 and 1951 the agricultural tax, bonds, and credit creation provided the major financing for capital formation which only amounted to roughly 5 percent of GNP. The agricultural tax, collected in kind, supported most of the PLA and civilian labor that worked to restore the railroad system and prewar factories. During the mid-

Potential Financial Sources for Capital Investment	Allocation of Funds for Production of Capital Goods	Final Composition of Capital Goods (I) and Consumer Goods (C)
1. Taxes: agriculture, industry, and other sources. 2. Profits and depreciation reserves of firms and organizations. 3. Bonds. 4. Credit creation. 5. Foreign credit.	1. Produce exports to import capital goods. 2. Import capital (Turnkey projects) on credit and pay later. 3. State budget allocations to enterprises and organizations. 4. Enterprise and organization spending for resources to produce capital goods.	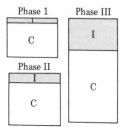

FIGURE 7–1. Schema for Financial Sources and Capital Formation in China's Socialist Economy

1950s the state allocated an increasing share of funds to export raw materials and farm products to the Soviet Union to repay the short-term credit that country gave China to import a variety of industrial turnkey projects that became the core of a new machine tool and metallurgical industry. The state also set high targets for enterprises and rural cooperatives from profits and depreciation reserves to pay for resources to produce capital. As a result, by 1956 the ratio of capital formation to GNP already rose to 14 percent—a very high rate for a country with less than 100 U.S. dollars per capita income. At the same time, however, the state managed to modestly expand the supply of consumer goods as figure 7–1 shows in phase II. During the 1960s and 1970s, in spite of political disturbances, which periodically caused industrial setbacks, the state gradually raised the capital formation to GNP ratio to between 23 and 30 percent—depending upon which year's prices are used to estimate GNP. The supply of consumer goods still rose very modestly to permit a very gradual rise in consumer welfare. These trends can be inferred to figure 7–1 by singling out the different financial sources for the allocation of production of capital goods at different historical periods. The final composition of capital goods and consumer goods produced was one of rising share of final output consisting of capital goods and a very modest growth in supply of consumer goods.

Financing Capital Formation

The distribution of income among rural households in the 1930s had been extremely unequal, in fact, very similar to that of the less-developed countries in the third quarter of this century.[8] One estimate of the degree of inequality places the top 20 percent of households earning 50 percent of rural income and the lowest 20 percentile obtaining only 5 percent. The Communist land reform redistributed income to greatly reduce this inequality, perhaps by as much as one-third, as measured by the decline in Gini coefficient of inequality.[9] Yet regional income inequality throughout the country still persisted, for land reform had not altered that in the least. A more equal distribution of rural household income meant that if the state could convince villagers of the justness and necessity for taxes to be paid, organized resistance from special groups was likely to be feeble or not forthcoming. Villagers might even tolerate higher taxation if each household perceived that the new tax burden was shouldered equitably by all.

New Tax on Agriculture   The party began imposing a new agricultural tax, collected in kind, in every area that came under its control. Cadres set this tax according to the "normal" harvest yield of the area so that tax levels varied according to land fertility. But within a given area, the new tax was established on a progressive basis according to household income level as measured in per capita grain that households earned. The minimum tax rate began at 3 percent for 75 kg. of grain per capita and reached a maximum of 42 percent for 725 kg. of grain per capita and above. This new tax weighed more heavily on wealthier households whereas the traditional land tax had been a proportional tax. Moreover, the new tax was certainly much heavier than the old land tax. In 1949 Finance Minister Po I-po reported that all taxes took 20 percent of grain production, which amounted to roughly 22 million tons out of a total production of around 110 million tons.[10] By 1950 the state increased its collections to 25 million, a 13 percent increase, whereas overall production only increased by around 9 percent. The state also expanded its taxation over the well-known "black lands"—that is, the lands that formerly had never been taxed because their owners never registered for tax purposes. Two factors probably enabled the government to extract tax at a much higher rate than before the war. First, the land reform had muted any potential opposition likely to be expressed by large landowners. Second, grain production was rapidly increasing and the general expectation was that production would continue to grow because peace and security had finally been restored to the countryside. This tax proved crucial for the regime to control inflation and supply grain to the PLA and labor mobilized to revive production and restore factories and railroads. In 1950 the tax amounted to nearly 42 percent of national budget receipts, and during 1948–49 it was even much higher. Therefore, the Communist party, in striking contrast to the Nationalist party before it, relied much more upon agricultural taxation in its early years for financing economic activities.

Grain Quota System Agriculture continued to finance capital goods' production through the compulsory grain quota system the party introduced in November 1953 and through the state's sale of industrial goods to rural areas at prices much higher than the goods that rural households sold. In 1953 the state initiated its first five-year plan, increased investment 84 percent above the 1952 level, and expanded exports by 28 percent.[11] Furthermore, the urban population had increased by 6 million people, an 8.4 percent jump since the end of 1952. The poor 1953 harvests and the state's depletion of grain stocks meant that if an industrial spurt was to take place, the rural sector would have to supply more to finance it. Therefore, the state decided to set grain quotas, which required households to sell at state-controlled grain markets or to state marketing agents. These fixed prices were usually 20 to 30 percent below market prices at the time. The state greatly increased its grain purchases in the next two years at twice the growth of grain production.

Meanwhile, during the early and mid-1950s industrial goods continued to sell at higher prices than agricultural goods so that the state benefited from these favorable terms of price exchange. However, the state progressively permitted the improvement of the terms of trade for agriculture at the same time it extracted even more produce by tightening its controls over family farming. By 1957, for example, industrial prices as compared to farm product prices had declined nearly 30 percent since 1950, and this trend continued through the 1960s so that the purchasing power of rural households gradually rose.

Commune Production Teams and an Eight-Grade Wage Structure The elimination of family farming came in 1956 by establishing agricultural cooperatives in every village of the country so that households no longer received income payments other than wages. Under this new arrangement the party initiated another policy to increase capital formation rather than continuing to increase grain quotas at fixed prices. Under the new commune system production teams agreed to set high investment targets for rural capital accumulation. This step freed state funds for economic activities outside agriculture. The party encouraged this decision by its nationwide campaign to "learn from Ta-chai," a movement that is described further on in this chapter. In the urban sector state organizations and enterprises for such areas as industry, transport, and marketing financed an increasing share of their capital goods' production from profits and depreciation reserves—an arrangement made possible by the establishment of an eight-grade wage structure in 1958. The wage rates in this system did not change from 1966 until 1977, at which time wages for specific grades were increased some 20 to 30 percent. These state policies to finance more capital accumulation in the rural and urban sectors and occasionally to subsidize one or the other sector so that both sectors could advance in balance with each other showed remarkable flexibility and imagination by the state.

We can look at these arrangements to finance capital goods' production in the following way. By 1962 organizational reform in agriculture had run its course. The commune and its production brigades and production teams operated on a fairly decentralized basis to allocate resources and produce goods, but they still adhered to certain cardinal principles of how their earnings were to be used. In essence, every commune set a very high financial target for reinvestment. A high reinvestment ratio quickly increased the supply of commune farm capital and the number of small-scale industries. Meanwhile, in urban industrial enterprises the eight-grade wage system allowed workers to obtain wage increases only by improving their skills to perform different tasks. The wages for each grade never increased over a twelve-year period. As factories and organizations also set high financial targets for reinvestment, they too increased their supply of capital goods. The profits of industries producing consumer goods were merely transferred to the state and then reallocated to industries producing capital goods.

The price and wage policies initiated by the party produced these results: low wages and high profits. A recent study by Jung-chao Liu indeed confirms that such policies meant pricing industrial products high and keeping costs—especially wages—low. In this way the state diverted considerable resources to investment for capital formation, export, defense, and government activities.[12] Liu's statistical evidence compares China's and India's profit-wage ratios for the late 1950s. The profit-wage ratio was much higher in China than in India for all industries, with the exception of coal.

Trade and Capital Formation

While China's total foreign trade as a percentage of its GNP remained slightly less than 4 percent throughout the period—except in 1958–59 when it reached 4.3 percent—we should not be misled to think that small percentages do not matter in economic development. In China's case, trade served as a powerful engine for capital accumulation. When a newcomer to industrialization imports complete industrial plants designed to supply products to a core of new and old industries that also produce capital goods, the supply of new capital will greatly increase. First, these *turnkey plants* will embody the most advanced technology from the supplying country, and they then serve as a model for domestic firms to learn from. Second, the supply of new capital produced from these new plants enables other industries to repair and replace their equipment and parts so that their production can be continuous. The cumulative gains that spring from these new industries cannot be measured, but in China's case they must have been very significant in the 1950s and later in the 1970s.

Capital Imports and Credit from Russia   During the 1950s about 45 percent of China's imports came from the Soviet Union, which supplied complete industrial plants numbering between 150 and 200. Of these, 63 were machine-tool and engineering plants; 24 were electric power plants; 3 plants produced iron and steel, and the others were for nonferrous metals, chemicals, aviation, electronics, and so on.[13] At the same time over ten thousand Soviet technicians and scientists swarmed throughout China to assemble these plants and instruct Chinese technicians and engineers in their operation and repair. Prior to 1954 China did not have the means to import enough of these turnkey projects, and in order to do so, the Soviet Union supplied short-term credit with interest. By 1965 China had received roughly 2,290 million U.S. dollars worth of Soviet aid, but she repaid this through exports amounting to 1,550 million U.S. dollars and foreign exchange payments to the Soviet Union of around 740 million U.S. dollars. Soviet credit had allowed China to install new industries much more quickly than if it had built these plants on its own to launch an industrial drive.

Imports from United States, Europe, and Japan   China's ideological break with the USSR around 1961 and severe setbacks in agriculture forced her to import more from Western Europe and Japan but to buy modestly. Not until 1972 did China resume large capital imports. Between 1972 and 1974 she contracted with Japan, the United States, and Western European countries for 2,342 million U.S. dollars in purchases of complete plants. These included 5 iron and steel plants, 3 complete power-generating plants with 43 turbines and generators, 2 oil rigs, 24 survey and supply vessels, 4 offshore drilling platforms for oil exploration and extraction, 30 chemical fertilizer plants, and 38 petrochemical and synthetic fiber plants.[14] By importing turnkey plants and learning their operation and maintenance, the Chinese are avoiding long-term dependence on outsiders. They have learned to repair these and reproduce others like them from the industrial capacity and modern technology they now have. In 1978 the Chinese went on another world market buying spree. In March they signed a trade pact with the Japanese committing Japan to purchase 47.1 million metric tons of Chinese crude oil by 1982, when the agreement will end. Japan will also buy 150,000 tons of coal in 1978 and 2 million tons a year by 1982. In return China plans to use the estimated 10 billion U.S. dollars from energy sales (1) to finance an array of industrial plant purchases ranging from steel mills to color-TV factories and a synthetic leather plant, and (2) to acquire Japanese expertise and capital goods for modernizing the railway system. In April and May China also shopped for coal mining machines, railway equipment, trucks, and petrochemical capital goods in Western European markets.

Capital Formation and Intermediate Industries

Intermediate industries that produce certain goods for direct consumption, such as energy or railroads, but still supply commodities mainly for other industries are typically called *producer goods industries*. These producer goods industries are often confused with capital goods industries. While some producer goods industries such as cement factories and machine-tool firms are capital goods industries, the two categories of industrial enterprises should be kept separate. We have already defined capital goods, and these should not be confused with the large assortment of commodities produced by intermediate industries for use in other industries. Yet capital goods like structures, equipment, tools, and machines are important for the growth of intermediate industries, and the expansion of capital goods is generally correlated with that of the growth of intermediate industries. Certainly a greater supply of capital makes possible the rapid growth of intermediate industries.

The machine-tool industry had rapidly expanded in the 1950s. In fact it appears to have grown so rapidly that by 1960 many plants could not find ready customers for the outpouring of drills, lathes, and presses.[15] Other industries had not expanded rapidly enough to provide the steady demand for the machine-tool industries. Therefore, in the 1960s machine-tool industries underwent considerable readjustment. The state reallocated skilled labor to other plants, and managers reduced productive capacity. The output mix even changed; many factories began producing pumps, farm machines, and petrochemical machinery. Two examples of how intermediate industries expanded show that rapid capital accumulation made possible rapid industrial expansion.

Railroad Restoration and Expansion First, the state gave very high priority to restoring and expanding the railroad system. Nearly one-fifth of all projected expenditures for capital construction in the First Five-Year Plan went to railroads.[16] New trunk lines quickly made their appearance. The line between Ch'eng-tu and Pao-chi soon linked Szechwan to Peking via other trunk lines. The 500-mile Chengtu-Kunming line, which followed, then brought southwest China under Peking's firm control. A vital trunk line to Lanchow in Kansu and then to Urumchi in the heart of Singkiang province integrated the far northwest into the national economy. These and others lines expanded the railroad system so that by 1955, 16,708 miles of railway lines were in operation, compared to only 13,494 miles in 1949. As a result, the freight tonnage hauled on this system by 1954 had doubled over that of 1950. By the late 1950s the railroad boom ended, and for the next decade and a half little expansion of either highways or railroads took place. Diesel engines gradually replaced some coal-burning locomotives, but old and new continued to coexist and haul freight. By the late 1970s the railway system clearly did not meet the needs of the economy, and new plans projected expansion with improved efficiency.

Energy Consumption   By the mid-1970s new reserves of coal, natural gas, and petroleum had been discovered, so that China's energy reserves seem comparable with those of the USSR and the United States. Consumption of energy in China also remained much lower than in these advanced countries. During the early 1970s, solid fuels accounted for more than three-quarters of the total primary energy consumption. But in the United States, on the other hand, they accounted for only 19 percent, and in the USSR for 39 percent.[17] By 1974 China generated 108 billion kw. of electricity, compared to only 7 billion in 1952; it produced 35 billion cubic meters of natural gas, compared to none in 1952; and it produced 63 million metric tons of petroleum, but only .4 million tons in 1952. By restricting energy consumption, exploring for new sources, and expanding the supply of new equipment to tap these sources, China should be able to fulfill its current needs and also rapidly expand oil exports to finance some of its imported capital goods.

Rural Capital Formation

We can observe two processes of capital formation in the countryside that distinguish Chinese rural development from that of other countries—both past and present. First, China launched its own "green revolution" without technological borrowing from abroad. Second, since 1958 communes have allocated considerable resources to develop small-scale industry on a huge basis, which has not been matched by any developing country today. Both processes depended upon the growth of capital goods. To be sure, commodities such as new seeds, chemical fertilizer, and farm machinery are not classified as capital goods by our definition of capital. Agricultural economists point out, however, that these same goods embody new technology and increase the productivity of either land or labor or both. We will relax the definition of capital goods and consider these industrial intermediary products as "farm capital."

The Green Revolution on a Limited Scale By the late 1960s certain farming areas began developing new cropping patterns so that the sown area greatly increased. Three crops per year instead of two became typical throughout east central and southeast China. Two crops per year instead of one and a half crops became widespread throughout the north. In localized areas where new cropping patterns emerged, a *green revolution* had begun. We define this term to mean that total output per sown area each year increased more rapidly than the combined inputs of land, labor, and capital. Such development meant that in these localized areas, food grains exceeded population demand, and thus a reserve was created for the support of a rapidly growing animal husbandry industry. For the first time in China's agrarian history the supply of farm animals, such as hogs and poultry, rose more rapidly than the human population. While some experts might deny that a green revolution had occurred for all of China, these new, localized, rural developments seem to deserve the term. Although only very limited areas of China have developed in this way, it is still worthwhile to try and answer the question of what caused this cropping revolution.

First, the supply of early-ripening, high-yield, and disease-resistant seeds increased for rice, cotton, and wheat.[18] An excellent agro-research foundation of seed development, soil study, and disease classification already had emerged prior to 1949. The new state expanded these research institutes and agricultural colleges during the 1950s, and by the mid-1960s new seeds had been developed, tested, and even distributed for production. For example, new wheat varieties had brought smut and other diseases under control by the late 1960s. New rice varieties accelerated the maturing stage so that two rice crops became possible, and in Kiangsu and Chekiang these two could be followed by wheat or millet.

Second, communes greatly expanded irrigation, drainage, and organic fertilizer application. In the north, tens of thousands of tube wells supplied water to the fields and thus irrigated up to 70 percent of the cultivated land for Hopei and perhaps 40 percent for Shensi. In northern Honan an area covered by thirteen counties sowed around 333,000 ha. of wheat in 1965 and produced 500,000 metric tons, but nine years later this same area produced nearly a million metric tons on the same sown area. This doubling of yield to nearly 3,000 kg./ha. had been achieved by commune work teams laboring during the off-farm months to expand irrigation facilities and apply more compost fertilizer to the fields. Such examples can be multiplied repeatedly to describe the large increase of food grain yields achieved during the last fifteen years, and the same factors consistently played a role: increased irrigation and more organic fertilizer.

Small-Scale Industries   A conspicuous feature of imperial China had been the coexistence of rural handicraft with farming. Household labor switched from one to the other, and often a division of family labor by sex allowed both activities to continue side by side: women spun and wove cloth; men tilled the fields. By 1960 the communes had become the organizational means to promote small-scale industries. These small enterprises utilized rural labor that might not be fully employed at farming. Rural labor did not migrate to large cities but found industrial employment close to home. These same industries produced such farm capital as farm machinery, chemical fertilizers, and construction materials—that is, the important industrial commodities that otherwise would have required shipping long distances by an overextended railroad system. Small-scale industries also coordinated the state's plan to mechanize at least two-thirds of the farming stages between soil preparation and harvesting by furnishing communes with much of their equipment, tools, and even the machines to begin mechanizing agricultural work.

The rapid proliferation of small-scale factories in virtually every market town of the country naturally proved very costly and inefficient.[19] Many plants wasted raw materials. Far more labor was employed than was usually needed. High unit costs marked the early operation of most of these factories. But through a learning-by-doing process and through copying the methods of the more successful communes, factories gradually improved their efficiency, effectively made better use of their capacity, and introduced innovations hitherto thought impossible. More and more of these small firms supplied industrial goods to the communes and generated a sizable flow of wage income to commune workers. Therefore, the persistence of traditional economic patterns continues to the present as the rural landscape becomes increasingly dotted with tractors, rice transplanters, and electric lines.

ECONOMIC ORGANIZATION AND CONTROLS

In order to save a high proportion of GNP to divert resources to capital goods' production, the state had to limit the supply of goods and services for final consumption, curb the spending of purchasing power that accumulated in households, and encourage workers on farms and in industries to labor hard, live frugally, and postpone consumption until the future. New economic organizations and controls had to be created to reallocate resources to capital goods' production and industrial growth, restrict consumer demand, and elicit work effort. The state and party introduced policies of considerable flexibility, created new organizations that proved independent yet compliant to state and party demands, and relied upon procedures, such as the "campaigns" that had been fashioned during the civil war to mobilize the population to work harder but for modest remuneration. China's rich organizational heritage accounts for part of the reason why the party and state leaders demonstrated flexibility and a willingness to scrap an idea or operation if it proved unworkable. Yet the new concepts of organization and human behavior developed by Mao and his colleagues also greatly influenced post-1949 change. The blend of old and new forms continues down to the present. Mistakes also occurred, and as is the case in any rapid socioeconomic transformation, Chinese society also bore high costs of human suffering.

Until 1957 the state and party borrowed heavily upon the experiences and resources of the Soviet Union. We have already noted the importance of Soviet short-term credit, capital imports, and payment for these by food grain, raw material, and foreign exchange shipments to the USSR. On the experience side China relied upon the economic planning procedures developed in the USSR and modified them slightly to suit domestic conditions. After 1957, however, China turned its back on the Soviet Union, developed new policies based upon Chinese perspectives and experiences, and gradually altered and refined these as well.

Price-Fixing Planning Agency

By 1952 the state had a planning agency, new ministries to supervise all branches of the economy, a centralized financial system under a national bank, and a state budget that reallocated funds to provinces after collecting its planned revenues.

The planning agency set one- and five-year output targets for a specific number of commodities: only 28 commodities in 1952, 96 the next year, 235 by 1956 and 417 in 1958. The agency also drew up a material-input plan, which identified the amount of resources required to produce each unit of planned output. Finally, the agency conceived a financial plan by which enterprises received funds from the state budget to combine with their own investment funds. The First Five-Year Plan (1953–1957) projected 694 projects of which the Soviet Union constructed 156. These new projects, along with the expanded capacity of existing industries, naturally needed more labor, raw materials, storage, and distribution facilities. For resources to be reallocated to these industries, price control had to be introduced. The planning organs and ministries responsible for these planning processes fixed the prices of all material inputs and final goods.[20] Factor prices included four elements: costs of production, depreciation, profits, and taxes paid at the factory. Similarly at the wholesale and retail levels the price markups included additional taxes, profits, unit costs, and transportation expenses. Contrary to the Soviet experience, Chinese planners set the prices of intermediate industrial products—that is, producer goods—quite high after the Korean War. As a consequence, firms earned high profits, which reduced the need of state subsidies for subsequent new production. But planning organs had to continually appeal to firms to make cost-reducing innovations because the firms' price-setting policies alone served to cover costs even when they operated inefficiently.

State Controls on Wages and Resources

Along with administered pricing, each enterprise had a labor plan specifying the number of workers they could hire and the annual wage fund not to be exceeded. Mounting pressures at year's end and when each five-year plan drew to a close drove many firms to hire more labor than they normally needed. Up until 1957 urban wages remained well above rural wages and thus attracted a perpetual stream of workers to cities. By 1957 the state readily saw that further controls were necessary to limit this migration, and if possible, even reverse it. Planners and ministries revised the wage rate system into the well-known eight-grade wage structure, which remained intact until the 1970s. Economic units were ordered to stabilize their workforce number and only permit workers to leave for other jobs if evidence of demand and employment elsewhere were strictly provided. The physical allocation of labor became a harsh reality.

The Ministry of Commerce and Transportation had the responsibility for stockpiling and allocating food grain, fibers, and raw materials vitally needed for export by the cities and by industry. Between 1950–51 and 1957–58 state procurements of grain from the countryside—including the agricultural tax and fixed-marketed sales—rapidly rose from 65.18 billion catties to 96 billion catties, which represents an annual growth of 5.5 percent and a rate similar to the growth of food grain production for the same period. China imported very little grain during this decade but exported considerable food and raw materials to the socialist block countries. The state administered the prices of these important materials and physically allocated them to regions, cities, and firms requiring them.

Centralized Financial System and State Budget Revenues

The People's Bank of China, created in 1949, issued all currency, made short-term loans, and held deposits for households, firms, and state organizations. It immediately opened thousands of branch offices throughout the country to issue its notes, extend loans, accept deposits, and transfer funds for the state. The People's Bank merely served as a financial conduit—not as an institution to mobilize savings for capital investment.[21] The state budget rapidly expanded during the 1950s, and a high proportion of its outlays went for capital formation. All organizations, including the state budget, maintained balanced budgets, so that capital investment was entirely financed from current savings. The central bank, therefore, provided very little liquidity and did not hold financial assets representing the transfer of funds into capital formation. It issued only enough funds for households and enterprises to make everyday financial payments. Firms drew upon their deposits when paying pensions and wages. Firms purchased goods and services from each other by debiting and crediting their respective bank deposits. The central bank financed these transactions only if these firms were carrying out the current economic plan. Households deposited their savings in branch banks, and they withdrew funds to purchase consumer goods. The retail unit receiving these payments deposited the funds in its respective branch bank. This financial system prohibited large-scale cash spending and mitigated against any tendency toward deficit financing.

The state budget's revenues rose from 6,519 million yuan in 1950 to 17,560 million in 1952, and then to 29,703 million in 1957—a little more than a fourfold increase over the seven-year period. This collection performance certainly eclipsed all similar efforts to garner more revenue for the state in the late Ch'ing and Republican periods. Taxes on industry and trade, profits from the same, and depreciation reserves accounted for the largest source of budget receipts and rose from 67 percent in 1950 to 81 percent in 1956. The state spent a quarter of its budget or 1,702 million yuan in 1950 for economic projects; by 1956 it was spending around 53 percent or 16,727 million yuan for the same. Until 1952 or so, the state still resorted to note issue to finance a modest deficit—perhaps around 8 percent of the budget—but strict, balanced budgeting became the rule thereafter.[22]

The Harbin Economic Control System

Up until 1951 committees of party cadres managed economic organizations and enterprises to revive the economy, but central planning demanded tighter control over factories. The deputy mayor of Tientsin, Wu Te, reported in early 1953 that "if the leadership agencies have to judge conditions, determine policy, guide work, on the basis of their false reports, then this is most dangerous."[23] Enterprises had to report correctly their activities, or economic planning would fail. The party moved to install a new enterprise economic control system that would be more centralized and suited for tighter control: the *Harbin system*. This was a network of accounting offices with considerable power to check on plan fulfillment and periodically examine production conditions in enterprises. It first developed in Manchuria and then spread throughout the country. These offices sent accountants to watch over financial plans and dispatched control workers to supervise the quality of work; both agents worked with factory managers to help them make decisions. Midway through the First Five-Year Plan prominent party members severely criticized the Harbin system as too bureaucratic and inept. Enterprise control responsibility still remained concentrated in factory managers' hands until 1958 when the party scrapped the old Ministry of Control and introduced greater decentralization among enterprises. Politics had now taken command over the economy (*cheng-chih kua-shuai*).

Family Farming Reorganization

In agriculture two developments unfolded which partially prompted a drastic reorganization of family farming.[24] Land reform had not eliminated the traditional imbalance between land and labor in farming. The large landowners had disappeared—only to be replaced by a new stratum of small landholders who still did not have enough capital or labor to farm. As in the past these families solved the problem by selling or hiring labor, leasing or renting land and farm capital, and lending or borrowing credit. Private exchange flourished as before and in the eyes of the party threatened to create a new group of large landowners. Meanwhile, the rapid increase in farm production was showing signs of slowing. Food grain and cotton output had increased 145 and 293 percent respectively between 1949 and 1952 but rose only 102 and 90 percent between 1952 and 1953 and by the same amount the next year.

Collectivized Farming In late December 1951 the party ordered households to form mutual aid teams to share their labor, land, and farm capital during peak farming seasons. Party leaders believed in the inherent superiority of cooperative farming over family farming, but they disagreed on how quickly the new farming system should be installed. At first the progress toward mutual aid teams was slow. By late 1952 cadres could report that only two-fifths of all rural households had joined seasonal mutual aid teams. By 1954 these teams exceeded 10 million, but more farmers resisted the scheme; the year's harvest had been poor, and farmers resented the fixed-price–fixed-grain marketing policy introduced the year before. Party leaders viewed this with apprehension for they recognized the slowing down of farm production already mentioned and were well aware of the persistence of rural capitalism. A major debate within the top leadership erupted over the agrarian question. It centered on whether to continue a policy of gradualism or to find radical measures to speed up cooperativization. Mao Tse-tung resolved the debate in the spring of 1955 by rejecting gradualism, although it was the majority view, and ordering a crash program to collectivize farming. Every household had to relinquish its claim to land and farm capital and instead receive wages according to the work its members performed for the village cooperative.

The New Three-Tier Production System In the next eighteen months the transformation took place. In late spring of 1955 only 1 out of 10 households participated in any kind of team farming arrangement. By mid-1956, 6 out of every 10 households were involved in cooperatives, and by year's end almost 9 out of 10. These units contained several farming teams that ranged in size from 20 to 60 households depending upon village size. Although farmers resisted by slaughtering some of their livestock or refusing to join these teams, party control and pressure were too powerful for them to evade or obstruct, and by 1957 cooperativization had been completed. The party did not stop there, however. In late summer of 1958 it militarized village organizations by forming brigades of workers to complete capital projects and farm the land. This new step proved disastrous. Production was disrupted for the next few years, and a three-year decline in harvests compelled the state to import grain from abroad and allow a trickle of refugees to leave the country via Hong Kong. When brigades had been created, the party also revamped its administrative echelon at the county level by forming a new unit called the *commune*. In area, the commune roughly approximated a district within the county or what was essentially an old township with its market town and satellite villages. After some readjustment of unit size, the country ended up with about 74,000 communes—each with an average of 1,600 households. All villages were renamed brigades and referred to as *production brigades*. Many villages had been combined into larger units for this purpose. Within each brigade clusters of 20 to 60 households were organized into *production teams*. Typically, these teams were neighborhood groupings of households in each section of the village. These production teams now farmed the land in common, and they determined the planning of production and its distribution. This three-tier system of production team, production brigade, and commune or administrative seat became the new agrarian system and has remained as such until the present. Through the commune, the party exercises closer control over rural society than any previous Chinese state had been able to achieve.

Midway through the Second Five-Year Plan (1958–1962) the party ceased publishing statistics, and information on plans, their goals, and performances has been scarce ever since. Yet some new trends are observable. The terrible harvests between 1959 and 1961 convinced the state to devote more attention and resources to agriculture. Budget expenditures to communes increased so they could purchase more chemical fertilizers, construction materials, and capital goods to build small-scale industries. From 1962 onward rapid irrigation development and small-scale industrial growth have taken place in the countryside. The communes in the north have built tube wells and irrigated their fields; in the south they have constructed drainage systems. Small factories sprang up in nearly every commune; many produced farm machinery; others supplied chemical fertilizer and construction materials.

Ta-chai Work Ethic

In 1964 a new policy emerged, which continued until about 1978 within the context of greater state support to agriculture. The origins of the policy go back to February 1960 in Hsi-yang county and the small village of Ta-chai. In that year Ch'en Yung-kuei, the production team leader of Ta-chai, reported to the Shansi Communist Party Congress how his village had raised crop yields to unprecedentedly high and stable levels through a new kind of team spirit and organization. As Ch'en's story unfolded, it became apparent that what Ch'en and his companions had done was to organize groups of farmers to labor without reward during the winter months to build embankments of earth in ravines to prevent water runoff and to reclaim more land. In Ch'en's words, "by constructing large embankments in deep ravines that could hold the silt behind it was just like chiseling gold slabs. They prevented the run-off of water; water could be stored; and villagers could still plant good fields." Ch'en's charismatic leadership had mobilized the farmers in season after season so that numerous embankments had been built and dirt behind them filled in. In this way the village had expanded its cultivated land, stored water, and irrigated many new terraces. Although a five-day rainstorm had destroyed the fruits of their labor in August 1963, the villagers had refused any state assistances and entirely rebuilt their embankments within two years. The farmers had worked without remuneration, increased their savings, and purchased enough of their materials to build each embankment, and increase food grain yield and output to high, stable levels. The new income generated by these harvests had enabled this

Ta-chai brigade to rebuild all its households and make the village a model for the other brigades in Hsi-yang to imitate.

Word of Ch'en's report ultimately reached Peking and Mao himself. Mao was so impressed by the new work ethic of the Ta-chai villagers that he instructed party cadres to push a nationwide campaign to have all production brigades adopt the Ta-chai spirit of work and sacrifice. Ch'en Yung-kuei was promoted to the party's top central committee, and he toured the country and spoke publicly for the new policy. Published works as late as 1976 still stressed the importance of a new spirit of struggle and work, which ought to be adopted by all production brigades. This new spirit called for brigades to rely upon their own efforts and resources:

> If our funds are insufficient, we will rely upon our labor. If our tools are inadequate, we will work that much harder. By relying upon a revolutionary spirit of bitter struggle, we will not ask the state for even a penny, not a single material.[25]

Brigades should save, purchase, and produce their own farm capital. But the Ta-chai spirit also called for brigades to help their neighbors. Those brigades that had rebuilt their villages and increased farm production through irrigation and land reclamation ought to give funds and resources to other brigades, so they too could acquire the necessary farm capital to improve the land.[26] In late 1975 a national conference on the "learn from Ta-chai" experience convened and proposed that by the 1980s all counties must have their brigades practicing Ta-chai procedures and must have advanced toward mechanization of farming. Production brigades were to channel their savings to buy farm machinery or produce these themselves. Just as Ta-chai-type brigades had increased their irrigation and water control projects by ploughing back annual earnings to buy construction materials, the same belt tightening could be continued to increase the supply of farm machinery.

Industrial Reorganization

If the 1950s were the decade for great transformation in agriculture, the 1960s witnessed enormous organizational change in industry. Between 1964 and 1966 two models of industrial organization competed with each other, and party debate remained divided on which of these two models to adopt.[27] The central question, as had been the case in agriculture a decade before, was how to organize production to modernize and rapidly increase production? Should industrial enterprises be structured on a hierarchical basis with firm norms for maximizing profit, setting wages by piece rate, and separating functional tasks between supervisor and laborer? Or should enterprises be managed with more political discussion in which cadres participated on the production lines and workers took part in factory management? These two different approaches were reflected in the management of the Ta-ch'ing oil fields in Heilungkiang province of the northeast and the Tsitsihar Locomotive and Carriage Works in the city of Tsitsihar of the same province.

The Tsitsihar Model At the Tsitsihar plant, workers received bonuses for meeting or surpassing quotas. They did not take part in factory management. The cadres' management was made up of two groups: One supervised the workers; the other carried out administrative planning. Tsitsihar city was administered like all Chinese large cities. City planners regulated the various urban units. Surrounding communes fulfilled their quotas for the regional agricultural plan. Factories in the city were under the authority of their respective ministry for meeting their plan.

The Ta-ch'ing Model The situation at Ta-ch'ing was quite different. This oil field had been discovered around 1960. The top-level management worked closely with the production crews, and nonparty persons even participated at this level. The second-level managerial echelon consisted of three groups that often rotated with each other: one performed office work; another handled all sorts of problems in the oil field; the third worked with the drilling teams. Work teams conducted political studies and tried to innovate accordingly. For example, rather than construct one large city near the oil field, cadres and workers decided to build sixty separate but coordinated work-towns with 164 households in each. These units became the center for work, education, and amusement for workers, party personnel and their families.[28] Farming, industry, education, distribution, and military defense were coordinated within these living-working units. The workers tried to make Ta-ch'ing self-sufficient in food grain by reclaiming land and producing their own grain, vegetables, and livestock. By 1976 the 40,000 oil field workers had somehow managed to reclaim 21,000 ha. of land, produce 36,000 metric tons of grain, and raise around 110,000 head of hogs. They had built schools to house 110,000 students and had even set up vocational schools and a small college. It is not surprising that the Ta-ch'ing organizational model would later be singled out for all industry to follow in the late 1960s.

The Great Cultural Revolution

The Great Cultural Revolution (1966–1969) that swept China first struck artistic and academic circles and by mid-1966 rapidly moved to the factories. For the next three years factories were jolted